AF361351

# Buddhist Environmental Ethics

SUNY series, Perspectives in Contemplative Studies
___________
Judith Simmer-Brown and Harold D. Roth, editors

# Buddhist Environmental Ethics

## A Contemplative Approach

COLIN H. SIMONDS

Cover Credit: "Sunrise over the Himalayas, Nagarkot, Nepal," by Riley McKenna Simonds

Published by State University of New York Press, Albany



EU GPSR Authorised Representative:
Logos Europe, 9 rue Nicolas Poussin, 17000, La Rochelle, France
contact@logoseurope.eu

For information, contact State University of New York Press, Albany, NY
www.sunypress.edu

**Library of Congress Cataloging-in-Publication Data**

Name: Simonds, Colin Harold, 1994– author.
Title: Buddhist environmental ethics : a contemplative approach / Colin Harold Simonds.
Description: Albany : State University of New York, [2025]. | Series: SUNY series, perspectives in contemplative studies | Includes bibliographical references and index.
Identifiers: LCCN 2025020766 | ISBN 9798855804973 (hardcover : alk. paper) | ISBN 9798855804997 (ebook)
Subjects: LCSH: Environmentalism—Religious aspects—Buddhism. | Environmental protection—Religious aspects—Buddhism. | Environmental ethics.
Classification: LCC BQ4570.E58 S56 2025 | DDC 294.3/37—dc23/eng/20250614
LC record available at https://lccn.loc.gov/2025020766

*To my parents, Don and Gwen, for showing me
what it means to be a good human being
and your steadfast love and support*

# Contents

# Acknowledgments

Many people have helped me along my academic journey, and it would be impossible to name them all. I'm deeply grateful to those who guided this project from its inception to its completion. Ellen Goldberg, my doctoral supervisor and long-term academic mentor, was an invaluable source of wisdom and support. This book would not have come to fruition without her help. Likewise, I'm very grateful for the inspiration, advice, and comradery of Geoffrey Barstow, who came on as a second reader for my PhD dissertation and has continued to serve as a guiding force in my academic career. My gratitude also goes out to the many folks with whom I've shared conversations over beer and coffee at conferences, retreats, and at my home institutions. Academia can often be a lonely place, and these conversations have helped keep me encouraged and moving forward. In particular, my thanks go to Richard, Amar, Sharday, and Dustin for their encouragement, advice, and friendship as I worked on this project during my post-doctoral fellowship at Queen's University.

Outside of academia, I've had the great privilege to live and practice in several Buddhist communities throughout this project. The teachings I've received, contemplative practice I've undertaken, and people I've been fortunate to meet in these communities have greatly informed my understanding of Buddhist ethics, philosophy, and contemplative practice. My deepest thanks go to Lama Mark Webber for bringing me into the world of Tibetan Buddhism and for continuing to point out the way. Thank you also to the folks I've met at Rangjung Yeshe, the Woodenfish Foundation, and the Namgyal Yangzab Buddhist Community of Canada from whom I've had the opportunity to learn and practice alongside.

My thanks go to the editors and staff at SUNY Press for helping materialize this project. Thank you to Judith Simmer-Brown and Harold Roth for including this project in their Contemplative Studies series. Thank you also to the two anonymous reviewers for their time and their comments, which greatly shaped the final form of this work.

Finally, my thanks go to my friends and family for supporting me during this project and beyond. Thank you to my parents, Gwen and Don, my siblings, Grace and Andrew, and our companions, Otto and Hazel, who have provided refuge, comfort, and love throughout my life. Thank you to all my friends who helped shape me, both intellectually and personally, from high school to undergrad to Quin-Mo-Lac to grad school. I wouldn't be who I am, and this book would not exist without you all. Last, my deepest thanks and love go to my amazing wife, Riley, for always believing in me, for infallibly being by my side, and for fiercely loving Norbu and me.

Regarding the manuscript, this work builds from both my dissertation work and from some of my previous publications in academic journals. Sections of chapter 1 were previously published in "The Trouble of Rocks and Waters: On the (Im)Possibility of a Buddhist Environmental Ethic," *Environmental Ethics* 45, no. 3 (2023), and "Animal Ethics Are Environmental Ethics in Tibetan Buddhism," *Canadian Journal of Buddhist Studies* 17 (2025). Sections of chapter 2 were previously published in "Buddhist Ethics as Moral Phenomenology: A Defense and Development of the Theory," *Journal of Buddhist Ethics* 28 (2021). Sections of chapter 3 were previously published in "*Lta sgom spyod gsum*: A Tibetan Approach to Moral Phenomenological Praxis," *Journal of Buddhist Ethics* 30 (2023). Finally, sections of chapter 6 were previously published in "Toward a Buddhist Ecological Ethic of Care," *Religions* 14 (2023).

# Introduction

## Environmentalism Has Failed

On the fiftieth anniversary of the publication of Rachel Carson's *Silent Spring*, the book commonly seen as the catalyst of the modern environmentalist movement, David Suzuki began a harrowing op-ed with these words in the Vancouver newspaper *The Georgia Straight*: "Over the past 50 years, environmentalists have succeeded in raising awareness, changing logging practices, stopping mega-dams and offshore drilling, and reducing greenhouse gas emissions. But we were so focused on battling opponents and seeking public support that we failed to realize these battles reflect fundamentally different ways of *seeing our place in the world*. And it is our deep underlying worldview that determines the way we treat our surroundings."[1] Suzuki is stating that, despite these minor victories, the environmentalist project to radically change how humans *be* in the world has made slow progress.

Tibetan Buddhism is a tradition centered around changing precisely how we see our place in the world. Its rituals, philosophy, and contemplative practices are directed toward the transformation of a deluded, maladjusted experience of the world to a liberated, realistic experience of the world. We are now just over a decade after Suzuki's op-ed, and it feels like people are finally recognizing the harrowing imminence of climate change, but our worldviews have not shifted accordingly. Surely then, Tibetan Buddhism can be an important voice in today's efforts to address our environmental emergency. This book is my attempt to build this bridge between the Tibetan Buddhist philosophical and contemplative traditions and the more-than-human world and offer a contemplative approach to Buddhist environmental ethics.

Before exploring this intersection, we must first outline the contours of the crisis itself. Of course, the climatic situation is far worse than the building of mega-dams and the clear-cutting of old-growth forests. Zooming out to a planetary level, Rockstrom and colleagues' article "A Safe Operating Space for Humanity" outlines nine "planetary boundaries"; if they are crossed, "important sub-systems, such as a monsoon system, could shift into a new state, often with deleterious or potentially even disastrous consequences for humans."[2] They write, "We have tried to identify the Earth-system processes and associated thresholds which, if crossed, could generate unacceptable environmental change. We have found nine such processes for which we believe it is necessary to define planetary boundaries: climate change; rate of biodiversity loss (terrestrial and marine); interference with the nitrogen and phosphorus cycles; stratospheric ozone depletion; ocean acidification; global freshwater use; change in land use; chemical pollution; and atmospheric aerosol loading."[3] Among the boundaries mentioned, they worryingly state that climate change, the rate of biodiversity loss, and the nitrogen cycle[4] have already surpassed their respective boundaries, and the phosphorous cycle and rates of ocean acidification are rapidly nearing their respective thresholds. We're thus nearly, if not already, in a novel, permanent climactic reality.

This degradation of the more-than-human world stems from how both ordinary individuals and the institutions we make up conduct themselves on a day-to-day basis. But behind these actions are ideological structures that inform and guide these actions. Scholars have articulated many of these underlying ideologies (dominionism, anthropocentrism, and so forth) that have led to our abhorrent treatment of the natural world, and these might very well be key factors. But from a Buddhist standpoint, what's most important is how each of these ideological biases is an error in one's *view* that leads to a habitual error in one's everyday *action*. As Peter Singer wrote forty-five years ago: "Habit. That is the final barrier the Animal Liberation movement faces."[5] Clearly, habit remains a major barrier for all projects toward earth, animal, or total liberation—but perhaps it is the barrier of wrong *view* that should be torn down first.

There are many explanations for why these inaccurate and harmful views have persisted and continue to inform the habitual actions of the general public. Timothy Morton presents negative habitual action as an epistemic problem. In their presentation of global warming as a "hyperobject," they gesture to the inability for us humans to fully grasp the gravity of the ecological situation. Hyperobjects are phenomena that are "so massively distributed we can't directly grasp them empirically" (despite attempts such as those of Rockstrom and colleagues to do so),[6] and if we can't grasp them empirically, then we can't actually address them behaviorally. Likewise, Kari Marie Norgaard claims that there are psychological barriers involved in climate denial that prevent everyday individuals from addressing climate change in our daily lives. I will not attempt to uncover and articulate further ideological barriers to climate action—as Ted Toadvine notes: "Diagnosing the causes for our alienation from nature has been a favourite pastime of environmentalists over the past century."[7] Instead, I hope to show how a Tibetan Buddhist moral phenomenological approach to the more-than-human world can address the central error of wrong view across each of these ideological, epistemic, and psychological barriers.

## A Tibetan Buddhist Response

This book will look at these issues through a Tibetan Buddhist philosophical lens to present new philosophical and contemplative ways of responding to the degradation of the more-than-human world. Of course, I am not the first to direct the Buddhist tradition toward environmental ethics. Prior scholars have conducted classical religious ecological exegesis of the *sūtras*[8] and have assessed the general ecological relevance of Buddhist principles,[9] but many of these eco-Buddhisms fall into what Lori Gruen has problematized as a "totalizing ethical approach." She makes a convincing case that these abstract ethical theories are divorced from the complicated, "entangled" world we occupy and thus can actually elicit inaction rather than action. She follows ecofeminist Marti Kheel in her rejection of traditional forms of ethical argumentation as "truncated narratives" that wrench "an ethical problem out of its embedded context."[10] Buddhist practitioners and scholars have approached the question of the more-than-human world in various ways, including eco-apologetics, eco-constructivism, eco-ethics, eco-contextualism, and eco-criticism, and while many of these approaches and their resultant works have great practical merit, Gruen's critique suggests that they may only have limited effectiveness and can just as easily deter people from working toward positive relationships with the more-than-human world as they might encourage it.

But the Buddhist tradition isn't about totalizing narratives. I'm absolutely indebted to the scholars who have articulated excellent versions of what an eco-Buddhism might look like, but many of these eco-Buddhisms neglect the fluidity, embeddedness, and the context-specific nature of Buddhist ethics. As I hope to show, Buddhist ethics are concerned with experience, attentiveness, and care, and in the kinds of Mahāyāna Buddhism with which I engage, the principle of *upāya* directly rejects the kind of totalizing narratives critiqued by Gruen and found in some modern eco-Buddhisms. But eco-Buddhism needn't be a totalizing narrative. If we shift our attention from the ecological merit of purely philosophical, canonical principles to the experientially embedded contemplative tradition that is essential to the broader Buddhist project, then we can articulate a new kind of Buddhist environmental ethic that attends to the complexity of our ecological reality. In short, the Buddhist philosophical system that originated in India and continued in Tibet has rich traditions of logic, epistemology, ontology, soteriology, and a unique ethical system that has yet to be fully mobilized toward contemporary philosophical (and practical) concerns. This book will fill some of the gaps of previous Buddhist engagement with the more-than-human world and work toward a more fruitful dialogue between Tibetan Buddhism and environmental ethics.

To return to Suzuki, his article advocated for a *radical* environmentalism — one that addresses the underlying roots of the ecological crisis rather than treat its symptoms. He is calling for a phenomenological, perceptual shift as a response to the ecological crisis that has heretofore been largely left outside of environmental discussions. There *are* some instances of this perceptual approach to environmental ethics in Western philosophical literature such as when Arne Naess states, "I am not much interested in ethics or morals. I'm interested in how we experience the world. . . . Ethics follows from how we experience the world."[11] That said, Naess's emphasis on experience is largely ignored in both Western and Buddhist environmental ethics. Thankfully, however, there is a potent interpretation of Buddhist ethics that mobilizes this very kind of phenomenological shift toward ethical ends and, as Naess recommends, approaches ethics through experience. This interpretation is called "moral phenomenology," and I will show how this ethical approach can be applied to environmental contexts to address many of the issues outlined above and to craft an environmental ethic based upon how individuals experience themselves and the more-than-human world. This experiential approach to ethics can directly address that final habitual barrier identified by Singer, habit, and can dramatically shift how individuals naturally experience, understand, and act in the world.

The project of this book is to mobilize this moral phenomenological interpretation of Buddhist ethics toward the ends of environmental ethics. To do so, it will first outline the philosophical foundation for a Buddhist concern for the environment. Then, it will articulate a defense and development of the interpretation of Buddhist ethics as moral phenomenology by surveying prior scholarship on moral phenomenology and addressing key issues in its theory. It will then look to the Tibetan contemplative framework of *lta sgom spyod gsum* (view, meditation, action) as a unique method for enacting a moral phenomenological ethic and will use this framework to nuance the many aspects of moral phenomenology in general. Once this theory and its praxis have been thoroughly articulated, this book will then be able to direct this ethical system toward contemporary issues facing the more-than-human world and address the experiential roots of the environmental crisis. In doing so, it will offer a novel way of engaging the climate emergency and present a new approach to Buddhist environmental ethics.

## Methodology

When I began writing this book, there was a heated methodological discussion in a Buddhist studies Facebook group. It began when a scholar asked for resources addressing the divide in the field between those who practice strict philology, translation, and historical studies and those who interrogate said Buddhist material through the lens of critical theory or hermeneutics and take part in a creative enterprise to engage Buddhist material with modernity. This scholar framed this tension by stating that the former group often accuses the latter of muddying up a clear tradition and that the latter group accused the former of lacking critical self-reflection and perpetuating a myth of scholarly objectivity. The comments ended up devolving into ad hominem attacks from both sides, and the discussion was largely unproductive outside of showing that this divide indeed exists in a very clear way.

There was, however, one notable dialogue that arose from this discussion concerning Donald S. Lopez Jr.'s 2016 article, "Developments in Buddhist Studies, 2015."[12] Lopez's paper works to unpack a 1966 quote from Holmes Welch that states: "Obviously, the philologist, the philosopher, the student of comparative religion, and the social scientist, each remaining what he [sic] is, must try to understand the others' approach to Buddhism, study the others' discipline, and collaborate in a concrete way so that the results of research may suffer less from the shortcomings that each now finds in the work of the other."[13] In my view, each of these approaches to the study of Buddhism must be considered when beginning a project. While these fields can of course be engaged in tandem, they are often at odds with one another in terms of their methodology and their overall objectives. This, however, needn't be the case. One can begin with philological study and engage this historical Buddhist tradition with critical theory, contemporary philosophy, and the unique issues of today. And this interdisciplinary approach to Buddhist studies has recently developed into its entire own subfield: Buddhist critical-constructive reflection.

Prior to this somewhat lengthy term being developed, a small subset of Buddhist academics began exploring what they called "Buddhist theology" as a self-reflexive Buddhist answer to the kinds of theological studies happening in other religious traditions in the Western academy. While Buddhists in Asia had developed sophisticated institutions, traditions, and discourses around the critique, understanding, and application of core Buddhist concepts, Buddhist *studies* in the academy had largely remained concerned about what *others* did in the *past*. Rarely did it assume the perspective of the tradition itself and think through contemporary ideas from a Buddhist perspective. Those who *did* do this kind of work occupied the periphery of the field until a collection was published in 2000 titled *Buddhist Theology: Critical Reflections by Contemporary Buddhist Scholars*. This collection explores what it means to conduct "Buddhist theology" and offers some examples of scholars *doing* Buddhist theology. While the use of the term *theology* to describe a self-conscious kind of Buddhist reflection has generally fallen out of favor, some of the explorations of the volume are remarkably relevant to this present study. For example, José Cabezon writes:

> The vast and diverse resources of the Indo-Tibetan tradition, it seems to me, could provide any scholar with ample raw material for constructive theological work. Its commitment to systematic, open and rational inquiry is in accordance with the academic theologian's analogous methodological requirements. Additionally, its rich hermeneutical insights, and its generally skeptical attitude regarding the role scripture should play in theological discourse, give the theologian the kind of freedom necessary to make ancient doctrine relevant to contemporary circumstances. Finally, its attempt to balance theory and practice — the conceptual study of doctrine and its internalization in meditation — serves as a continual reminder that the Buddhist theological task must take both into account, and that it can be reduced to neither.[14]

My hope is to do just this and apply the resources of the Indo-Tibetan philosophical and contemplative tradition toward one of the most pressing issues that we face today.

In 2006, the Buddhist Critical-Constructive Reflection Group was established at the American Academy of Religion as a venue for scholars to engage in this theological approach to Buddhist studies and "participate both in the modern critical study of religion *and* in the religion under study."[15] The term *Buddhist critical-constructive reflection* replaced *Buddhist theology* because of the incongruity of *theos* with Buddhism's understanding of gods, but the spirit of the discipline remained the same. Two years later, John Makransky, coeditor of *Buddhist Theology*, would publish a foundational paper in *Global Buddhism* outlining the history, methods, and goals of this approach to Buddhist studies. In this paper, Makransky identifies two main purposes of the Buddhist critical-constructive movement: "to apply critical academic findings to inform current Buddhist understanding"[16] and "to explore how Buddhist thought and practice may address pressing needs of modern societies and inform current issues."[17]

When it comes to the study of Buddhist environmental ethics, most recent articles have leaned heavily into the former pursuit of Buddhist critical-constructive reflection and eschewed the latter. Perhaps as a reaction to some of the normative claims of Buddhism being an "exceptionally green religious tradition," recent scholarship has taken up quite critical stances towards eco-Buddhism. Many have argued that Buddhism falls short of the ecocentric axiology necessary for full environmental ethics, that interdependence is an insufficient philosophical position for motivating ecological work, and that Buddhism is more concerned with overcoming the natural world rather than living as a harmonious steward of the land.[18] Of course, this hasn't stopped contemporary Buddhists from engaging questions of the environment. Far from it. But recent academic scholarship seems to have ignored the constructive role it can play. Therefore, this book will work to provide a constructive response to some of these recent critiques and look at how a holistic environmental ethic can be built from the contemplative practices of Tibetan Buddhism.

During this project, I was a research affiliate at Rangjung Yeshe Institute in Kathmandu and was active as practitioner, retreatant, and translator with the Namgyal Yangzab Community of Canada, both of which situate themselves in a Drikung Kagyu[19] lineage. I was also a postdoctoral fellow at Queen's University, an adjunct professor at the University of Ottawa, and an assistant lecturer at the University of Alberta. I therefore bring to this work both my lived experience as a practitioner of Tibetan Buddhism and my training as a scholar of religion and Buddhist philosophy to engage in an academic process that is both critical and constructive. To explore Buddhist environmental ethics, I am considering the academic scholarship in religious studies, religious ecology, and environmental philosophy while at the same time engaging the Tibetan Buddhist tradition as not simply an object of study but also a lived religion to be presented as an equal interlocutor in discussion. Thus, the purposes and methodologies of the Buddhist Critical-Constructive Reflection Group greatly inform my work. I apply a critical lens to the sources and texts I use for constructing a Buddhist environmental ethic while simultaneously exploring how the Buddhist tradition can be a major source of generative thought for addressing contemporary issues.

Another way of understanding this methodological approach is by calling it by perhaps a more familiar term: *Buddhist philosophy*. Rather than simply look for what other philosophers have said about the present subject in the past (which early studies of Buddhist philosophy focused on), I will follow Jay L. Garfield's methodological call and *do* Buddhist philosophy. In the postscript to his work *Engaging Buddhism: Why It Matters to Philosophy*, Garfield contrasts the "exegetical project of figuring out what Buddhist philosophers said" with actually taking up the Buddhist philosophical position oneself, and he defines *doing* Buddhist philosophy in the following way: "[It is] the attempt to address serious philosophical problems, of interest in their own right, some arising from the Buddhist tradition itself, some from the West, in conversation with the Buddhist tradition, taking it seriously as a source of puzzles and of insights, and taking its horizon of concerns seriously as a backdrop for philosophical reflection."[20] This is precisely what this book will do. By taking up the position of Tibetan Buddhism and bringing it into dialogue with environmental ethics, I will be able to reflect upon their respective problems in new ways and provide novel insights into the questions each tradition brings forth. Rather than attending only to the historical realities of Tibetan Buddhism and its philosophical tradition (which would be *studying* Buddhism), I will look at how contemporary Buddhism is both challenged by and can productively respond to contemporary issues concerning the more-than-human world.

## Chapter Overview

In sum, this book works to articulate a novel, contemplative articulation of Buddhist environmental ethics. To do so, it must accomplish two main aims: It must detail, defend, and develop a contemplative, experiential approach to Buddhist ethics, and it must apply this theory of Buddhist ethics to our more-than-human world. Chapter 1 therefore begins this project by outlining some of the challenges and potentials of the eco-Buddhist project to contextualize the rest of the book. It first reviews some of the normative approaches to eco-Buddhism found in popular Tibetan Buddhist works that center compassion and interdependence in their ecological ethics before assessing some of the critiques of this apologetic approach by critical scholars of Buddhist environmentalism. Ultimately, this chapter directly addresses the concerns of these scholars and argues that an authentic and robust environmental ethic can be constructed from Buddhist principles. It argues that a Buddhist environmental ethic emerges quite naturally from the combination of the goal of liberating all sentient beings from *duḥkha* (suffering, dissatisfaction, or unease), an understanding of *duḥkha* as dependently arising, and a recognition that the environment is a major cause of this *duḥkha*. This chapter thus shows how a Buddhist concern from the environment can indeed be constructed from Buddhist principles and lays the foundation for a contemplative approach to Buddhist environmental ethics.

Chapter 2 begins outlining what a contemplative, experiential approach to Buddhist ethics looks like by defending and developing the categorization of Buddhist ethics as a moral phenomenology. It first details some of the ways Buddhist ethics have been classified by other scholars as either consequentialist or as a virtue ethic to provide a foil for the discussion. It then explores how moral phenomenology has been understood in Buddhist contexts and considers the evidence scholars have provided in their arguments for this moral phenomenological interpretation. Then it looks to the Tibetan Buddhist tradition for evidence of a moral phenomenological approach to Buddhist ethics to further develop this theory. Having developed this interpretation, this chapter addresses issues that emerge from a moral phenomenological approach to ethics from a Tibetan Buddhist perspective to strengthen and defend this interpretation from possible critiques. Finally, this chapter briefly examines the use of the term *moral phenomenology* in Western philosophical settings and looks at how the notion of ethical comportment might allow for this Buddhist understanding of ethics to be dialogued Western systems of thought.

Chapter 3 builds from chapter 2 and seeks to offer a practical addendum to the theory of moral phenomenology through the contemplative framework of *lta sgom spyod gsum*, or "view, meditation, action." It first investigates how the framework has been defined and used both descriptively and practically in Tibetan primary texts. It then nuances this usage by identifying key aspects of this framework's deployment in Tibetan contexts, including how view is prioritized among the three steps of the framework, what particular "view" these texts are referring to, how the unity of view and action is the intended fruition of contemplative practice, and how there is a specific order of operations in the implementation of this contemplative framework. This chapter then relates *lta sgom spyod gsum* directly to the ethical project of moral phenomenology and demonstrates how it can be mobilized as the practical arm of this unique, contemplative Buddhist ethical theory.

Chapter 4 nuances the former two chapters and looks at the specific role of meditation in the contemplative framework of *lta sgom spyod gsum*. It outlines *śamatha*[21] (calm abiding) practice, with specific reference to Kamalaśīla's[22] *Bhāvanākrama*[23] and Tsongkhapa's commentary on the text, as the foundational meditation practice that develops the ability to concentrate on views in *vipaśyanā*[24] (insight) practice. It then outlines *vipaśyanā* as the meditative practice that brings intellectual views into one's experiential fold and explains how the framework of listen, reflect, meditate[25] is method for doing so. It then explains precisely how these modes of meditation fit into the moral phenomenological project. This chapter then explores the role of direct meditative experience as the mechanism by which intellectual understanding becomes a fully embodied, perceptual understanding during contemplative practice. It situates the meditative experiences occasioned by Tibetan Buddhist meditation in the broader academic discourse on mystical states and argues that the meditative experience conditioned by intellectual study and constructed by contemplative practice is the catalyst for ethical transformation in this moral phenomenological system.

Chapter 5 applies this fully developed moral phenomenological approach to ethics to the environment. It explores how some of the ecologically relevant principles of Tibetan Buddhism can be mobilized toward a comprehensive Buddhist environmental ethic through moral phenomenology and its related contemplative framework. It suggests what an applied moral phenomenology would look like and identifies some of the fundamental ontological and epistemic issues facing the more-than-human world that can be addressed through this ethical approach. It then identifies the particular views, both provisional and ultimate, that could lead to positive ecological awareness, including emptiness, *duḥkha*, and interdependence, but also certain views found in environmental philosophies such as deep ecology, ecofeminism, and new materialisms. By identifying these views, this chapter thus allows for Buddhist environmental ethics to be implemented through contemplative means and for moral phenomenology and its practical framework of view, meditation, action to be mobilized toward ecological ends.

Chapter 6 then develops this moral phenomenological approach to Buddhist environmental ethics by looking at the specific role of contemplative practice in this ecological context. It first lays out how *śamatha* and *vipaśyanā* should be understood in an ecological context and investigates their respective roles in occasioning ecological awareness. This chapter then surveys other potential methods for experiencing ecological views found in contemporary environmentalisms including deep listening, contemplative walking, cultivating sustained attention to natural phenomena, and spontaneous encounters with nonhuman ecological agents. Despite these varied contemplative methods for bringing about ecological awareness, this chapter concludes that the formal methods of *śamatha* and *vipaśyanā* present the best opportunity for bringing about an ecological moral phenomenology due to its precision and consistency. Finally, it thinks through how *action* might manifest in a Buddhist environmental ethic, looks at the Dalai Lama, Gary Snyder, Dr. Gail Bradbrook, and Windhorse Farms as examples of this experiential Buddhist eco-ethic, and thinks through the question of eating animals as a test case for a moral phenomenological environmental ethic.

Finally, this book concludes by reviewing the earlier chapters and emphasizing the novel contribution that moral phenomenology and the contemplative framework of *lta sgom spyod gsum* can make in theorizing and implementing Buddhist environmental ethics. It compares this approach to other presentations of Buddhist environmental ethics in the field to highlight the specific issues that this kind of eco-Buddhism can uniquely address. It then responds to some of the potential critiques of such an approach and offers future avenues for this contemplative approach to Buddhist ethics to be directed in both the scholarship on Buddhist ethics and in the lives of everyday practitioners. Ultimately, it is my hope that this book presents a compelling case for a renewed attention not only to Tibetan Buddhism but contemplative practice in general as a source of generative thought for environmental ethics.

1

# Liberating All Sentient Beings

## Foundations of Buddhist Environmental Ethics

### Mapping Buddhist Eco-Ethics

This book is of course not the first to mobilize the Buddhist tradition toward an environmental ethic. We can trace the threads of popular eco-Buddhism back to the 1950s, and there has been much scholarly work done on Buddhist environmental ethics in the last thirty years. But despite this wealth of literature, there are still ongoing, long-lasting disputes as to whether or not eco-Buddhism is a legitimate project, whether ecological concern is consonant with Buddhist values, and whether or not Buddhism has anything novel to actually contribute to our contemporary ecological situation. In order to best situate a contemplative approach to Buddhist environmental ethics, we should thus go over some of these questions and establish what I consider to be the foundation of a Buddhist concern for the environment.

In his paper "An Assessment of Buddhist Eco-Philosophy," Donald K. Swearer surveys the eco-Buddhist philosophical literature published up until 2005 and classifies it along five useful lines. These classifications follow: eco-apologists, eco-critics, eco-constructivists, eco-contextualists, and eco-ethicists.[1] First, eco-apologists are those who view the Buddhist tradition as inherently environmentally friendly and articulate their philosophical arguments from this position. Second, eco-critics such as Ian Harris,[2]

15

Lambert Schmithausen,[3] and more recently, Daniel Capper[4] reject this normative claim and critique the project of bringing together ecology and Buddhism. Third are the eco-constructivists who also reject the normative claim that Buddhism is inherently green but who nonetheless see value in constructing ecological ideas from Buddhist sources. Fourth, eco-contextualists assume the position that environmental thought must be context specific and that generalized eco-Buddhisms must be eschewed for more place-based environmental movements. Fifth, and most relevant to this current project, is eco-ethics. Swearer identifies a cohort of Buddhist scholars who approach the topic of the environment from an eco-ethicist position and who rely on the system of Buddhist ethics as a means to engage questions of the environment. Those who work from this position use normative ethical theories such as deontology, virtue ethics, and consequentialism to address questions of the environment from a Buddhist position. In doing so, they somewhat challenge the notion that Buddhism is inherently eco-friendly and that, for it to be an effective force in environmental discourse, the system of ethics specific to Buddhism must be relied upon over general pan-Buddhist principles.

Within these five approaches to Buddhist eco-philosophy, there is a major tension between those who present a normative view of Buddhism as an inherently green religion and those who are critical of such a claim. This tension between the normative green Buddhist position and a kind of systemic, critical Buddhist eco-ethics is most clearly expressed in Simon P. James's article "Against Holism: Rethinking Buddhist Environmental Ethics." His main contention surrounds what he calls the "unity thesis" of Buddhist environmentalism, which he frames using formal logic thusly:

> Premise 1. A holistic view of the world, according to which humans are regarded as being "one" with nature, will necessarily engender environmental concern.

> Premise 2. The Buddhist teaching of emptiness represents just such a holistic view of the world.

> Therefore, Buddhism is an environmentally-friendly religion.[5]

James contests this framing by arguing that both premise 1 and premise 2 are false, but he nonetheless regards the conclusion as true. However, it is true not because of the logic of normative eco-Buddhism but because of the Buddhist tradition's ethical system and its potential application to issues of the environment.

I agree to some extent with James's valuation, but I might frame the problem in a different way. Most eco-Buddhist thinkers concern themselves with *axiology* rather than ethics or with *values* rather than morality. Of course, these areas are closely related as our actions typically follow our values, but there is an important difference between finding ways that Buddhism *values* nature and finding ways to *morally respond to* the environmental crisis. In my reading, the majority of eco-Buddhist literature is concerned with the former, which limits their applicability to the present ecological situation. Even in articles that purportedly concern themselves with environmental ethics we find this emphasis on value over behavior or action. For example, John J. Holder's "A Suffering (But Not Irreparable) Nature: Environmental Ethics from the Perspective of Early Buddhism" outlines "six of the main points central to an early Buddhist environmental ethic,"[6] all of which deal with particular *valuations* rather than behavioral outcomes. He states that the early Buddhist valuation of *duḥkha*, ecosystems, virtues, nonanthropocentrism, nonwild nature, and aesthetics can inform a Buddhist approach to the environment. What this approach looks like, however, is left unexplored.

That said, there are several works that apply the characterizations of Buddhist ethics as a virtue ethic, consequentialist ethic, or even deontology to the environment. These works concern themselves less about how nature or the environment is valued in Buddhist settings and more about how the kinds of behaviors, virtues, and actions encouraged by Buddhist ethical systems can be applicable to our current environmental crisis. Some of this work on eco-Buddhist virtue ethics, consequentialism, and deontology is of great quality and offers useful ways of thinking about the Buddhist approach to the environment. In general, these approaches can be split into two major streams: rule-based approaches to the environment and character-based approaches to the environment.

The rule-based approach to Buddhist environmental ethics is most clearly seen in the work of Padmasiri De Silva. De Silva's major work on the subject is his book *Environmental Philosophy and Ethics in*

*Buddhism*, where he surveys concepts of nature in Buddhism and the general approaches to Buddhist ethics before bringing these strands of thought together in a chapter titled "Buddhist Environmental Ethics" specifically. In this chapter, De Silva first brings up the idea of applied ethics in the context of population, pesticides, deforestation, and extinction before moving on to a sustained discussion on the general principles of a Buddhist environmental ethic. He draws heavily from the life-based ethics of Paul Taylor and the ecological ethics of J. Baird Callicott in his interpretation of Buddhist sources but does so only to "make an assessment of the different strands of thinking in the Buddhist discourses that provide perspectives on the human-nature orientation, rather than to attempt a comprehensive Buddhist theory of environmentalism."[7]

De Silva is quite clear in what he sees as the foundations for a Buddhist environmental ethic. He writes that "the moral implications of killing, inflicting suffering on living creatures, and developing a non-violent attitude to the natural environment forms a coherent moral perspective."[8] To this end, the Buddha repeatedly admonished to "keep away from activities that would unintentionally injure living creatures,"[9] such as traveling during the rainy season and engaging in agriculture in addition to more explicit acts such as hunting, killing, and so forth. De Silva seeks to prove this thesis of a "coherent moral theory" by looking at five themes "which are related to the issues about the destruction of life" and on which the Buddha commented: "blood-sacrifices, warfare, agriculture, meat eating and suicide."[10] In his analysis, the Buddhist stance on each of these issues leads to a kind of ethical theory characterized by a value of life. Further, this value of life leads to particular rules that are placed on the monastic and lay population in order to preserve the maximal amount of life. We might therefore say that De Silva's life-based ethical interpretation leads to a rule-consequentialist position that he then maps onto the Buddhist ethical system.

While De Silva's work is quite interesting, a far more common approach to Buddhist environmental ethics uses the interpretation of Buddhist ethics as a kind of virtue ethics to ground its thought. Those writing on Buddhist virtue-ethical approaches to environmentalism draw from the theory of scholars such as Damien Keown, Charles Fink, and James Whitehall and extend their interpretive framework to contemporary questions surrounding the environment. Keown himself has engaged in this work in his 2007 article "Buddhism and Ecology: A Virtue Ethics Approach." In this piece, he first acknowledges some of the pitfalls of Buddhist environmental thinking before claiming that an understanding of Buddhist ethics as virtue ethics can be used to navigate the environmental crisis. He begins by explaining the Aristotelian roots of virtue ethics before applying this ethical system to the Buddhist setting and finally using this lens to address ecological questions.

Keown points to early Buddhist ideas of non-greed and contentment as "foundational values that support ecological concern" and spells out some of the ecological implications of *ahimsa* (nonviolence). None of these points is entirely novel. We can see nongreed and nonviolence mentioned many times throughout the eco-Buddhist literature. However, where Keown *does* present a novel argument is in his restructuring of these virtues as a cohesive environmental ethic. By presenting a virtue-ethical approach to Buddhist environmental ethics, Keown is proposing that developing the virtues found in Buddhism is the way to navigate the environmental crisis. In other words, he goes beyond earlier writers who looked at the ecological implications of nonviolence or nongreed and asserts that these developing these virtues is the path to environmental ethics par excellence. In doing so, he follows Frasz's presentation of virtue ethics in ecological contexts and quotes him saying, "The thrust of environmental virtue ethics is to foster new habits of thought and action in the moral agent—not just to get the immediate decision made right, but to reorient all actions henceforth in terms of holistic, ecologically based ways of thinking."[11] Thus, although Keown concedes that the virtues of an enlightened being "do not bring the power to solve ecological problems," he nonetheless sees these virtues as profoundly reorienting such that they "may guide us in grasping the issues at stake and in accepting or rejecting possible courses of action under consideration."[12]

This virtues approach to Buddhist environmental ethics is further developed in monographs by Pragati Sahni,[13] Simon P. James,[14] and David E. Cooper[15] and has largely been the dominant ethical approach to Buddhist environmental ethics in the

Western academy. Their work is quite compelling and actually has many resonances with what I will articulate as a contemplative approach to Buddhist environmental ethics. However, I contend that by characterizing Buddhist environmental ethics through the conventions of Western ethics, the Buddhist tradition loses some of its unique qualities (as I will argue in the following chapter) and hence its novel applicability to our contemporary ecological issues.

## Critiques of the Eco-Buddhist Project

This is where a contemplative approach to Buddhist environmental ethics, articulated on its own terms, can fruitfully enter the discourse and perhaps offer something new. But prior to laying out what this contemplative approach looks like, we must address a more fundamental question: Why would a Buddhist care about the environment in the first place? Put differently, how would a Buddhist frame their concern for the environment in terms familiar to their tradition? The above works largely take for granted the notion that Buddhist ethics would include the natural world in its moral purview and therefore sometimes find inadvertent company in the eco-apologetic camp. However, as recent critiques have made clear, the Buddhist tradition is in no way *inherently* ecological, and some scholars have argued that a Buddhist environmental ethic is actually untenable. Should we wish to articulate a contemplative Buddhist environmental ethic, these critiques must therefore be addressed.

The earliest of these eco-Buddhist critiques arose in the 1990s in the work of Ian Harris and Lambert Schmithausen and centered around the doctrinal goals of early Buddhist practice. Rather than become "one with the natural world" as some eco-Buddhists encouraged,[16] these scholars noted how early Buddhist practice was aimed at overcoming and transcending the material world and all its natural elements. As Lambert Schmithausen states: "I for one find it hard to deny that the overwhelming majority of the canonical materials suggests that in early Buddhism it was just a *matter of course* to strive, in the first place, for one's own self-perfection and release."[17] Despite this historical rejection of natural phenomena, Schmithausen nonetheless holds open the possibility that Buddhism may be able to authentically respond to the environmental problems of today.[18] In contrast, Japanese scholar Noriaki Hakamaya holds no such optimism. Hakamaya wrote an extremely critical response to Schmithausen's early work on the possibility of an authentic Buddhist response to environmental issues titled "Buddhism as a Criticism of Physis/Natura." In it, he states that Buddhism explicitly negates nature and "seems to advocate, uncompromisingly and with emotional commitment, a *negative* attitude towards nature"[19] based on the "otherworldliness of 'canonical' Buddhism."[20] Thus, any attempt to craft a positive ethic toward the environment out of Buddhist source material is, according to these scholars, necessarily a modern innovation. Harris does concede that "it is unhelpful to characterize [eco-Buddhism] as a deviation from traditional norms," and "it would be far closer to the truth to see [eco-Buddhism] as an example of a vigorous tradition engaged in a healthy process of reflexive apologetics."[21] Nonetheless, elsewhere he makes clear that "Buddhism's ultimate aim is to escape from the restrictions imposed by our position as beings-within-the-world," and "concern for the animal kingdom can happily be taken along as baggage on the path to perfection, but at some stage it will be left at the side of the road."[22] Thus, far from holding a positive view of the natural world, these scholars claim that canonical Buddhism is "not, in essence, an ecological religion" and can at best be seen as ambivalent and at worst seen as completely negative in its comportment to the more-than-human world.[23]

The philological critique of these scholars is further strengthened by recent historical works on the material relationships between humans and nonhumans in Buddhist settings. For example, Johan Elverskog's *The Buddha's Footprint* shows how canonical Buddhist positions on the relationship between wealth and merit spurred a protocapitalist market economy that compelled a willingness "to exploit not only the natural world for monetary gain but also the people who lived in proximity to the resources."[24] Similarly, Elverskog argues that the Buddha's preference for "the beauty of the human manipulation of nature"[25] over the beauty of wild nature supported massive agricultural development across Buddhist Asia. He writes that the cultivation and trade of rice, sugar, cotton, and tea had "earth-shattering environmental consequences"[26] and argues that, as a result of the increase of monasteries in city centers, "the environmental impact of Buddhist urbanization was immense."[27] Even in cases where Buddhist principles likely *should* have encouraged positive action towards the more-than-human world, the material history of Buddhist cultures maintained this exploitative relationship. As Geoffrey Barstow shows in his book *Food of Sinful Demons*, vegetarianism was a highly respected if somewhat exceptional practice in historical Tibetan Buddhism, where it was seen as an expression of a practitioner's deep realization of compassion. However, both cultural and economic pressures superseded the religious impulse toward mass vegetarianism in Tibet, where meat was lauded not only as a necessary evil but as a positive good by the Buddhist laity and monastics alike.[28] Thus, both the principles found in canonical Buddhism and the material history of human-nonhuman relationships in Buddhist societies push against the popular narrative of Buddhism as an eco-friendly religion.

Both this philological critique and this historical critique are directed toward Buddhism as it existed in the past. However, the third major critique of eco-Buddhism found in contemporary scholarship is directed toward the *potential* of Buddhism to construct an environmental ethic today or in the future. Scholars such as Ian Harris and Daniel Capper have brought into question the relevance of the Buddhist notion of *pratītyasamutpāda*[29] (dependent origination, interdependent arising, interdependence[30]) as a foundation on which to build an authentically Buddhist environmental ethic. Their critique takes place on two major axes: (1) the false equivalency of *pratītyasamutpāda* and ecology, and (2) the ethical flattening of this ontological position. Regarding the first, Harris has shown how there was historically no word for "nature" (as it is understood in contemporary green discourse[31]) in Buddhist languages[32] and that *pratītyasamutpāda* simply lacks the semantic range capable of capturing the terms *nature* and *environment*. As Harris writes, "Modern environmentalist thinking makes much of the interdependence of things in the natural world, and it is certainly true that the doctrine of *pratītyasamutpāda* is in tune with a world view which accepts complex, interdependent relationships. However, there is a problem associated with making a comparison between Buddhism and environmentalist thinking which the scholars mentioned above fail to acknowledge. The Buddhist analysis of things, be they animate or inanimate, is far more radical than that adopted by Western ecology."[33] Thus, according to Harris, the common eco-Buddhist impulse to draw from *pratītyasamutpāda* for environmentalist inspiration is philologically and linguistically inappropriate.

But Harris' above critique goes beyond mere semantic difference. Elsewhere, he expands this critique to claim *pratītyasamutpāda* is an inappropriate *philosophical* basis for ecological thought. He puts this critique quite bluntly when he writes: "Buddhist environmentalism aims to open up the possibility of a better ordering of man's relations with the natural world in its infinite diversity and complexity, yet its adherence to the Hua-Yen principle of interdependence negates its social and eco-activist agenda, for if all depends on all then the black rhino depends on the hydrogen bomb, the rain forest on the waste dump."[34] He is not alone in his skeptical attitude toward the ecological potential of *pratītyasamutpāda*. Daniel Capper echoes this statement when he writes that "if we must value everything because everything is interconnected . . . then we must protect ocean radioactivity as well as dolphins, atmospheric carbon as well as parrots, and anthrax as well as human probiotics."[35] What Harris and Capper are alleging is that *pratītyasamutpāda* creates a flattened ontology incapable of supporting any kind of discriminating ethic (a position I will challenge below). This ineptitude of interdependence actually goes further than mere semantic incompatibility but may compel an *indifference* to the plight of the more-than-human world. Musing again on the rhino, Harris writes:

> For the environmentalist the potential demise of these noble creatures is a matter of sadness and concern. To counteract this possibility, measures will be taken to protect the species by mitigating the destructive forces at work in the rhino's habitat. . . . In this sense, environmentalism represents a "fight against pollution and resource depletion." A Buddhist is unlikely to view things in this way. . . . Change, dissolution, suffering and death are the hallmarks of all conditioned things. At the deepest level, what we take to be a rhino is nothing more than a

> complex series of momentary *dharmas* which have come together in a certain pattern. . . . The rise and fall of all things, whether they be mountains or animals is part of the inexorable process Buddhists call *samsara*.[36]

In other words, rather than inspire environmental action, reflecting on the extinction of the rhino may compel us to simply pursue Buddhist practice to escape *saṃsāra*[37] altogether. Thus, even in contemporary constructions of eco-Buddhism that recognize the novelty of their position, Harris and Capper argue *pratītyasamutpāda* does not provide a sufficient ground for environmental thought and practice.

To borrow some terminology from Swearer, these eco-critics direct their remarks primarily to those engaged in eco-apologetics and eco-constructivism. For the most part, these are compelling critiques and are worth considering. However, rarely do we find that eco-critics respond to those engaged in Buddhist eco-ethics. The one exception to this is Daniel Capper. In *Roaming Free like a Deer*, Capper first establishes a goalpost for what constitutes an "authentic" environmental ethic and then evaluates the potential for historical and contemporary Buddhisms to fulfil his given criteria. To determine what constitutes a satisfactory environmental ethic, Capper turns to two major philosophers in the field: Holmes Rolston III and Arne Næss. He therefore engages two distinct approaches to environmental ethics in the land ethic and deep ecology respectively. While the particulars of these theories and their ethical prescriptions are quite distinct, Capper nonetheless sees them as important touchstones for contemporary environmental ethics and uses them each to highlight two major aspects of environmental thought.

According to Capper, the most important aspect of an environmental ethic is the preservation of a sustainable biosphere. To define environmental ethics, he writes, "The full biosphere . . . must be ecocentrically sustainable in terms of meeting the needs of both humans and nonhumans today while not sacrificing ecological needs of tomorrow."[38] To substantiate this definition, he turns to Rolston's articulation of the land ethic, which states that a sustainable biosphere is "a baseline quality of environment" founded on the ecocentric notion of "land as community" and that this community necessarily includes air, water, soil, forests, rural lands, wildlands, wildlife, and renewable resources.[39] Capper also quotes Rolston to assert that "the bottom line, transcultural and nonnegotiable, is a sustainable biosphere . . . of the full Earth" because "our integrity is inseparable from Earth integrity."[40] Capper thus posits (by way of Rolston) a holistic, land-based environmental ethic focused foremost on the integrity of the whole ecosystem and secondarily at the individual beings within it. When this is used as a means for assessing Buddhist approaches to the more-than-human world, Capper concludes that the tradition falls short of promoting such an ethic. He writes that the Buddhist tradition has strong elements that support a concern for animal welfare but that it is limited "in terms of realizing Rolston's sustainable biosphere."[41] Rolston himself makes a major distinction between an animal rights approach and a broader environmental ethic in *A New Environmental Ethics*. Reflecting on Mark Sagoff's claim that "environmentalists cannot be animal liberationists" and "animal liberationists cannot be environmentalist,"[42] Rolston writes,

> Environmental ethics will object that in an ethic based on sentience, and stopping there, most of the biological world has yet to be taken into account . . . an animal-based ethics can value everything else only instrumentally with reference to higher animals, who form only a small fraction of living things. . . . This is too short-sighted. . . . An animal rights or welfare ethic, if it stops there, is blind to the still larger effort in environmental ethics to value life at all its ranges and levels; indeed to care for a biosphere Earth.[43]

Thus, this holistic articulation of the land ethic and a sustainable biosphere as the quintessence of environmental ethics presents a major challenge for a Buddhist ethical approach to the more-than-human world, which traditionally relies upon sentience of individual beings as the single qualifier for moral consideration.

Furthermore, Capper's critique of Buddhist environmental ethics extends beyond this emphasis on holism as he highlights the trouble that an ethical valuation of individual rocks and waters poses to Buddhist ethical formulations. He writes, "For most

Buddhists, notions of reincarnation result in the targeting of compassion toward animals but not toward plants, minerals, or water, resulting in a limited biocentric orientation. . . . This limited biocentric attitude substantially lacks the ecocentric elements required by a full environmental ethic, which must recognize that plant, mineral, and water resources, too, need to be valued in order to create ecosystem health."[44] Not only do these abiotic elements need to be valued in Capper's articulation of environmental ethics, but they need to be valued *intrinsically*, as in Arne Næss's deep ecology.[45] Capper makes this point explicitly when he writes, "With intention and *for their own sake*, Rolston extends ethical value to abiotic elements of the environment such as gases, water bodies, and stones as part of enhancing total ecosystem health."[46] This is perhaps curious given how there exists a philosophical tension between holistic community-based ethical constructions and ethics directed toward individual beings or phenomena as evidenced in Sagoff's claim that "animal liberationists cannot be environmentalists" and so forth. Nonetheless, we do indeed see Rolston use the language of "intrinsic value" in quite extensive ways. He traces the use of intrinsic valuation of natural phenomena to the articulation of the land ethic in the work J. Baird Callicott and in environmental virtue ethicists like Robert Chapman and ultimately concludes with how the environmental ethicist should understand valuation, writing, "Humans are not so much lighting up value in a merely potentially valuable world, as they are psychologically joining ongoing planetary natural history in which there is value wherever there is positive creativity. While such creativity can be present in subjects with their interests and preferences, it can also be present objectively in living organisms with their lives defended, and in species that defend an identity over time, and generate the storied achievement of natural history."[47] Interestingly, this presentation of intrinsic valuation deviates significantly from Capper's use of it. Rolston ascribes intrinsic value to *life*, but not to abiotic phenomena like rocks and waters. He does, however, push back on the statement "we do not have duties to rocks, air, ocean, dirt, or Earth; we have duties to people, or sentient things"[48] but does so through an appeal to the instrumental value of rocks and waters to the flourishing of a sustainable biosphere. Nonetheless, we can understand how the intrinsic valuation of rocks and waters in certain environmental ethical formulations like deep ecology can be a difficult bar for classical Buddhist ethics to meet, and how even the intrinsic valuation of plant life may be a major challenge for traditional Buddhist ethics, which center sentience as their primary qualifying characteristic.

In other words, both the holistic approach to environmental ethics found in the land ethic and the intrinsic valuation of abiotic phenomena in articulations like deep ecology make it quite difficult to construct a truly environmental ethic out of the Indo-Tibetan Buddhist ethical tradition.[49] Buddhist ethics, like all of Buddhist philosophy, is organized around the central concept of *duḥkha*. Beings experience dissatisfaction, stress, or suffering, and Buddhist thought and contemplative practice are directed toward identifying and addressing the source of this malaise. *Duḥkha* is a phenomenological reality that is necessarily experienced by individual sentient beings, and this makes the experiences of individual sentient beings the primary concern of a Buddhist ethic.[50] If, as Capper claims, the intrinsic valuation of abiotic phenomena like rocks and waters is a requirement of an environmental ethic, then directing Buddhist ethical formulations to this end indeed would be impossible at worst and a deviation from traditional norms at best. Similarly, the preservation of an abstract system such as a holistic understanding of "land" or the maintenance of biodiversity *for their own sake* would be impossible to defend using traditional Buddhist ethical formulations, which center individual sentient beings. By these metrics, it seems Capper's contention that the prioritization of sentience in Buddhist moral theory amounts to a "compassionate concern for animals that sponsors Buddhist actions for animal welfare" but "substantially lacks the ecocentric elements required by a full environmental ethic"[51] is true. Thus, beyond Harris, Schmithausen, and Elverskog's critiques of *historical* Buddhist orientations toward the natural world, it appears that any present or future environmental ethic based on Buddhist moral theory is philosophically untenable.

## A Defense of Buddhist Environmental Ethics

However, in the midst of these critiques, I would nonetheless argue it is methodologically inappropriate to evaluate a Buddhist environmental ethic by these standards. As we have seen, in the broader field of Buddhist ethics, scholars such as Barbra Clayton,[52] William Edelglass,[53] and Jay L. Garfield[54] have begun pushing back against the common exercise of subsuming Buddhist ethics to a Western ethical categorization. This is due to how, as Garfield states, "Buddhist moral theorists see ethics as concerned not *primarily* with actions, their consequences, obligations, sentiments or human happiness, but rather with the nature of our *experience*."[55] It therefore does not fit neatly into virtue ethics, consequentialism, or deontology despite the attempts of scholars to do so. Indeed, in our attempts to make it fit neatly into Western ethical theories, we not only distort some of the fundamental ethical assumptions of the tradition but miss most of what makes it unique. Likewise, if we begin from Western environmental ethics and attempt to subsume Buddhist ethics to this standard, we not only run into philosophical incongruities but miss out on a potentially forceful articulation of environmental ethics. Thus, to avoid these two errors, we must begin from Buddhist principles and explore how the modern understanding of the environment looks through its philosophical lens.[56]

The first major point to make is that any attempt to construct an ethic based on *intrinsic* value is akin to building a house on a crumbling cliffside. It may stand for a while (and it may provide some practical shelter from the literal storm of environmental catastrophe), but it will inevitably fall into the sea when subjected to philosophical analysis. In particular, it will fall when subjected to a Madhyamaka negative dialectical analysis. In his *Mūlamadhyamakakārikā*, Nāgārjuna shows how all phenomena are ultimately empty of intrinsic, independent existence by refuting the four possible modes of causality. In its opening verse, he writes:

> Not from itself, nor from other,
> Nor from both, nor from no cause,
> Does anything whatsoever, wherever and whenever arise.
> Such a thing does not exist.[57]

In brief, Nāgārjuna argues that for an independent thing to come into existence, it must be caused, and this causation can happen in one of four ways: (1) it can cause itself, (2) another independent thing can cause it, (3) both another thing can cause it and it can cause itself, or (4) it can be caused by nothing. In his analysis, he finds each of these possibilities unsatisfactory and, this being the case, claims phenomena are therefore empty of independent existence; they only can be found to exist in a relative, dependently co-arisen way. His text shows how this emptiness of intrinsic or independent existence applies to both phenomena and the qualities of phenomena, including motion, the senses, agenthood, suffering, *nirvāṇa*, and, in the end, all views. This, however, is not a nihilistic negation of the existence of all things but a recognition of their radical relativity. Later in the text, Nāgārjuna writes:

> That which arises in dependent origination
> Is explained as emptiness.
> That, being a dependent designation
> Is itself the middle way.
> That being so, a thing which is not dependently arisen
> Does not exist.
> Therefore, a thing that is not empty
> Does not exist.[58]

In other words, phenomena are empty of independent existence but exist in dependence on a confluence of myriad causes and conditions of which they, in turn, are a cause and condition.

This is the Madhyamaka understanding of *pratītyasamutpāda* — radical relativity and complete interdependence. Any notion of "intrinsic valuation" is therefore absurd. There is no independent thing to which one can ascribe independent value. In a Western philosophical context, Anthony Weston has made a similar critique of intrinsic value and its inappropriate move to value phenomena "in absolute isolation."[59] He argues it is more appropriate to "consider a more holistic picture conception according to which values are connected in a weblike way" and writes that "the notion of 'intrinsic value' is almost a *contradiction* precisely because it insists on cutting values off from their relations with others in order to consider them 'just in themselves.' "[60] In a Buddhist context, however, to construct an environmental ethic on the intrinsic valuation of natural phenomena is a fundamental philosophical error. This is not to say value cannot exist, but it must be understood as a relative characteristic of relative phenomena. I would argue that not only is this relative value a sufficient baseline for environmental ethical speculation, but it is the *only* possible baseline for environmental ethics. In other words, not only is intrinsic value not a necessary prerequisite for an environmental ethic as Næss, Rolston, and Capper may contend, but it is itself ontologically untenable when analyzed from a Madhyamaka Buddhist philosophical position. A Buddhist environmental ethic would therefore need to begin by ascribing *relative* value to rocks, waters, trees, and the atmosphere just as it would ascribe relative value to sentient beings.[61]

Second, the notion of preserving the land, an ecosystem, or the global biosphere *for its own sake* would similarly be critiqued from a Buddhist philosophical position. This ascription of intrinsic valuation to a holistic picture of the biosphere would meet the same philosophical end as the intrinsic valuation of independent entities in the natural world. Of course, like individual rocks and waters, these holistic understandings of ecology would hold *relative* value to the well-being of sentient beings. This relative valuation may push back against classical formulations of the land ethic, which state that "a thing is right when it tends to preserve the integrity, stability, and beauty of the biotic community [and] it is wrong when it tends otherwise,"[62] but in fact approximates some of the sentiments of earlier presentations of an (perhaps inadvertently) instrumentalized sustainable biosphere like Capper's contention that "the full biosphere . . . must be ecocentrically sustainable in terms of meeting the needs of both humans and nonhumans today while not sacrificing ecological needs of tomorrow."[63] However, aside from this similarity, the Buddhist philosophical tradition would hesitate to prioritize the integrity of the whole at the expense of its parts largely because of the lack of distinction between the two. In the Tibetan tradition, there is a term, *snod bcud*, that literally translates to "container" (*snod*) and its "contents" (*bcud*). Typically, this is used as a metaphor for the world and the sentient beings therein, but it also has been used by contemporary Tibetan teachers to refer to an environment and its inhabitants and to advocate for environmental consciousness in Buddhist communities.[64] There is an important distinction, however, between the way this metaphor is employed in Tibetan contexts and the way that ecosystems, environments, or the biosphere are understood in popular environmentalist discourse. In articulations of the land ethic, the land and its inhabitants are obviously understood to be related to one another in a mereological sense, but they are nonetheless treated as distinct entities. The holistic land is one thing, the individual beings and phenomena that make it up are another, and the former is prioritized over the latter. This is not the case in the Buddhist understanding of *snod bcud*. Just as Nāgārjuna shows how cause and effect are mutually produced in a dialectical fashion and therefore only exist in relation to one another, so too do the container and its contents only exist in relation to one another. In the absence of one, there is the absence of the other because they are mutually produced. Thus, not only are the land, the ecosystem, or the biosphere only relatively valued like individual rocks and waters, but the distinction of a system apart from the individuals that make it up is necessarily rejected in favor of a dialectical understanding of the environment and its inhabitants.

I would argue, however, that this rejection still leaves open the possibility of an environmental ethic that attends to the biosphere while remaining squarely rooted in Indo-Tibetan Buddhist moral theory. In Mahāyāna traditions, the goal of religious practice is to liberate *all* sentient beings from *all duḥkha*. Even if we understand this goal to be impossible,[65] this *bodhisattva*[66] vow to liberate all sentient beings nonetheless compels an altruistic comportment and an ethic of care toward the beings one comes across in their day-to-day life. If sentient beings are taken as the sole arbiter of moral value, and we read Buddhist moral theory as more of an animal ethic than an environmental ethic as Capper contends, the philosophical maxims of the tradition necessitate that we attend to the myriad dependently originated causes and conditions that contribute to the furthering or alleviation of *duḥkha*. These causes and conditions of course involve environmental factors in both their individual (rocks, waters, air) and holistic (biosphere, ecosystem, land) sense. When all of these factors are presented together, being the goal of liberating beings from *duḥkha*, *duḥkha*'s arising in *pratītyasamutpāda*, and an understanding of the environment as a cause and condition of this *duḥkha*, we can indeed arrive at an authentic Buddhist environmental ethic true to the tradition's core ethical principles. This may contradict the ambivalence or negative comportment toward the natural world that Schmithausen identifies in early Buddhism, but we easily can explain why this is the case. Early Buddhism promoted the goal of *arahant* (individual liberation), whereas the Mahāyāna tradition I am operationalizing here promotes the goal of becoming a *bodhisattva* and liberating all sentient beings. To achieve the goal of Early Buddhism, attending to the natural world is unnecessary and may even be unhelpful.[67] However, to actively work for the liberation of sentient beings from the grips of *duḥkha*, we *must* attend to the natural world, abiotic phenomena, and ecological formations at every scale.

Thus, the philosophical critiques of contemporary eco-Buddhisms subside quite naturally. If there are no sentient beings left living, then it does not matter what happens to the oceans, the ozone, or the ice caps. However, if there is even a *single* sentient being left in *saṃsāra*, one would still have to attend to the myriad nonsentient phenomena that would support this being in the matrix of dependent origination. In this formulation, *pratītyasamutpāda* and the philosophy of emptiness may radically relativize causality, but they certainly do not flatten all ethical value. This understanding of interdependence thus challenges both Harris's and Capper's reading of *pratītyasamutpāda* as a flat ontology wherein all phenomena are of equal ontological status by virtue of their implication in *pratītyasamutpāda* and are therefore of equal moral worth. Interestingly, this issue of ethical flattening is commonly addressed in the fields of new materialism and object-oriented ontology, which wrestle with the implications of, to quote Timothy Morton, "there [being] hardly any difference between a person and a pincushion."[68] In these cases, however, this kind of ontology can in fact compel ecological thought and a tenderness to nonhuman others. This is because of how human *conatus* is still a factor, regardless of how we may theorize the ontological status of individual objects.[69] Similarly, interdependence is not a theory divorced from human experience and, in the Buddhist context, is inextricable from the reality of *duḥkha*. Dependent origination points to the causal matrix and the radical relativity of all phenomena, but a discriminating awareness of what to adopt and what to reject in terms of their soteriological efficacy and their contribution to the *duḥkha* of sentient beings is maintained as a crucial point of Buddhist practice. Divorcing interdependence from its embedded context and ignoring the way it is understood to compel compassionate action is inappropriate, and together they indeed can be used to construct a robust, authentic Buddhist environmental ethic.

With this in mind, the proper treatment of the rocks, waters, air, soil, and other abiotic phenomena that make up our natural world can be seen as a precondition for alleviating the *duḥkha* of sentient beings. If the ocean is too acidic, the soil composition inappropriate, or the air filled with too much carbon, then sentient beings will amass greater amounts of gross *duḥkha*. Of course, biotic phenomena that fall outside of the traditional Buddhist understanding of "sentient being" would fall under a similar treatment. If we take interdependence, *duḥkha*, and compassion seriously, then it becomes soteriologically necessary to ascribe relative value to these phenomena and treat them with care. This would be the case with broader holistic ecological concepts as well. A sustainable biosphere, a healthy bioregion, a flourishing land, and stable biodiversity are necessarily ascribed relative value in this Buddhist ethical context due to how their disruption greatly harms the individual sentient beings therein. If these environmental assemblages and their integrity were ignored, then harm would befall sentient beings, and one would not be working toward the alleviation of the *duḥkha* of all sentient beings. I am not the first to suggest this necessity. John Clark makes this point clear in the Madhyamaka context when he writes, "For Nāgārjuna, a being can only be understood adequately as part of a system of relations. On the basis of such a philosophical position, there are good reasons to hold that our compassion for sentient beings must extend outward to the communities of life and the greater ecological wholes of which they are a part."[70] Thus, while the intrinsic valuation of nonsentient nature may be philosophically untenable in Buddhist contexts, and the preservation of a sustainable biosphere for its own sake would be incommensurable with Buddhist philosophy, their relative valuation and a motivation to care for these necessary factors of an environmental ethic are nonetheless present in a Buddhist environmental ethic due to how they form the relative causes and conditions of the *duḥkha* of sentient beings.

Interestingly, if we search Tibetan Buddhist texts, we can see this concern for abiotic phenomena embedded in the Buddhist contemplative tradition itself. For example, Gampopa's[71]

*Jewel Ornament of Liberation*[72] tells practitioners to first practice lovingkindness and compassion "with sentient beings as [their] object" and then practice lovingkindness and compassion "with phenomena as [their] object."[73] From a soteriological standpoint, there would be no reason to practice lovingkindness and compassion toward nonsentient phenomena if they were understood as independent entities because they would fall outside of the purview of Buddhist ethical concern. However, because they are *relatively* valued due to their implication in dependent origination, Gampopa instructs practitioners to extend their practice of compassion to abiotic or nonsentient phenomena. A simple act such as discarding waste in a lake can (fittingly) ripple out to affect the wellbeing of the fish in the water and the critters who rely on the shoreline habitat. It is therefore imperative to give the waste, the water, and the act of discarding the former in the latter ethical consideration. In this way, Gampopa promotes ethical attention to nonsentient phenomena such as rocks and water as an extension of the more classical Buddhist concern for the well-being of all sentient beings. We also can see this connection explicitly made with natural phenomena throughout the Buddhist world such as the *vinaya*[74] admonitions against sprinkling water known to contain living beings on the ground, knowingly destroying seeds and plant life, and digging up dirt, which may disturb beings in the soil.[75] Similarly, we find a concern for the preservation of rocky mountains and glacial waters in Tibet due to the *yul lha* and *klu*[76] that are understood to rely upon these natural phenomena for their homes.[77] Of course, this extension of relative value to the natural world was clearly insufficient to produce a mass historical environmental movement in traditional Buddhist settings, but we can nonetheless see how individual nonsentient phenomena such as water and mountains were given ethical consideration as a consequence of the central Buddhist concern for alleviating the *duḥkha* of sentient beings.

Conversely, what was patently *absent* in the Buddhist tradition before the Buddhist encounter with modernity was a concern for broader ecological concepts such as species, the land, the ecosystem, or the biosphere. Then again, these concerns were also absent from every other religious, philosophical, and ethical tradition before modernity because they are deeply informed by contemporary ecological science. Take, for example, the nine boundaries that Rockstrom et al. have delimited as a "safe operating space for humanity." Each of these nine boundaries, which include climate change, stratospheric ozone depletion, biogeochemical flow, biodiversity loss, and so on, is a factor of a sustainable biosphere and must be tended to in any contemporary environmental ethic. But there is a reason that these aspects of a sustainable biosphere are present in recent work by Holmes Rolston III and Daniel Capper and not in foundational works by Aldo Leopold or J. Baird Callicott: They were quantified in 2009. Thus, these contemporary articulations of environmental ethics reflect this updated understanding of ecological science and incorporate their findings into their philosophy. Similarly, these notions of land, ecosystems, and biosphere can easily be assimilated into a contemporary Buddhist environmental ethic despite them previously being absent. There is nothing in these notions that contradicts Buddhist philosophical principles, and they can in fact help the tradition better understand the causal matrix it is otherwise concerned with. These ecological concepts paint a clearer picture of the precise workings of *pratītyasamutpāda*, which allows Buddhists to more efficiently work toward the alleviation of the *duḥkha* of sentient beings through environmental means. This is not an uncritical equation of ecology with *pratītyasamutpāda* but a recognition of the many ecological processes that constitute the land and the biosphere that are implicated in the matrix of dependent origination like any other phenomenon and therefore must be attended to in Buddhist ethical contexts. And it is in this confluence of *duḥkha*, *pratītyasamutpāda*, and ecological science where we can locate a contemporary Buddhist care for the environment.

*Buddhist Animal Ethics versus Buddhist Environmental Ethics*

Still there might be those who may claim that the centering of sentient beings in my above articulation means that a Buddhist ethic strays from a classical environmental ethic. They might argue that Buddhist principles allow us to engage with an ethic of the more-than-human world only through an animal ethics lens, and that a holistic approach to environmental ethics is at odds with animal ethics. To illustrate this tension, we can think through a story from

Shabkar's life that has been scrutinized by several recent scholars. In his famous autobiography, the Amdo yogi recounts a story of him saving baby birds from a preying eagle and writes:

> When I was living at Tsonying, I noticed an eagle that, each spring day, caught three or four of the thousands of baby waterfowl that couldn't fly yet. The eagle tore out and devoured their hearts while they were still alive. Feeling intense pity, each year during those two spring months, I tried to protect the small waterfowl from the eagle. They soon understood that I was protecting them and would come and gather near me on the shore of the island. Whenever the eagle approached, they cried out miserably.
>
> One day I ran after the eagle wielding a slingshot; when the eagle saw me it faltered and fell into the water. It lay there flapping in the water, exhausted and it began to sink, looking right at me. I felt sorry for it, hauled it out of the water, and put it on the shore. When it had dried a little. I tied the slingshot around its neck and scolded it, saying, "When you're killing little birds, you're quite brave, aren't you? I tapped it several times on its beak and claws with a twig, and just left it there for a while, then freed it. It didn't come back for some time.
>
> One day the eagle came back and caught a fledgling. I rushed after it and when it landed on a boulder, I hit it with a stone from my slingshot, almost killing it. It flew off, leaving the baby bird sprawled on its back. I thought the little bird's heart had already been torn out, but when I picked it up, I saw it had just lost consciousness out of fear. Upon reviving, it looked at me and then scampered back into the water. Protecting them in this manner during those two years, I saved several thousand small birds.[78]

Rachel Pang notes how this wordy account is a case where Shabkar uses narrative to urge readers to treat animals with care and is a prime example of how Shabkar both practiced and advocated for animal ethics.[79] Capper, however, reads this account as a prime example of the limitations of Tibetan Buddhism for constructing an environmental ethic.

Commenting on this story, Capper notes how Shabkar's protection of these fledgling birds "provides a nice window into Buddhist animal-welfare sentiments" but nonetheless "lacks a systematic understanding of the natural world."[80] In his analysis, there is a stark difference between animal ethics and environmental ethics and Shabkar's account falls solely in the former ethical category. He writes that "this story involves sentimental compassions for baby animals but limited compassion for eagles . . . the entities that died for the sake of the fledglings' diet . . . or for the water or minerals that fed those entities."[81] Capper therefore concludes that the "Buddhist ethic of compassion," demonstrated in Shabkar's account, "does not make for a complete, viable environmental ethic" and "is constrained in [its] application to ecosystems."[82]

While Capper does not make this connection himself, his argument fits neatly within a historical debate in Western philosophy regarding the compatibility of animal liberation and environmental ethics. In general, there are two positions taken on whether or not animal ethics and environmental ethics are philosophically compatible (which I will call the compatibility thesis): a positive affirmation that they indeed are consonant philosophies, and a negative argument for their dissonance. At the advent of this debate, the dominant position was the latter. J. Baird Callicott established the initial contours of the debate with his 1980 article "Animal Liberation: A Triangular Affair" and fervently argued that animal liberation and environmental ethics (construed as a Leopoldian land ethic) are fundamentally incompatible. In his words, Callicott seeks to "distinguish sharply environmental ethics from the animal liberation/rights movement both in theory and practical application and to suggest, thereupon, that there is an underrepresented but very important, point of view respecting the problem of the moral status of nonhuman animals."[83] This bifurcation between the ethical approaches lies in how moral considerability is distributed to nonhuman entities differently in each philosophical tradition. Callicott reads the animal liberation approach as amounting to an extension of moral humanism or humane moralism which "has consistently located moral value in individuals and set out certain metaphysical reasons for including some individuals and excluding others."[84] In contrast, his Leopoldian environmental ethics "locates ultimate value in the 'biotic community' and assigns differential moral value to the constitutive individuals relate to that standard."[85] Thus, animal ethics and environmental ethics are incompatible because of their differing modes of valuation. The former prioritizes the wellbeing of individual nonhuman animals whereas the latter prioritizes the integrity of an ecological whole, and these necessarily come into conflict when analyzing issues of overpopulation, invasive species, meat consumption, and so forth. Ethics are therefore a "triangular affair" such that standard anthropocentric ethics, animal ethics, and environmental ethics are considered to be mutually exclusive and at odds with one another. The rejection of the compatibility thesis was furthered in Mark Sagoff's 1984 article "Animal Liberation and Environmental Ethics: Bad Marriage, Quick Divorce" where we find perhaps the strongest denouncement of a possible alliance between animal ethics and environmental ethics. Without equivocation, he writes "environmentalists cannot be animal liberationists" and "animal liberationists cannot be environmentalists."[86]

The first affirmation of the compatibility thesis occurred in Mary Anne Warren's article "The Rights of the Nonhuman World" which directly addressed and responded to Callicott's earlier work. She recognizes the source of incompatibility that Callicott points out, but nonetheless holds that "a harmonious marriage between these two approaches is possible provided that each side is prepared to make certain compromises."[87] She sketches this compromise thusly:

> In brief, the animal liberationists must recognize that although animals do have significant moral rights, these rights are not precisely the same as those of human beings; and that part of the difference is that the rights of animals may sometimes be overridden, for example, for environmental or utilitarian reasons, in situations where it would not be morally acceptable to override human rights for similar reasons. For their part, the environmentalists must recognize that while it may be

acceptable, as a legal or rhetorical tactic, to speak of the rights of trees or mountains, the logical foundations of such rights are quite different from those of the rights of human and other sentient beings.[88]

In Warren's view, animal ethics and environmental ethics are therefore distinct enterprises. However, rather than be seen as incompatible (as Callicott or Sagoff might), Warren argues that they are in fact *complimentary*. She writes:

> Each helps to remedy some of the apparent defects of the other. The animal liberation theory, for instance, does not in itself explain why we ought to protect not only *individual* animals, but also threatened *species* of plants as well as animals. The land ethic, on the other hand, fails to explain why it is wrong to inflict needless suffering or death even upon domestic animals, which may play little or no role in the maintenance of natural ecosystems, or only a negative role.[89]

In this case, while animal ethics may not be commensurate with environmental ethics they are not only compatible but are necessary interlocutors. Both have gaps in their theory and their practice which the other can meaningfully address. For this reason, Warren concludes that "only by *combining* the environmentalist and animal rights perspectives can we take account of the full range of moral considerations which ought to guide our interactions with the nonhuman world."[90]

In an interesting turn of events, Callicott was swayed by Warren's arguments and amended his position in an article titled "Animal Liberation and Environmental Ethics: Back Together Again." He affirms that "Warren recommends . . . a wholly reasonable ethical eclecticism" before articulating his own compatibility thesis. In Callicott's later piece, he recognizes that while "animal welfare ethicists and environmental ethicists have overlapping concerns,"[91] if we wish to truly establish a "lasting alliance" between these two ethical trajectories then we "require the development of a moral theory that embraces both programs and that provides a framework for the adjudication of the very real conflicts between human welfare, animal welfare, and ecological integrity."[92] To this end, he argues that Mary Midgely's conception of an animal ethic based on social relations with nonhuman animals and Leopold's land ethic "share a common, fundamentally Humean understanding of ethics as grounded in altruistic feelings."[93] He writes that both animal liberation and environmental ethics "share a common ethical bridge between the human and non-human domains in the concept of community" and that by combining Midgely's notion of mixed community with Leopold's notion of the biotic community we can arrive at a holistic "metahuman moral community" which can serve as "the basis of a unified animal-environmental ethical theory."[94]

If we were to fit Capper into this debate, it is clear that he would find company in Mark Sagoff and in early J. Baird Callicott. His evaluation of Shabkar's encounter with the fledglings makes clear that he places Buddhism squarely within the realm of animal liberation and, consequently, *at odds* with environmental ethics. His critique of has two main points: that Buddhism sponsors compassionate action for animals but not the environment, and that Buddhism cannot attend to the complexities of ecosystems with many preying individuals. Rephrased in the language of the animal liberation and environmental ethics debate, Capper argues that Buddhism is to be considered an animal ethic instead of an environmental ethic and that there is a fundamental conflict between its emphasis on individual beings' welfare and notions of collective wellbeing like the land ethic or a sustainable biosphere.

Given my above refutation of Capper's critique of Buddhist environmentalism, it may not come as a surprise that I again disagree with Capper on the characterization of Buddhist ethics as solely animal ethics and his implicit rejection of the compatibility thesis. In turn, one might think that I therefore agree with Mary Anne Warren and the later Callicott and affirm the compatibility thesis in the same way that they do. While I do indeed see animal ethics and environmental ethics as being compatible, I do so in a different way than Warren and Callicott posit. Warren and Callicott argue that the separate ethical enterprises of animal liberation and environmental ethics are complimentary, but, if we begin from Buddhist ethical principles, I argue that animal and environmental ethics are in fact the *same*.

There is precedent for this kind of position in the Western philosophical tradition. In an article titled "Animal Ethics are Environmental Ethics," Dale Jamieson rejects the bifurcation between the fields and argues that, contrary to Callicott, Sagoff, and (in my view) Capper, animal liberation necessarily results in a concern for the nonsentient environment. Central to his argument is that "a deep green ethic does not require strange views about value" such as the value of collectives like species, ecosystems, and mineral formations having "mind-independent" or "inherent" value.[95] Instead, Jamieson argues that "an animal liberationist ethic, rooted in traditional views of value and obligation, can take nonsentient nature seriously."[96] To do so, he critiques one of the fundamental claims of normative environmental ethics, writing "were there no sentient beings there would be no values but it doesn't follow from this that only sentient beings are valuable."[97] In Jamieson's ethic, there is a necessary distinction between primary and derivative value. He writes that "creatures who can suffer, take pleasure in their experiences, and whose lives go better or worse from their own point of view are of primary value," and that nonsentient factors (like those found in the environment) which can affect this primary value must also have a derivative value.[98] Importantly, however, Jamieson notes that "the distinction between primary and derivative value is not a distinction in degree of value, but rather in the ways different entities can be valuable,"[99] and writes that "although nonsentient entities are not of primary value, their value can be very great and urgent," and can even "trump the value of sentient entities."[100] As a result of this method of valuation, Jamieson argues that animal liberation ethicists and environmental ethicists hold many of the same normative views because of how "many of our most important issues involve serious threats to both humans and animals as well as to the nonsentient environment; because animal liberationists can value nature as a home for sentient beings; and because animal liberationists can embrace environmental values as intensely as environmental ethicists, though they see them as derivative rather than primary values."[101] There is therefore a theoretical convergence as well as "convergence at the practical and political level" such that, in his formulation, animal ethics should be read *as* environmental ethics.

When *duḥkha* is understood in the context of *pratītyasamut-pāda*, we can begin to see how a Buddhist animal ethic necessitates a concern for nonsentient nature in Buddhist settings. If Buddhist philosophy asserted that phenomena are independent of one another, then one might be able to address *duḥkha* as an isolated experience of sentient beings and ignore nonsentient phenomena altogether. But this is of course not the case. Since all phenomena arise in dependence upon one another, the ecological stability of the nonsentient river affects the fish, waterfowl, and land mammals that rely on its cleanliness for food, habitat, and hydration. This means that nonsentient nature *must* be valued because of how it supports the flourishing or contributes to the *duḥkha* of sentient beings. One must care for the river because if it gets polluted or becomes too acidic, this will create more *duḥkha* in sentient beings, and this extension of value would apply to all nonsentient phenomena in both wild and domestic spaces.

To use the language of Jamieson, a derivative value for the nonsentient environment can quite easily emerge out of the primary value of sentient beings. *Duḥkha* forms the basis for Tibetan Buddhism's primary valuation of sentient beings, but *pratītyasamutpāda* necessitates a derivative valuation of nonsentient nature. Jamieson writes that "were there no sentient beings there would be no values but it doesn't follow from this that only sentient beings are valuable," and this is precisely the Buddhist approach to an ethic of the more-than-human world. To briefly restate this position, if all sentient beings were free of *duḥkha* and left *saṃsāra*[102] altogether, then it would not matter what happens to lakes, mountains, or soils. These nonsentient features of the environment would no longer hold any bearing on the *duḥkha* of sentient beings and would therefore no longer possess derivative value. However, if even a single sentient being is living on Earth, then a Tibetan Buddhist practitioner would be obliged to care for the nonsentient environmental supports of that being's flourishing.


## The Challenge of Predation to Eco-Buddhism

Capper's critique, however, contains an important third point: that there is a fundamental conflict between its emphasis on individual beings' welfare and notions of collective well-being like the land ethic or a sustainable biosphere and that Buddhism is incapable of addressing this conflict. As he writes, "The compassionate concern for animals that sponsors Buddhist actions for animal welfare, however, also imposes a limit on the tradition in terms of supporting a sustainable biosphere, given that this attitude cannot, as it is, result in a viable environmental ethic that attends to the complexities of ecosystems with many preying individuals."[103] In the realm of animal and environmental ethics, this is called the "problem of predation" and has been taken up by many esteemed theorists who arrive at a diversity of positions. I would respond to this claim by stating that it is not correct to say that Buddhism *cannot* address the problem of predation in a systematic, universal way but rather that it *will not*. Thinking through this problem will perhaps allow us to begin to see the novelty of the Buddhist approach to the more-than-human world that we will turn to in the following chapter.

As we will see, I forward Buddhist ethics as a nonabsolutist enterprise. Rather than rely on a single set of rules for addressing each ethical dilemma as a Kantian or utilitarian ethicist might do, the Buddhist ethical tradition offers a particularist approach to ethical development and ethical action. Many scholars have articulated this nonabsolutism from a number of angles, including Peter Harvey's gradualism,[104] Barbra Clayton's ethical contextualism,[105] William Edelglass's moral pluralism,[106] or my defense of Garfield's moral phenomenology in the next chapter. Regardless, what separates these nonabsolutist Buddhist approaches from more universalist Western approaches to ethical decision making is the Buddhist tradition's emphasis on *upāya* (skillful means). *Upāya* posits that the *bodhisattva* on the mission to liberate all sentient beings from all *duḥkha* is permitted to do even what is not ordinarily allowed if doing so will result in the alleviation of *duḥkha*.

Applied to the context of animal liberation and environmental ethics, this idea would allow the Tibetan Buddhist practitioner to respond to an issue such as overpopulation or invasive species with nuance. To refrain from taking life is the first of the Buddhist precepts, but eradicating an invasive vine or killing several deer so that hundreds do not starve may be appropriate in certain situations. In other situations, they may not be. To give a milder example, forcibly relocating an invasive mammal to its native ecosystem would surely cause a lot of *duḥkha* in its capture, transport, and readjustment to its new surroundings, but causing that *duḥkha* may be necessary to preserve ecosystem dynamics, which, if disrupted, would cause great amounts of *duḥkha* for great amounts of beings. Speaking abstractly about universal rules for either the problem of predation or broader tensions between animal and environmental ethics "wrenches an ethical problem out of its embedded context,"[107] to borrow the language of ecofeminist Marti Kheel, and this abstraction ignores the myriad emotional relationships, communities, and relational exchanges between beings that can contribute to both the exacerbation or alleviation of *duḥkha*. If *duḥkha* was taken as an individualized phenomenon, then perhaps we might arrive at some universal principles to apply to every situation, but it's not. *Duḥkha* is an interdependent phenomenon, and we therefore need to approach ethical situations skillfully, with *upāya*, from this Tibetan Buddhist perspective. Jamieson writes that "although nonsentient entities are not of primary value, their value can be very great and urgent" and can even "trump the value of sentient entities."[108] In the Tibetan Buddhist context, this contention appears to hold quite well. Derivatively valued entities such as watersheds, coral reefs, and rainforest ecologies that affect the well-being of innumerable beings may hold more ethical value than the *duḥkha* of a single banana slug, ant colony, or grey squirrel and therefore may hold more gravity in our decision making. But these decisions would have to be made according to the social, ecological, and material contexts of the given situation.

To return to the story of Shabkar's protection of the fledglings on which Capper builds his critique, it is completely reasonable to read Shabkar's scolding of the eagle and protection of the baby birds as being appropriate in that particular ethical situation. Perhaps in other situations, it may be inappropriate to intervene in animal predation. In a more extreme case, there are situations where one could imagine the introduction of predator species to a new environment, or the active culling of invasive species may be justifiable through a Buddhist environmental lens. To pass judgement on such situations in an abstract, universalist manner is to impose standards on Buddhist ethics that it may not recognize as valid. Thus, while the problem of predation may challenge a

Buddhist environmental ethic (as it does Western environmental ethics), it certainly does not prevent an effective and authentic Buddhist environmental ethic from being articulated.

In fact, the particularist approach of a contemplative Buddhist environmental ethic may offer novel insights into the problem of predation that generally has been approached in absolutist terms. The rule-based and character-based articulations of Buddhist environmental ethics that we quickly parsed at the beginning of this chapter may lead to definitive answers on whether or not it is appropriate to intervene in the predator-prey relationship, but a contemplative approach would necessarily attend to these situations in a context-specific matter. Likewise, a Buddhist approach to our more-than-human world may offer novel interventions into other questions that arise in animal and environmental ethics. Regardless, it is clear that the environment must be included in Tibetan Buddhism's ethical purview, even if we rightly understand it to be centered on sentience. When *duḥkha* and *pratītyasamutpāda* are taken together with our contemporary understanding of ecological systems, the environment has a major role to play in the well-being of sentient beings and therefore has immense derivative value. But, as I argued at the beginning of this chapter, simply attending to values is not enough. A full environmental ethic should tell us how to go about our lives as we move through our more-than-human world and should be grounded in some kind of normative ethical theory. Thus, to fully arrive at a contemplative approach to Buddhist environmental ethics, we must begin by articulating a normative Buddhist ethic on its own terms — and it is to this articulation of Buddhist ethics as a moral phenomenology that we now turn.

2

# Moral Phenomenology

## A Theory of Buddhist Ethics

### Past Classifications of Buddhist Ethics

To properly articulate a contemplative Buddhist environmental ethic, we need to first understand what a general Buddhist ethic looks like, and much work has been done over the last several decades to classify the tradition's ethical system in various ways. Some such as Damien Keown, Charles Fink, and James Whitehill see Buddhist ethics as a kind of virtue ethic. In Keown's view, Buddhist ethics parallel those of Aristotle in four distinct ways: (1) the similarities between *eudaemonia* and *nirvāṇa;*[1] (2) psychology in Buddhist and Aristotelian thought; (3) intention and will; and (4) each tradition's desire for "the good." He writes, "Both Aristotle and the Buddha were alike in eschewing metaphysical notions and instead directing their attention to the practical and empirical. The central concern of both is with the telos of human nature and the means of attaining it."[2] Thus, for these scholars, characterizing Buddhist ethics as a virtue ethic allows us to best understand the tradition.

Charles Goodman favors a different kind of interpretation: that of consequentialism. Goodman explores sources across the Indo-Tibetan Buddhist landscape and looks at three distinct periods of ethical thought: the Theravāda, the Mahāyāna before Śantideva,[3] and the Mahāyāna after Śantideva. He reads the Theravāda and

47

the Mahāyāna before Śāntideva (for which he uses Asaṅga[4] as an exemplar) as a rule-consequentialist ethic wherein the practitioner follows a prescribed set of rules because these rules produce the best consequences when most people follow them. Contrastingly, he analyzes the ethical style of Śāntideva and those who come after him as act consequentialist, wherein practitioners approach each situation on their own terms and act in a way that maximizes the good (in this case the development of compassion and alleviation of *duḥkha*). He is largely alone in his interpretation, but much of the evidence he provides is solid and intriguing, and his interpretation is an important counterpoint to the classification of Buddhist ethics as a virtue ethic.

These interpretations are useful and respectively highlight important aspects of the Buddhist approach to ethics. However, scholars have also begun to take up a compelling argument that Buddhist ethics do not actually resemble *any* form of Western ethics. As Peter Harvey writes: "Overall, the rich field of Buddhist ethics would be narrowed by wholly collapsing it into any single one of the Kantian, Aristotelian or Utilitarian models, though Buddhism agrees with each in respectively acknowledging the importance of (i) a good motivating will, (ii) cultivation of character, and (iii) the reduction of suffering in others and oneself."[5] Barbra Clayton also makes this claim toward the end of her book *Moral Theory in Śāntideva's Śikṣāsamuccaya*. Overall, she views Śāntideva's work (and the Mahāyāna tradition more broadly) as similar to a virtue ethic but concedes that the presence of *upāya* sufficiently complicates things to the point where no consistent characterization can be found. She weighs her options thusly: "To call [Śāntideva's] morality a situation ethic, as Keown suggests as a possibility, would not adequately convey the central importance of the gradual cultivation of certain character qualities in his thinking. Equally, to call it an Aristotelian-type virtue ethic would not capture the fact that there is a 'utilitarian aspect' to this morality, such that a maximizing principle seems to be in effect for the bodhisattva in certain cases, and in association with the concept of karmic fruitfulness."[6] Fittingly, after working through these contrasting positions, her discussion turns to pondering the possibility of a single, homogenous approach to Buddhist ethics. She poses and tentatively answers the following question: "Do the results of this research support the notion, reflected for example in Keown's work but arguably throughout the literature on Buddhist ethics, that Buddhist ethics as a whole can be treated homogeneously? At first glance, it would appear not."[7] However, if there is not a possibility of a homogenous approach to Buddhist ethics, then we are left with a particularist approach wherein different parts of Buddhism are necessarily treated differently, and the tradition itself is bereft of a consistent whole. Clayton brings up this dilemma in her conclusion, writing, "The danger involved with the particularist approach as I see it is thus to prematurely end the investigative work, by assuming from the outset that because moral views are always complex that no consistency can be found, and is therefore not worth looking for."[8] This danger is a real one and would limit not only scholarly engagement with Buddhist ethics but also the strength of Buddhism's voice in global philosophy and politics. Thankfully, rather than abandon this exercise completely, scholars have begun to formulate how a Buddhist approach to ethics might look if we were to begin not from a Western ethical standpoint, but from the tradition itself.

## Jay Garfield's Moral Phenomenology

If we begin from Buddhist principles to articulate a uniquely Buddhist ethical system, we arrive at what has been termed a *moral phenomenology*. This Buddhist moral phenomenological approach to ethics has been gestured to by Buddhist teachers across traditions, but its explicit identification did not come until Jay Garfield's 2010 article "What Is It Like to Be a Bodhisattva?" In this article, Garfield looks at Śāntideva's *Bodhicaryāvatāra*[9] to see how phenomenology and morality collide in this text. Five years later, Garfield would write *Engaging Buddhism: Why It Matters to Philosophy*, wherein he dedicates a chapter to looking at how this phenomenology-centered ethics plays out not only in the writings of Śāntideva but also across various Buddhist traditions. Together, these two works form the core of the case for Buddhist moral phenomenology and can be used to tease out this ethical system.

To first give some background, Garfield comes to moral phenomenology through his observation that there is a distinct quality to Buddhist writings on morality that eludes perfect Western categorizations. In the case of the *Bodhicaryāvatāra*, he writes, "Śāntideva's understanding of how to lead such a life is distinctive, and is very different from accounts of the moral or the exemplary life familiar in the Western tradition."[10] This sentiment also carries over to a more general reading of Buddhist ethics, as evident in Garfield's introductory statement: "In Buddhist philosophical and religious literature we find many texts that address moral topics, and a great deal of attention devoted to account of virtuous and vicious actions, states of character and lives. However, we find little direct attention to the articulation of states of principles that determine which actions, states of character or motives are virtuous or vicious, and no articulation of sets of obligations or rights."[11] Thus, overall, Garfield contends that "Buddhist moral theorists see ethics as concerned not primarily with actions, their consequences, obligations, sentiments or human happiness, but rather with the nature of our experience."[12] His argument for a moral phenomenological approach to Buddhist ethics emerges from a reluctance to subsume Buddhist ethics under a Western ethical tradition. Instead, Buddhist ethics should be considered "a moral phenomenology concerned with the transformation of our experience of the world, and hence our overall comportment to it."[13]

According to Garfield, moral phenomenology is a ubiquitous mode of ethics across all Buddhist traditions past and present. In the Theravāda tradition, he locates moral phenomenology in the *brahmavihārās* (Four Immeasurables)[14] and their attention to how particular experiences mediate interpersonal relationships.[15] In terms of *karuṇā*,[16] he writes that adopting a compassionate attitude is "more than an act of recognition; it is also to adopt a mode of comportment to the world, a mode in which the welfare and suffering of others is that which is ascertained in perception, in which sentient beings are perceived intentionally *as suffering*, and in which the actions that are readied in the perceptual cycle are actions designed to alleviate suffering."[17] Ultimately, he argues that compassion is "tied directly to the phenomenology of perception as well as to the ideology of the four noble truths and of dependent origination."[18] There are a couple of things to unpack in this presentation that are important to understanding the relationships among view, perception, and action. On this account, compassion arises not only from a particular *kind* of perception but a particular *object* of perception. The direct perceptual experience of the Four Noble Truths, *duḥkha*, *samudaya*, *nirodha*, and *marga*, causes the feeling of compassion from the experiential recognition of *duḥkha*[19] in oneself and in others and the possibility of its cessation. Similarly, a direct perceptual experience of *pratītyasamutpāda* orients an individual toward *action* because they can directly see how particular actions have particular consequences, all of which are implicated in the *duḥkha* of self and other. For these perceptual encounters to truly install a comportment of compassion in an individual, they cannot be one-off events but a consistent lens through which one views the world (adopted, say, through contemplative practice).

A similar sentiment carries over to the other *brahmavihārās* as well. Garfield characterizes *mettā*[20] as "an attitude of spontaneous positive emotion and well-wising toward others," which "focuses intentionally and cognitively not specifically on the suffering of others, but on positively promoting their welfare."[21] This complements compassion that is concerned with the alleviation of negative states rather than the promotion of positive ones. Nonetheless, Garfield states that, like compassion, "[lovingkindness] is not a reflective attitude, but a perceptual set."[22] This perceptual reading can be found with the third *brahmavihārā* as well. *Muditā*, or sympathetic joy, is the unfabricated happiness in the well-being of others and is commonly seen as the antithesis of envy or jealousy. In Garfield's formulation, sympathetic joy is again "not simply a post-perceptual cognitive judgment and appraisal, but part of a perceptual set, a way of being embedded in the world."[23] And finally, Garfield sees equanimity (*upekṣā*)[24] as again being something that concerns itself primarily with a perceptual engagement with the world. He states that equanimity is the process in which "we dislodge the sense that the world revolves around us or even the sense that the events in our immediate environment resolve around us" which, in turn, "allows us to care about what happens per se, not about its impact on *us*."[25] And like the other *brahmavihārās*, Garfield calls equanimity "perceptual sets, ways of experiencing and taking up with the world."[26] Thus, these qualities are framed as *perceptual modes* by Garfield such that the focus of ethics is on an individual's *experience* of the world rather than their actions per se. By taking up these lenses, one's actions will *spontaneously* accord with these ethical ideals such that no moral calculus is necessary.

Garfield also identifies a similar approach in Mahāyāna Buddhism. He sees the Mahāyāna ethical tradition as a drive for "a universal concern for the enlightened welfare of all sentient beings and to the cultivation of states of character that reflect this awareness and commitment."[27] While the latter half of this definition might lead one to believe that Mahāyāna ethics are indeed virtue ethics, the final portion needs be emphasized to understand Garfield's position. Yes, the cultivation of states of character are recognized as a component of this ethical framework, but these states of character are *reflections of a particular awareness* or *perceptual mode*. Thus, he brings Mahāyāna ethics back to a focus on moral phenomenology. And like his presentation of moral phenomenology in the Theravāda tradition, Mahāyāna ethics rests on the perceptual cultivation of *karuṇā* as the "central moral value and the model of the bodhisattvas caring."[28] Where this cultivation eludes a virtue ethic interpretation, however, is in the mode of cultivation. One does not directly cultivate an attitude of care. Rather, it is a by-product of an experiential appreciation of *pratītyasamutpāda*. This is absolutely key to understanding Buddhist moral phenomenology both theoretically and practically. Garfield lays out this relationship thusly:

> Care, grounded in the awareness of our joint participation in global life, hence, from the Mahayana perspective, is the wellspring of the motivation for the development of all perfections, and the most reliable motivation for morally decent actions. Care is also, on this view, the direct result of a genuine appreciation of the emptiness and interdependence of all sentient beings. Once one sees oneself as nonsubstantial and existing only in interdependence, and once one sees that the happiness and suffering of all sentient beings is entirely causally conditioned, the only rational attitude one can adopt to others is a caring and careful one.[29]

Important to this presentation is how suffering is bad per se regardless of *whose* it is and that, in this tradition, "to fail to take another's suffering seriously as a motivation for action is itself a form of suffering and is irrational."[30] This is because the *duḥkha* one experiences is bound up with the *duḥkha* of others and, likewise, one's own liberation is contingent upon the liberation of all other beings.

## *Bodhicitta*: The Goal of Moral Phenomenology

For Garfield, no other work gets this point across more clearly than Śāntideva's *Bodhicaryāvatāra* and its emphasis on the cultivation of *bodhicitta*. *Bodhicitta* is at the heart of both the *Bodhicaryāvatāra* and the Mahāyāna path in general. This can clearly be seen in the words of Chatral Sangye Dorje:[31] "The enlightened wish to benefit others and the *bodhicitta* of application are essential because they are at the root of the Mahāyāna."[32] *Bodhicitta* is also one of the Sanskrit terms typically left untranslated in English scholarship due to its semantic variability. For example, Francis Brassard has shown how *bodhicitta* can refer to a desire for enlightenment, an object of concentration, a cultivation of awareness, an aspect of renunciation, an aspect of conversion, and an aspect of contemplation.[33] Nonetheless, after dedicating an entire book to parsing these various aspects of the term, he ultimately concludes that "the best translation I can . . . imagine for *bodhicitta* is *bodhicitta*."[34]

Despite this alleged untranslatability, we can nonetheless define the term operationally. Khunu Lama Tenzin Gyaltsen,[35] who himself transmitted the *Bodhicaryāvatāra* to His Holiness the Dalai Lama, gives the following definition:

> Supreme bodhicitta is desire to
> clear every fault from each and every sentient being
> and to produce infinite good qualities in each of them.
> Even among the wondrous this is wondrous![36]

Here, we can see the *intentional* or *perceptual* character of Buddhist ethics even in this classical definition. *Bodhicitta* in this brief account involves the wish to perfect other beings—a wish that emerges from a deep perceptual realization of *pratītyasamutpāda* or *śūnyatā*. Moreover, a distinction is made in Tibetan settings between *bodhicitta in aspiration* and *bodhicitta in application*.[37] The former is a perceptual or intentional set in which one generates the *wish* for the removal of flaws and development of good qualities in others. Dilgo Khyentse Rinpoche calls it "compassion directed impartially toward all sentient beings, without discriminating between those who are friends and those who are enemies."[38] In order to realize this goal, it is necessary to become fully liberated oneself, therefore aspirational *bodhicitta* also is the wish to achieve complete awakening for oneself so that one can subsequently help others do the same. *Bodhicitta* in application is, curiously enough, often defined as the *pāramitās*. In *Words of My Perfect Teacher*, Patrul Rinpoche separates these into two categories: "Generosity, discipline, patience, diligence, and meditative concentration are the first five *pāramitās* which are of the aspect of the practice of skillful means. Wisdom is the sixth *pāramitā* and concerns the accumulation of primordial wisdom."[39] And yet, these must be practiced concurrently and cannot be separated, as is evident in Dilgo Khyentse Rinpoche's statement: "These two bodhicittas, the skillful means of compassion and the wisdom of voidness, should never be separated. They are like a bird's two wings, both of which are necessary for it to fly; you cannot achieve enlightenment through compassion alone, nor through the realization of voidness by itself."[40] By this account, even the action-oriented virtues of generosity, patience, and so forth are *necessarily* tied to a perceptual experience of emptiness. Thus, when analyzing the *pāramitās* in light of the Tibetan emphasis on *bodhicitta,* they can best be seen as the consequences of a particular perceptual mode and a particular way of experiencing both oneself and one's relationship to the entire world of sentient beings.

This accords well with Garfield's employment of the term. He writes: "Bodhicitta is a complex psychological phenomenon. It is a standing motivational state with conative and affective dimensions. It centrally involves an altruistic aspiration, grounded in compassion, to cultivate oneself as a moral agent for the benefit of all beings."[41] Moreover, this motivational state has associated obligations. It "demands the development of skills in moral perception, moral responsiveness, traits of character, insight into the nature of reality so deep that it transforms our way of seeing ourselves and others, and what we would call practical wisdom."[42] Garfield finds evidence for this position as he parses Śāntideva's text. At the start of the *Bodhicaryāvatarā*, "Śāntideva begins by considering how, having developed aspirational bodhicitta, one cares for and nurtures the attitude; he then turns to how one develops the concentration required to maintain introspective awareness of one's own motivational and affective states."[43] However, toward the end of the text, we see a more poignant case for *bodhicitta* being a form of moral phenomenology. Garfield writes,

> The final chapters of the text address the role of meditation in stabilizing the qualities and ways of seeing cultivated earlier, and finally the importance of a particular kind of wisdom as the foundation of the engaged bodhicitta that is the foundation of awakened life—that is, the ability to see all phenomena—including oneself, that to which one is intimately related, and other moral agents—as empty of inherent existence, as interdependent and as impermanent. For Śāntideva, the culmination of ethical practice is a cognitively rich perceptual skill—a new way of experiencing oneself in the world.[44]

Thus, *bodhicitta* has not only conative and affective dimensions but also a *perceptual* or *experiential* dimension, and the cultivation of *bodhicitta* involves reworking one's *default perceptual mode* to orient it toward seeing oneself and all phenomena as interdependent, impermanent, and ultimately empty of intrinsic existence. The close relationship between this cognitively rich perceptual mode and the affective and conative states it can engender is what makes moral phenomenology unique among ethical theories.

## A Working Definition of Moral Phenomenology

Moral phenomenology is therefore an ethical theory centered on the *experience* of an individual where *perception* and *affect* are the loci of moral development. It rests on the assertion that action stems from an individual's experience of the world and that to change one's experience of the world is to change one's behavior. It entails a radical change of an individual's moral behavior by going directly to the root of *experience* rather than refining one's ability to conduct a moral calculus or developing secondary qualities that themselves emerge from the grounds of experience. As such, moral phenomenology primes actors to respond *spontaneously* to situations as they present themselves in a manner which accords with their broader realization of their situatedness in myriad relationships, communities, ecosystems, and so forth.

Key to this kind of ethical theory is what we might call a "default perceptual mode." This is the lens through which we see the world and involves both our bare sense experience and, more importantly, the way we label and process that sense data through our acquired conceptual frameworks. It is the way in which we experience the world as it happens, in the present, without reflection. And while it certainly involves concepts, these concepts and their associated affective states are instantly applied as indivisible from the sensory experience itself. Important to my employment of this term is how default perceptual modes are *fluid* in that they are not biologically determined but adapt to the conceptual contexts an individual develops in. These default perceptual modes can also be influenced throughout one's life and in dependence upon the conceptual frameworks one encounters and subscribes to.

This is a key idea in the Buddhist tradition (though not explicitly referenced) and is essential to its project of transforming the *duḥkha*-pervaded experience of an ordinary being to a liberated experience of a buddha. In Tibetan Buddhism, the fundamental cause of *duḥkha* is *avidyā*[45] (ignorance, misapprehension, or not properly seeing). It is our misapprehension of ourselves and of phenomena writ large that leads us to cling to them as permanent, independent entities, and it is this clinging that causes *duḥkha*. This *avidyā* characterizes the way in which ordinary sentient beings (i.e., those who have not progressed on the Buddhist path) perceive the world. We feel as though we have a self, and we interact with phenomena as though they are independent entities. However, under analysis, no self is to be found among the *skandhas* that make us up,[46] and phenomena are found to have no substantial, independent essence. Therefore, the solution to *duḥkha* in many schools of Tibetan Buddhism is to correct this fundamental misapprehension of self and of phenomena. Such an approach involves installing a particular *ontological view* (in this case, *anātman* or *śūnyatā*) as one's default perceptual mode through contemplative practice, overriding the earlier default perceptual mode that led to undesired outcomes. As a result, an intimate relationship between ontology and ethics becomes apparent. Similarly, a moral phenomenological approach to ethics takes *avidyā* as the root of unwholesome actions and seeks to refine an individual's ethics through a reorientation of their default perceptual mode via the introduction of different ontological positions. As such, there is also a similarly intimate relationship between ontology and ethics to the point where the experiential realization of particular ontological positions is *itself* ethical.

## Daniel Aitken's Account of Moral Experience and Transformation

The first academic work to expand on Garfield's moral phenomenology was Daniel Aitken's 2017 PhD dissertation titled "Experience and Morality: Buddhist Ethics as Moral Phenomenology." The dissertation reads as a detailed unpacking of Garfield's work in its assessment and dismissal of virtue ethics and consequentialism, but it includes two key additions to moral phenomenological theory: (1) an account of perception and its role in the ethical project of moral phenomenology and (2) a decisive identification of the moral problem and its solution in a moral phenomenological framework. These two points fill out Garfield's work and take it from the realm of speculative interpretation to formal ethical theory with clear problems, methods, mechanisms of action, and results.

The first of these, an account of perception, is integral to the moral phenomenological project. Moral phenomenology is directed at a transformed one's perception or experience of the world, so a precise understanding of perception and its relationship to ethics is an asset to moral phenomenological theory. Central to Aitken's discussion is how perception is "not a passive process" but is instead "always accompanied by other mental activity, which makes it a part of an active interpretive process."[47] This somewhat contrasts Western notions of perception wherein the object perceived presents itself to our senses as raw data. In the Buddhist context, "perception is always accompanied by other mental activities that shape the context of our experience."[48] He grounds this claim in Asaṅga's *Abdhidharmasamuccaya* and its classification of mental actions. The first of these groupings are the "Five Constantly Operative Mental Processes"[49] that accompany each mental event and are hence integral to all accounts of perception. They are (1) feeling,[50] (2) ascertainment,[51] (3) intention,[52] (4) contact,[53] and (5) attention.[54] Together, these five factors form the basis of all experience and are therefore the grounds from which action stems. These mental factors are therefore also the realm in which moral phenomenology operates. Aitken writes, "For these Buddhist psychologists, these five mental activities are essential properties of awareness, and without all five, experience would be incomplete. . . . An appreciation of how contact, feeling, ascertainment, intention, and attention operate to create our experience of the world reveals how the way we take up the world is central to Buddhist ethical practice."[55] He also provides a rough schema for how these mental factors operate in the Buddhist tradition:

> The function of contact is not simply to provide the impetus for bare sensory perception, but to provide the ground for feeling. Feeling gives experience an affective dimension. Every moment of experience is colored as pleasant, neutral, or unpleasant, which gives rise to the most basic form of psychological motivations described in Buddhist texts as the movement of the mind to or away from objects. That we are attracted to some things and repulsed by other things has obvious implications for Buddhist action theory and ethics. These feelings are not simply reactions to pre-existing characteristics; they help form and are formed by ascertainment. Ascertainment, the way we think about objects, involves a process of interpretation and classification. The way we think about objects and the way we feel about the contents of our experience affects where we place our intention and attention.[56]

Thus, because of these factors that are involved in each moment of perception, he claims that our perceptual engagement with the world is charged with moral significance.

If we return to Garfield's presentation, we can recall his placement of *bodhicitta* at the apex of the moral phenomenological system and his definition of *bodhicitta* as "a standing motivational state with conative and affective dimensions" that "centrally involves an altruistic aspiration, grounded in compassion, to cultivate oneself as a moral agent for the benefit of all beings."[57] Thus, it may seem that the conation of intention and the affect of feeling are viable candidates for moral phenomenology. But is this the case? In Garfield's view, which he constructs from the views of a plurality of Mahāyāna thinkers, compassion is "a direct result of a genuine appreciation of the essencelessness and interdependence of all sentient beings."[58] In other words, this conative and affective mode emerges from a particular ontological view. It emerges from the way one *directly understands, labels, conceptualizes,* or *frames* one's perceptual experience. Thus, while we may certainly make ethical progress by attending to the perceptual processes of intention and feeling, the crux of moral phenomenological transformation lies elsewhere: in ascertainment.

What Aitken translates as "ascertainment" is the Tibetan term *'du shes*, which, of course, can be translated a number of ways. Perhaps its most common English translation is "discrimination," but it also can be used to refer to "conception," "apprehension," "consideration," "discernment," "recognition," and "perception." Each of these describes a particular kind of perception in which things are set apart, labeled, and understood as discrete entities with particular characteristics. *'Du shes* is the faculty that allows us to see the world in particular ways and is the means through which we arrive at the aforementioned "genuine appreciation of the essencelessness and interdependence of all sentient beings."[59] Therefore, I claim that it is in our ascertainment or discrimination that we find the ability to enact a moral phenomenology. Through changing the structure of our discriminating awareness, we change our core experience of ourselves and all phenomena. Through changing our ascertainment, we change our conative and affective approaches to the world and, hence, change our entire ethical comportment. Ascertainment is inextricable from contact, attention, feeling, and intention, and changing the way we discriminate between or conceptualize phenomena affects our entire mode of experience. Therefore, I suggest it is in discrimination or ascertainment that we find the locus for moral phenomenological transformation.

While Aitken does not single out ascertainment in his presentation of moral phenomenology, the way he understands the fundamental ethical problem that moral phenomenology addresses lends itself to this conclusion. He grounds his argument for the accuracy of a moral phenomenological interpretation in Āryadeva's[60] *Four Hundred Verses*[61] in which, as Aitken writes, "Āryadeva maintains that confusion pervades vice, and, conversely, a correct view undermines vice and accords with virtue."[62] Thus, immorality is rooted in a mistaken perception of reality. To be more precise, Aitken follows Āryadeva in claiming that our perception of phenomena as "permanent, pure, pleasurable, and essentially existent" is the cause of vices "such as fear, attachment, desire, and pride."[63] These four mistaken characteristics are how phenomena appear to ordinary individuals, but they are the exact opposite of how phenomena actually *exist*, according to the Buddha. They are the inverse of the "marks of existence," a foundational Buddhist concept that is primarily found in Maitreya's *The Foundation for Yoga Practitioners* in the Tibetan tradition. This text states that all phenomena are marked by (1) impermanence; (2) a lack of an independent, pure Self; (3) *duḥkha* or dissatisfaction; and (4) being empty of an independent essence.[64] Thus, immorality emerges from a misperception or *mistaken ascertainment* of reality and the feelings of fear, desire, and so forth that accompany it.

It is perhaps then unsurprising that the solution to this problem is a reorientation of one's perception or "the elimination of unhealthy mental states through resolving the confusion that pervades them."[65] As Aitken writes, "Since confusion is the mental state that pervades and fosters vice, both the epistemological and moral antidote is wisdom, accurate metaphysical knowledge."[66] Rather than perceive phenomena as permanent, pleasurable, and essentially existent, seeing them as impermanent, suffused with *duḥkha*, and empty of inherent existence will guard against desire, fear, anger, and other negative emotions that lend themselves to immoral behavior. Interestingly, on top of these obvious antidotes, Āryadeva also points to dependent arising as a view that overcomes mistaken perception in his text *Four Hundred Verses*, which states,

Just as touch exists in the skin,
delusion exists in all mental states;
therefore, by overcoming delusion,
all afflictive emotions are also overcome.
If one perceives interdependent origination,
delusion will not arise.
Therefore, through all the diligence applied to this,
that discourse should be explained as it is.[67]

This passage gestures to the impetus for Āryadeva writing his *Four Hundred Verses* in the first place. An astute understanding of dependent arising or emptiness is necessary for reorienting one's perception to the reality of phenomena and, in turn, of reorienting one's ethical behavior through overcoming afflictive emotions. This emphasis is reinforced later in Āryadeva's work, where Aitken quotes him saying, "It is preferable to slip even from ethics than from [proper view] in any way. Through ethics one goes to heaven; through view one goes to the highest state."[68] These kinds of strong statements are what leads Aitken to the conclusion that "Śāntideva's and Āryadeva's Buddhist ethical practice is the development of metaphysical knowledge and epistemic accuracy."[69] Thus, Aitken provides strong support for a moral phenomenological interpretation of Buddhist ethics and a strong case for knowledge acquisition, through its ability to restructure one's ascertainment or discrimination, as the primary means of changing one's perception and, hence, behavior.

## Moral Phenomenology in the Vajrayāna

Garfield and Aitken find evidence for a moral phenomenological interpretation of Buddhist ethics primarily in the Śrāvakayāna (or Theravada) and Mahāyāna traditions, but we can also find ample evidence for this classification in the Vajrayāna[70] tradition as well. For example, the Samaya[71] Vows are pledges one takes upon receiving initiation into the mandala of a particular tantric deity in Vajrayāna practice. Once given the ritualized empowerment[72] to practice a particular form of deity[73] yoga, one is required to uphold these vows and protect them from deterioration. There are different variations on these vows,[74] but most of the formulations consist of fourteen root downfalls and eight gross downfalls, which constitute a breach of one's pledge.[75] For this discussion, the root downfalls are more relevant than the gross downfalls, so we will limit our discussion to the former. In Tibetan systems of highest yoga tantra, the fourteen root downfalls are

1. disparaging the lama;

2. transgressing the words of the sugatas;

3. speaking ill of one's dharma brothers and sisters;

4. abandoning love for all sentient beings;

5. abandoning bodhicitta;

6. disparaging the doctrine of one's own school or the dharma systems of others;

7. sharing secret information to the uninitiated;

8. treating one's aggregates (skandhas) with contempt;

9. abandoning the view of natural purity and emptiness;

10. showing only affection to the wicked;

11. conceptualizing phenomena as actually existent;[76]

12. creating doubt in those who have faith;

13. breaking the vows one has taken; and

14. disparaging women.[77]

These fourteen can be categorized into downfalls of three kinds: body, speech, and mind. To act discordant to the words of the *sugatas*[78] in the *sūtras*, to treat one's *skandhas* with contempt, to find friendship in those who are unwholesome, and to break vows one has taken (such as the five precepts) can all be seen to be actions of the body. To disparage one's teacher, disparage one's sangha, disparage dharma traditions, disparage women, share secret information to those uninitiated, and introduce doubt to those who have faith can be seen to be actions of speech. Finally, to abandon love, abandon bodhicitta, abandon the view of emptiness, and see empty phenomena as actually existent are all actions of the mind or *views*. It is this last grouping that gives us evidence for a moral phenomenological interpretation.

Broadly speaking, we might characterize consequentialism with actions and virtue ethics with personal qualities, each of which can claim the proscriptions against particular actions of body and speech as their own. However, this moral emphasis on not abandoning particular *views* (actions of mind) eludes both ethical formulations. Where it *does* fit quite neatly is in a moral phenomenological framework that prioritizes particular experiences or perceptual modes as its ethical emphasis. It deals with *ascertainment*, *discrimination*, and the conceptual process that informs our perception of the world. These downfalls concerning the mind involve affective, conative, cognitive, and perceptual dimensions that compel practitioners to take up and maintain a particular *experience* of the world lest they incur a root downfall.

Further, it would be useful to break down these four downfalls concerning the mind in terms of the dimensions they address. The proscription against abandoning love for all sentient beings deals with the affect of a practitioner. We can easily make sense of this proscription even without any complex moral phenomenological analysis. Lovingkindness is a moral good found in every iteration of Buddhism, so its inclusion here is unsurprising. The proscription against abandoning *bodhicitta* concerns the conation of a practitioner and similarly makes sense given the emphasis of *bodhicitta* in the Mahāyāna and the Vajrayāna. The final two proscriptions, however, are quite interesting. The admonition to not abandon the view of emptiness and to not conceptualize phenomena as actually existent concerns itself with how practitioners understand the world, perceive phenomena, and experience themselves in relation to others. In effect, these two proscriptions are an ethical appeal to *ontology*. Seeing oneself, others, and all phenomena as empty of inherent existence and not reifying external phenomena or internal experience as ultimately, intrinsically real is given moral weight in these downfalls. We can understand this being the case due to their ability to guide an individual's experience to relatively sound behavior and ultimately desirable liberation.

At face value, this might not make a great deal of sense. Especially in Western contexts, emptiness has a reputation of being nihilistic or world denying due to the connotations of the term, but this understanding is largely misconstrued. Emptiness is the common English translation of the Sanskrit word *śūnyatā* and the Tibetan term *stong pa nyid*. To make lexical sense in English, emptiness requires a qualifier as to what it is empty *of*. With this in mind, the clearest way to describe emptiness is as the emptiness *of* independent, intrinsic existence. The term *śūnyatā* and the philosophy surrounding it are some of the most hotly contested elements of Buddhism, and a detailed historiography of these debates is beyond the scope of this book. However, it is nonetheless useful to highlight a key element of *śūnyatā* to understand the root downfall of abandoning its view: its equation with *pratītyasamutpāda*.

This equation of *śūnyatā* and *pratītyasamutpāda* can be traced back to at least the core text of the Madhyamaka school of Buddhism, the *Mūlamadhyamakakārikā*,[79] in which Nāgārjuna[80] states:

> Whatever arises in dependent origination,
> that is explained to be emptiness.
> That is a dependent designation,
> so that itself is the middle way.
> For that reason, there are no existing phenomena
> which are not dependently arisen.
> Therefore, there are no existent phenomena
> which are not empty.[81]

In other words, phenomena are empty because they arise in dependence on other phenomena. They are fully relative. They emerge from causes and conditions and are themselves causes and conditions for all other phenomena. Each aspect, quality, particle, and so forth that constitutes a particular phenomenon is entirely interdependent. There is absolutely no essence or individuality that stands apart from cause and condition. Because of this, they are empty of intrinsic, independent existence. This equation of *śūnyatā* and *pratītyasamutpāda* is such a crucial point that its realization caused the famous Tibetan scholar Tsongkhapa's enlightenment experience. After this experience, he wrote his *Praise for Dependent Relativity*, in which he states,

"All of this is empty of essence" and
"from this arises this effect"
these two determinations mutually
do not obstruct but assist one another.[82]

Thus, it is only through the emptiness of independent existence that phenomena can dependently arise, and it is because phenomena arise in interdependence that they are fundamentally empty of any intrinsic identity. It is for this reason that we can read the proscription against abandoning the view of emptiness as an ethical maxim. To hold emptiness as one's view is to hold the profound interconnectedness of all phenomena as one's view, and this in turn informs how one acts in the world.

This leads to another characteristic commonly ascribed to *śūnyatā*, which is especially relevant to our discussion on moral phenomenology: its ability to elicit compassion in those who directly experience the view. Again, if we take emptiness as some sort of nihilistic absence, then this claim may seem absurd. However, understanding emptiness as being synonymous with dependent origination helps contextualize this claim and helps posit its validity. The relationship between emptiness and compassion is most clearly made in the poetic Sanskrit phrase śūnyatā-karuṇā-garbham. In Tibetan, this reads as *stong nyid snying rje'i snying po can*, which Robert Thurman says, "may be the most beautiful phrase ever in Tibetan."[83] He translates the phrase as "voidness is the womb of compassion,"[84] but a clearer translation of the Tibetan might read "emptiness is endowed with an essence of compassion." In either case, compassion is seen as the result of a genuine appreciation of emptiness. Thurman sources this phrase back to Nāgārjuna's *Ratnāvalī*,[85] which includes this phrase in its discussion of the different kinds of teachings the Buddha shared with different kinds of beings.[86] In this text, the phrase is typically translated as "having an essence of emptiness and compassion,"[87] but in isolation (as Thurman takes it) it points to a direct relationship between emptiness and compassion. The phrase also appears in Sakya Pandita's *A Clear Differentiation of the Three Codes* (Tib. *sdom pa gsum gyi rab ru dbye ba*), where, in this context, its meaning is closer to that of Thurman's than in the *Ratnāvalī*.[88] In Sakya Pandita's text, the phrase *stong nyid snying rje'i snying po* is indeed a phrase unto itself and gets translated by Jared Douglas Rhoton as "emptiness which has as its essence compassion."[89] Again, when we understand the emptiness of phenomena as synonymous with the radical interconnection of all things, it makes sense that it has an essence of compassion. If we were to directly, experientially appreciate how our happiness and dissatisfaction is bound in that of others and how every action of body, speech, and mind has profound far-reaching consequences on the well-being of others, we would naturally take up a conative mode that places a compassionate care for others as our central concern.

I would argue that this phrase is perhaps the greatest single piece of evidence for a moral phenomenological interpretation of Buddhist ethics. The centrality of emptiness in Mahāyāna Buddhism and the proscription against giving up its view in the Vajrayāna are inherently ethical because of their ability to reorient an individual to a compassionate affective and conative disposition. As Nāgārjuna and Sakya Pandita write, emptiness has the nature of compassion. Thus, to realize emptiness is to assume a compassionate disposition. This relationship between emptiness and compassion can also be found in the yogic traditions of India and Tibet. For example, one of Saraha's[90] texts on Mahāmudrā, *Spontaneous Song of View, Meditation, Action, and Fruition*,[91] includes the following:

> The union of Mahāmudrā which transcends concepts,
> bliss, clarity, non-thought, like space,
> is vast and all-pervasive, the nature of great
> compassion.[92]

While this passage does not explicitly reference emptiness, the way in which Saraha portrays the nature of mind as beyond concepts evokes a Prasaṅgika-Madhyamaka approach to phenomena.[93] This, he claims, is itself the nature of great compassion. When the fundamental state of one's mind is realized (as bliss, clarity, and nonthought), a vast compassion emerges alongside it. We can see a similar linkage occurring in Mipham Rinpoche's Dzogchen text *The Essence of Mind*.[94] He writes,

> Regarding that which is called "the nature of mind,"
> it is the original naked face of the unconditioned
>     *rigpa*[95]
> which must be recognized through the blessings and
>     oral instructions of the lama.
> If one were to ask what this is like,
> it is empty of essence, without any fixed frame of
>     reference —
> it is naturally luminous, effortlessly established,
> it is all-pervading, unobstructed compassion,
> it is the pure awareness in which the three *kāyas* are
>     inseparable.[96]

In this Dzogchen context, we have a clearer equation of emptiness with compassion than in the verse from Saraha. The nature of one's mind is emptiness, luminosity, and compassion. We might say that, in this case, compassion is not an epiphenomenon of emptiness and instead assert an ontological claim that the nature of mind is itself empty of intrinsic existence and utterly compassionate. The Samaya Vows are more directly related to these yogic traditions than they are to the Madhyamaka philosophical system, so it is fitting that in these yogic traditions we also find an equation being made between emptiness and compassion. Both the Mahāmudrā songs of Saraha and the Dzogchen work of Mipham Rinpoche help us understand why the proscription against abandoning the view of emptiness exists and help us make the case for an ethic of moral phenomenology in the Vajrayāna tradition as well.

It is for this reason that we find contemporary Buddhists such as Joanna Macy claiming that a "full recognition of the true nature of the self as interconnected with all life . . . is essential because it can serve *in lieu of* ethics and morality."[97] I would assert that it is not that this recognition serves *in lieu* of ethics and morality but that it itself *is* an ethic—a moral phenomenological ethic. If we were to understand moral phenomenology as it is exclusively articulated by Garfield and Aitken, then Macy's statement might be slightly mysterious. It may be evident that Macy is referring to a kind of moral phenomenology, but the relationship between interconnectedness and morality are not fully spelled out in their work. However, when we look at how *śūnyatā* and *pratītyasamutpāda* are related in the Madhyamaka tradition and how these are seen to compel compassionate behavior in the Madhyamaka, Mahāmudrā, and Dzogchen traditions, we are able to paint a clearer picture of why Macy is making the above claim. Through analyzing the Samaya Vows, the phrase *śūnyatā-karuṇā-garbham*, and by looking at related ideas in the Mahāmudrā and Dzogchen traditions, we find a compelling case for a moral phenomenological approach to ethics in the Vajrayāna tradition in addition to the evidence found by other scholars in the Theravāda and Mahāyāna traditions.

## The Problem of Reclusion in Moral Phenomenology

Finally, there are two major problems that might easily come to mind when we talk about a moral phenomenological approach to ethics and that should be addressed if we want to articulate a contemplative approach to environmental ethics. They are what I term the "problem of reclusion" and the "temporal issue." The problem of reclusion can be stated thusly: If moral phenomenology centers around cultivating a particular *experience* of the world (through study and meditation as we will see in the following chapter), then it follows that an individual is motivated to remove themselves from the world until they are able to fully cultivate that experience. Of course, this might not be universally the case, but the way in which ethical cultivation appears to be a disengaged process leads to this potential problem. Further, if one looks at the history of Buddhist practice (on which this moral phenomenology is built), one would see recluses, retreatants, and wandering vagabonds being lauded as exemplary practitioners. Obviously, one is unable to actively work to alleviate the *duḥkha* of sentient beings if they simply lock themselves in a cave and do not actually engage with them. However, in this moral phenomenological context, one is equally unable to do so if they do not have the sufficient realization to be able to skillfully act in accordance with the needs of others.

This problem comes up directly in the Buddhist literature. The most poignant narrative in which this problem of reclusion can be found is the famous story of Asaṅga[98] and Maitreya.[99] Asaṅga wished to meet and receive teachings from the bodhisattva Maitreya, so he entered retreat to meditate on compassion and acquire the requisite merit for Maitreya to appear to him. After twelve years in seclusion without even an auspicious dream to tell him he was on the right track, he became dejected and left in defeat. Then, Asaṅga

> came across a starving dog, dragging its maggot-infested hind legs behind it. Despite the dog's attempts to bite him, Asaṅga was overwhelmed by compassion, and for want of anything to feed the dog, he cut a piece of flesh from his own leg for it to eat. He then turned his attention to its appalling wounds, but soon realized that all attempts to remove the maggots might save the dog but would kill the maggots. The only solution he could think of was to use his tongue to coax the maggots out of the stinking flesh. Shutting his eyes, he bent down to do what he could to heal the animal, only to find himself licking the dust by the side of the road. When he opened his eyes, he found the dog had disappeared. In its place, before him stood Maitreya.[100]

It was only after putting his compassion into *action* that Maitreya appeared, which indicates that compassion must be put into practice in order for it to have any meaningful effect. As related earlier, the mind of enlightened compassion, *bodhicitta*, is often presented as having two parts: aspiration and application. While in retreat, Asaṅga was cultivating a *bodhicitta* of aspiration, but it is clear that this was not enough for Maitreya to validate his practice. It was only when aspiration was married with application that the initial aspiration had any meaningful effect. If, as Garfield writes, *bodhicitta* is the desired result of Buddhist moral phenomenology, one must therefore go beyond mere aspiration and actually cultivate the applied side of *bodhicitta* else it remain undeveloped.

Interestingly, this suggests that a mental experience of compassion alone is ethically (and, in the Buddhist context, soteriologically) insufficient. Moral experience on this account must be reified through concrete actions of the body to establish its ethical validity and efficacy. At face value, this might be obvious. There is a clear difference between feeling compassion for a beggar as you pass them on the street and taking concrete actions to alleviate their poverty, whether that means giving them some subsistence directly or donating to a local shelter. However, a moral phenomenological account places more importance on experience than consequences or actions themselves. Thus, we might arrive at the conclusion that, in fact, the experience of compassion supersedes the concrete action. Asaṅga's story, however, demonstrates how this experience must be *enacted materially* to be deemed ethical. Even if particular experiences are the focus of a moral phenomenological approach to ethics, they are only moral insofar as they inform, direct, and compel action. Rather than remain purely idealistic and portray the experience of compassion in a retreat setting as ethically sufficient, this story shows how a proper moral experience must be one that is involved in the affairs of the world. One can only develop a full experience of *bodhicitta* if one develops both its aspiration and application, and one's phenomenological experience can only be deemed ethical insofar as it compels action. Thus, while short-term study and meditation retreats may be encouraged for developing an ethically sound experience of the world, total long-term reclusion does not follow from a moral phenomenological approach to ethics and is actually antithetical to its ethical project.

## The Temporal Problem in Moral Phenomenology

Alongside this issue of reclusion, we have a related problem: the temporal issue. If moral phenomenology calls for the cultivation of a particular experience, and that experience takes time to accurately establish as one's default perceptual mode, then what is one to do prior to its establishment? Moral phenomenology is built from the claim that our behavior stems from our experience of the world and that if one establishes a particular experience with appropriate conative and affective dimensions, then ethical action will necessarily follow. However, this also means that, until we establish a perceptual/affective/conative mode akin to *bodhicitta*, if we simply allow our actions to naturally follow our deluded experience of the world, then we run the risk of acting in morally inappropriate ways. Even if one subscribes to this sort of ethic and is in the process of putting it into practice, their behavior will not yet fully accord with the ethical view (such as interdependence) that they are working to realize perceptually. Therefore, how is one supposed to guard against this unethical behavior en route to the actualization of a moral phenomenology?

Perhaps this limitation arises in other kinds of ethical formulations such as virtue ethics, wherein prior to perfecting a virtue such as generosity, an individual may still act out of greed. There is, however, a difference here. In virtue ethics, one develops their moral character through their *actions* and gradually acclimates to whatever is regarded as proper moral character (defined by particular virtues). In moral phenomenology, however, *action* is always chronologically secondary to *view*. Thus, until one actually *experiences* the world in the right way, one does not necessarily *conduct* themselves morally. This is because the spontaneous compassionate conduct to which moral phenomenology aspires comes from the perceptual realization of a particular view. Therefore, installing that view as one's perceptual mode through study or meditation takes precedent to acting in specific ways and developing moral character.

If we look for Buddhist resources to address this limitation, we can find a useful response in Nāgārjuna's *Ratnāvalī*. In the second section of the text, which addresses the causes of higher rebirth and enlightenment, he writes:

> Therefore, as long as one does not understand
> this teaching which clears away clinging to the self,
> Until then, devote oneself to the practice
> of generosity, moral discipline, and patience.[101]

If we read this passage with moral phenomenology in mind, the solution to the temporal issue becomes clear. Ultimately, Buddhist moral phenomenology aims to reorient an individual to ethical behavior through the perceptual recognition of concepts like *anātman*, *pratītyasamutpāda*, and *śūnyatā*. However, Nāgārjuna says that the development of generosity, discipline, and patience is necessary *until* these concepts are experienced directly, and one is able to appropriately carry oneself in the world with resultant spontaneous and natural compassion. Essentially, Nāgārjuna is suggesting that one relies upon virtue ethics *until* they directly see the selflessness of phenomena that may serve in lieu of ethics these more specific, prescriptive ethics. Thus, following Nāgārjuna's quote, we may claim that these are *provisional* insofar as they are only relied upon up until one installs the correct view as their default mode of perceiving the world.

This idea of "provisional ethics" is not foreign to the Tibetan tradition—it can clearly be seen in its understanding of the *three vows*.[102] The three vows are the monastic Prātimokṣa Vows,[103] the Mahāyāna Bodhisattva Vows,[104] and Vajrayāna Samaya Vows,[105] respectively. As one progresses down the path of practice, one reprioritizes one's ethical commitments such that Bodhisattva Vows take precedent over Prātimokṣa Vows, and Samaya takes precedent over both. This reprioritization is most clearly seen in the Mahāyāna concept of *upāya* (skillful means), which explicitly calls for the breaking of certain rules if done with a compassionate mindset and is for the benefit of others. Śāntideva's *Bodhicaryāvatārā*, one the most highly regarded texts in the Tibetan tradition, makes this clear. It states,

> Having understood in that way,
> a bodhisattva must continuously exert themselves for
>     the benefit of others.
> The bodhisattva who sees this extensively and pos-
>     sesses compassion
> is granted the ability to do even what is prohibited.[106]

In other words, Śāntideva notes how the necessity of liberating others from *duḥkha* takes precedent over abstaining from sexual conduct, alcohol, lying, and so forth as long as one has a compassionate motivation behind one's actions. One who has committed oneself to the bodhisattva path may break some of the conventional rules Buddhists follow if, in doing so, they contribute to the liberation of other beings.

Moreover, as one progresses from the Prātimokṣa Vows through the Samaya Vows, the *moral theory* captured by the vows changes as well. We might call Prātimokṣa Vows deontological since they give clear rules one must follow and are more concerned with the rules themselves than the consequences of these actions or the virtues they develop. Bodhisattva Vows and the practice of the Mahāyāna are directly related to the *pāramitās* and *upāya*, which can easily be characterized as dealing with virtue ethics and consequentialism respectively. Finally, Samaya Vows deal with actions of body, speech, and mind but are also uniquely concerned with *experience* in a manner consonant with moral phenomenology. Thus, in the case of the three vows, we might say that, throughout the course of their study and practice, individuals in the monastic Tibetan tradition move from a deontological approach to ethics to a virtue ethics or consequentialist approach before establishing a moral phenomenological approach to ethics.

Of course, it would be foolish to claim that once one achieves a realization of emptiness, one abandons their earlier Prātimokṣa and Bodhisattva Vows. In fact, Tibetan philosophers were constantly guarding against a nihilistic view of emptiness that would negate the validity of the Four Noble Truths and ethics altogether. There is also evidence that, despite their low doxographical position, those who aspired to uphold their Prātimokṣa Vows (despite being involved in Vajrayāna practice) were regarded as exemplary practitioners.[107] In my interpretation of these vows, I am not suggesting that if one takes the Bodhisattva Vows, then they are given license to wholly abandon the Prātimokṣa Vows and conventional deontological approaches to ethics (although exceptional cases like Drukpa Kunley[108] might paint this picture). Rather, what I am suggesting is that, as one progresses down the Buddhist path, one relies less and less on ethical formalities and more and more on one's natural ethical comportment to the world. The affective states that the Bodhisattva Vows elicit supersede the rationalized abstentions of the Prātimokṣa Vows, and in its call to maintain an experience of emptiness, the direct phenomenological orientation of the Samaya Vows supersede both. Many Buddhist texts also suggest that it is only through ethical discipline that one actually develops the meditative capacity to realize emptiness in the first place, making these earlier ethical formulations found in the Prātimokṣa and Bodhisattva Vows not only provisional but *necessary steps* toward the realization of emptiness and the establishment of a moral phenomenology. It is for this reason that we find a host of rules to follow and virtues to develop in this ethical tradition that I am characterizing as otherwise experiential and spontaneous—they are to guard the practitioner against wrongdoing *until* they fully establish bodhicitta as their default perceptual mode, after which they needn't rely on them. Thus, to respond to the temporal issue, it seems as though our solution is to be found right in the structure of the three vows themselves. Until one has come to completely experience the world through the lens of emptiness/interdependence, one must provisionally rely upon other ethical forms (explicit rules, virtue ethical formulations, or consequentialist calculi) to structure one's ethical world.

## Moral Phenomenology in Western Philosophical Contexts

Prior to concluding this discussion on moral phenomenology, it is worth noting that moral phenomenology is not *necessarily* unique to the Buddhist tradition. The Western philosophical tradition has a history of thinking about "moral phenomenology," though its understanding of the term is largely distinct from the ethical theory we just parsed. The first work to use the term *moral phenomenology* was Maurice Mandelbaum's *The Phenomenology of Moral Experience*, which defines moral obligation as a *force* of *felt demand* with respect to particular *direct moral obligations* and draws primarily from the work of Emmanuel Levinas. Mandelbaum's project is a *descriptive* one rather than *prescriptive,* and he offers an explanatory model of moral experience rather than a kind of tangible program for moral behavior that what see in Buddhism's moral phenomenology. Overall, most of the Western literature that talks about "moral phenomenology" follows Mandelbaum in this kind of descriptive project.

That said, there are some who have thought through the convergence of moral phenomenology and ethical theory. For example, in "Moral Phenomenology and Moral Theory," Terry Horgan and Mark Timmons dialogue moral phenomenology with contemporary ethics and argue that the *experience* of morality is at direct odds with consequentialism. In their words, "The point is not that people never do such [utilitarian] calculating in cases of direct moral judgment, but that they just typically do not; moral experience in the case of direct moral judgments does not fit well with the account the consequentialist gives of obligation." They conclude, "To the extent to which one puts methodological weight on considerations of moral phenomenology, one will favor non-consequentialist views in normative ethics"[109]

The nonconsequentialist view they support is, perhaps unsurprisingly, virtue ethics. They argue that while "the first-person study of the experiential aspect of our moral life"[110] creates nothing but tension when dialogued with consequentialism, there are many compatibilities and possibilities for integrating the study of moral experience into a broader formulation of virtue ethics. Rather than look at how an ethic can emerge *out of* a first-person experience of the world (as we investigated in the Buddhist tradition), these two works look at how moral phenomenology can inform historical (Western) philosophical traditions. There is, however, one notion in Western moral phenomenology that takes a step in the direction of Buddhist moral phenomenology; that is ethical comportment. Horgan and Timmons's article only mentions this idea in passing when they state, "Perhaps one should allow (in addition to conscious moral beliefs, both deliberative and spontaneous) cases in which one responds in a morally appropriate way without consciously forming a moral belief at all—call this kind of experience, 'ethical comportment.' The idea is that in persons having a high degree of moral expertise, the phenomenology of their habitual responses to morally significant situations may not include making (or coming to have) a moral judgment as part of their experience."[111] They derive their notion of ethical comportment from an earlier work by Hubert and Stuart Dreyfus titled "What Is Morality? A Phenomenological Account of the Development of Ethical Expertise," in which the authors contrast the ethical deliberation present in consequentialist and virtue ethics with spontaneous ethical comportment and posit the latter as a potential ground for ethical theory. It is here that we find a potential bridge between Buddhist and Western moral phenomenologies.

Dreyfus and Dreyfus argue that ethical comportment (being the spontaneous *appropriate* reaction to moral situations that confront the individual) is a skill not unlike driving a car or playing chess. Like driving a car or playing chess, there are differences between the experience of a novice and an expert and according stages of experiencing moral situations as one progresses through the stages of ethical expertise. In their formulation, moral expertise begins with maxims (such as never to lie) with which an individual makes sense of situations, before revising those rules in particular situations (one should lie to save a life), and eventually abandoning the maxims altogether in favor of a natural attention to the particulars of a situation.[112] However, what is missing in their formulation is *how* one progresses from stage to stage. To phrase this lack as a question: What actions does one take to move from being a novice to achieving competency and expertise? As we will see in the following chapter, the Buddhist tradition can offer a necessary practical supplement to this kind of development.

Nonetheless, after their formulation of this kind of ethical expertise, Dreyfus and Dreyfus are led to defend Carol Gilligan's interpretation of care ethics.[113] Gilligan contrasts the "justice perspective" with the "care perspective" and associates the justice perspective with those who approach ethical dilemmas through a utilitarian calculus or a situation in which universals must be applied without prejudice. In contrast, the care perspective is "doing spontaneously whatever the situation demands"[114] based on the specific context in which a moral dilemma presents itself in and the relationships it involves.[115] While she does not use the term herself, Dreyfus and Dreyfus categorize Gilligan's approach as one that is built from an intuition of ethical comportment. Not only that, but they also see this kind of ethical theory as one that reflects the highest form of ethical expertise. They write, "When one measures Gilligan's two types of morality against a phenomenology of expertise, the traditional Western and male belief in the maturity and superiority of critical detachment is reversed. The highest form of ethical comportment is seen to consist in being able to stay involved and to refine one's intuitions."[116] Thus, Buddhist moral phenomenology indeed has some potential parallels in Western contexts. The serious treatment of ethical comportment by Dreyfus and Dreyfus and Gilligan's ethic of care demonstrates how attending to the imminent moral experiences of an individual can inform moral theory and itself be a source of ethical thought. While this notion of moral phenomenology is evidently a minority position in Western uses of the term, ethical comportment nonetheless provides a useful bridge from Western notions of moral phenomenology to the Buddhist kind articulated above. While this book concerns itself primarily with the Buddhist ethical tradition, this connection between Buddhist moral phenomenology and ethical comportment might allow for productive conversations to occur in the future both in the realm of metaethics and, as we will see later in this book, in our ethical approach to the more-than-human world.

Regardless, it is only in the Buddhist tradition that we find moral phenomenology constituting an ethical project involving a clear path for moral cultivation, a desired outcome, and clearly articulated link between our ontological views and our ethical lives. In the Buddhist tradition, moral phenomenology is a theory centered on the *experience* of an individual and rests on the assertion that actions stem from an individual's immediate experience of the world. It involves reorienting one's default perceptual mode and its associated conceptual and affective states to influence how one spontaneously responds to the situations one is presented with. As earlier scholars have pointed out, this approach to ethics can be found in the Theravāda and Mahāyāna traditions, but we have also seen compelling evidence that a moral phenomenological approach to ethics is consistent with the kinds of Vajrayāna Buddhism that we find in Tibet. Further, we have seen how Buddhism might respond to the problem of reclusion and the temporal problem that emerge when thinking through a moral phenomenological approach to ethics. What remains to be seen is how one actually develops ethically in this moral theory. To fill this gap, we must therefore look to how contemplative practice functions in the soteriological and ethical systems of Tibetan Buddhism.

3

# View, Meditation, Action

## A Contemplative Framework for Ethical Development

Tibetan Buddhist traditions center contemplative practice as the primary method for ethical development. Whether a practitioner positions themselves in the Mahāyāna tradition and meditatively cultivates generosity and compassion or in the Vajrayāna tradition and practices tantric visualization and deity yoga, contemplative practice is the cornerstone upon which one builds one's ethical capacity. However, this contemplative practice is not sim ply done in a directionless vacuum. Especially in the Dzogchen and Mahāmudrā lineages of Vajrayāna Buddhism, contemplative practice occurs in a strict framework of *lta sgom spyod gsum* (view, meditation, action), which guides and directs the practice toward pre-established, desired ends. Ethical development can surely occur outside of this particular framework, but I nonetheless hold that view, meditation, action presents the most expedient way for moral phenomenological transformation and is essential for applying Buddhist ethics to our more-than-human world.

## Original Context and Definition of *lta sgom spyod gsum*

The framework of view, meditation, action can be found across literary genres in Tibet. We can find Tibetan authors using the framework in *rnam thar* (hagiographies),[1] *dohas* (songs of spiritual experience),[2] aspiration prayers,[3] pith meditation instructions,[4] *sadhanas* (ritual practice texts),[5] and doxographies.[6] These texts and the framework's usage therein span the four major schools of Tibetan Buddhism, making *view, meditation, action* a ubiquitous term in the tradition. Further, we can find *lta sgom spyod gsum* in some of the seminal Indian texts from which Tibetan Buddhism developed. For example, the Indian *mahāsiddha* Saraha,[7] who played an important role in establishing the Mahāmudrā tradition of Vajrayāna Buddhism, has a song titled "Spontaneous Song of View Meditation, Action, and Result" that addresses various aspects of the path of Mahāmudrā. Most of this song speaks to Mahāmudrā in general and gives general instructions on the practice. There are, however, specific references to view, meditation, action as a closed framework such as when he sings: "In brief, by acting in whatever way benefits the practice of view, meditation, action, one acts according to the natural state, yoga."[8] Thus, in Saraha's song, we have view, meditation, action used as both a general signifier for the various facets of Mahāmudrā practice and a specific framework therein.

Perhaps more important than its inclusion in a variety of Tibetan literary genres is how view, meditation, action is defined and understood in the Tibetan tradition. While examples are few, there are some instances of the framework *lta sgom spyod gsum* being packaged together in Tibetan dictionaries and given its own entry. For instance, Nobrang Orgyen's[9] *Compendium of Buddhist Terminology*[10] gives the definition of *lta sgom spyod gsum* as follows:

1. [View is] the *Sūtra-pitika* which explained the main points of the view of the Buddhist Dharma traditions.

2. [Meditation is] the *Abhidharma-pitika* which explained the main points of the method of training in meditative stabilization.

3. [Action] is said to be the three *pitikas* and the three texts, together with the *Vinaya-pitika* which explained the main points of right action.[11]

While this entry doesn't necessarily speak to the practical nature of the framework, the English parsing of *lta sgom spyod gsum* does.

One of the earliest examples of this can be found in Garma C. C. Chang's translation of Milarepa's[12] *Hundred Thousand Songs*, where he gives his own definition of view, meditation, action to help the anglophone reader understand what the framework means. Chang writes: " 'View' is the knowledge or principle upon which all meditations are based and religious activities conducted. 'Practice' refers to the yogic exercise of the View; 'Action' to a state in which the yogi is absorbed in the View while carrying out [their] daily activities."[13] Thus, we find a presentation of view, meditation, action wherein practice (read: meditation) involves yogic (or meditative) cultivation of the view, and action refers to behavior that accords with and stems from the view. Likewise, in several of his translations, Erik Pema Kunsang provides the following definition of view, meditation, action: "The philosophical orientation, the act of growing accustomed to that—usually in sitting practice, and the implementation of that insight during the activities of daily life. Each of the 'nine vehicles' has its particular definition of view, meditation and action."[14] Thus, we have two important aspects of *lta sgom spyod gsum* in Kunsang's definition. First is the clear practical relationship between view, meditation, and action in this definition. Meditation is growing phenomenologically accustomed to a particular philosophical position, and action is acting from that position. Second, he states that each of the nine vehicles has a distinct view, meditation, and action unto itself. Taken together, Kunsang seems to be suggesting that, despite these disparate views, meditations, and actions, each vehicle implements the framework in the same way. In other words, regardless of the specific views, meditative practices, and actions that are inserted into the framework, the relationship between the three components is universal.

If we wish to operationalize this framework in a moral phenomenological setting, we should understand the broad semantic range of each of the individual components of *lta sgom spyod gsum.* In Gegen Dorje Tharchin's 1950 dictionary commissioned by the University of Washington, *lta ba* is given the following entry: "its honorific form is *gzigs pa,* and it is the meaning of that which perceives the object of realization."[15] Thus, there is a sense of *perceiving* and a sense of an *object of perception.* These two connotations can be clearly seen in the entry for *lta ba* in Tibetan-English dictionaries. The Rangjung Yeshe dictionary entry states: "[philosophical] view, orientation, point of view, philosophical position [wrong] view / opinion, belief, heresy, speculative theory, ideology], theory, position, stand point, outlook, attitude, perspective, doctrine, opinionatedness, dogma, principles, ideology, teaching, insight, understanding."[16] Establishing *lta ba* therefore involves intellectually affirming a particular philosophical position, point of view, ideology, or theory. It is this sense of *lta ba* that is involved in the framework of view, meditation, action.

Next, *sgom pa* is typically translated as "meditation" but has a wider semantic range than the English term provides. Gegen Dorje Tharchin's Tibetan definition of *sgom pa* reads: "the mind resting single-pointedly. . . . It refers to the cultivation of *citta* (heart/mind) and so forth."[17] These can be seen as two of the main uses of the English term *meditation*. In Tibetan Buddhism, meditation is of two kinds: *zhi gnas* and *lhag mthong*, which are the equivalents of the Sanskrit *śamatha* and *vipaśyanā*, respectively. In English, the former term often gets translated as "calm abiding" and the latter as "special insight," which, as in Tharchin's definition of *sgom pa*, respectively involve single-pointed concentration and the meditative cultivation of particular views. Alongside the word *meditation*, Hopkins states that *sgom pa* can also refer to "cultivation," "progress," and "development,"[18] but Rangjung Yeshe gives even more English equivalents, including "training," "familiarization," "contemplation," "creative imagination," and "to become accustomed to."[19] Jim Valby offers further connotations of *sgom pa* such as: "making a living experience of," "concentrated attention to the nature of things," "close attention," "call up," "foster," and so forth.[20] From all of these related meanings, we can thus conclude that meditation refers to the act of single-pointedly focusing on a particular object in order to cultivate a perceptual familiarity with, contemplate the meaning of, or *make a living experience of* said object. Far from simply sitting in a quiescent state, *sgom pa* involves concentrating on a particular concept or *lta ba* to bring that view into one's default perceptual mode.

Finally, Hopkins translates *spyod pa* as "deeds," "behavior," "enjoy," "make use of," "practice," "act out," and "perform." To this, Rangjung Yeshe adds "to engage in," "behave," "carry out," "participate in," "be involved with," and "commit." Tharchin echoes some of these sentiments in his Tibetan entry, including: "theory and practice being separated from each other, clumsy action, precise action, elaborate action, confused action, and so forth."[21] So, we have two clear connotations to the term. In the first, *spyod pa* is used to denote action on a specific object as is the case with "enjoy," "make use of," "participate in," and so on. Second, we have a general sense of a continued *kind of acting* in the terms *conduct*, *behavior*, *action*, and *activity* in the dictionary entry by Tharchin. In the contexts where view, meditation, action constitute a particular framework of practice, it is typically this general and continued sense that *spyod pa* is referring to. Further, this use of *spyod pa* to denote action and behavior is especially important to the framework's utility in a moral phenomenological setting, so it is worthwhile emphasizing this long-term, behavioral sense of *spyod pa* the more specific sense of acting on an immediate object.

## Practical Uses of *lta sgom spyod gsum*

Zooming out from the individual terms, when *lta sgom spyod gsum* is used in Tibetan texts, it often performs one of two roles: it is either used as a descriptive device for organizing aspects of the Buddhist tradition (as in the earlier definition by Nobrang Orgyen), or it is used as a practical framework for didactic purposes. In terms of a moral phenomenological praxis, these descriptive uses of view, meditation, action do not give us a great deal to work with.[22] They are useful insofar as they provide us with some background as to how the framework was understood and deployed by particular thinkers throughout Tibetan Buddhism's history, but they do not give us much material for relating *lta sgom spyod gsum* to ethics. There are, however, many scholars and practitioners who use the framework in a practical sense wherein view, meditation, and action are intimately connected to one another as sequentially related parts of Buddhist practice. Since these practical, sequential uses of view, meditation, action are what can be mobilized toward moral phenomenological ends, we will parse some of these examples in detail.

First, we can find a strong example of *lta sgom spyod gsum* being used in a practical sense in the text of the ninth Karmapa, Wangchuk Dorje,[23] *Mahāmudrā: Dispelling the Darkness of Ignorance,*[24] where he writes,

> To be free from all notions of "apprehended" and
> "apprehender" and see one's true abiding mode is
> the view.
> To meditate without distraction on the meaning of
> that is the meditation.
> To be free from all actions and activities and main-
> tain that view during any of the four actions is the
> action.
> To be free from hopes and fears, such as the fear of
> falling to the lowest depths of saṃsāra or the desire
> for attaining the highest Buddhahood, and to be
> free from notions of action and agent in meditation
> is the fruition.
> You should understand the meaning of view, medita-
> tion, action, and fruition in that way and generate
> diligence.[25]

Here we find meditation being defined directly in relation to the view such that, in this presentation, meditation's function is to bring the view into the fore of one's experience of the world. This relationship between view and meditation can also be seen quite clearly in the *Prayer of Mahāmudrā* by the Third Karmapa Rangjung Dorje.[26] He writes:

> To cut through misconceptions of the ground is to
> have confidence in the view.
> To maintain that view without distraction is the cru-
> cial point of meditation.
> To train in all objects of meditation is the supreme
> form of action.
> May I possess the confidence of view, meditation, and
> action![27]

As in the case of Wangchuk Dorje, meditation is being defined as a specific practice of maintaining the view without distraction. Where Wangchuk Dorje's presentation differs from Rangjung Dorje's is in his presentation of action. Rangjung Dorje's action is training in all the facets of meditation, whereas Wangchuk Dorje's action is defined in relation to view such that all action should be done while simultaneously sustaining the view. Thus, alongside the view being integrated as a perceptual mode, it seems to also serve a *conative* function in this particular Mahāmudrā context.

A more straightforward use of *lta sgom spyod gsum* as a practical framework occurs in Dudjom Rinpoche's[28] *Light of Primordial Wisdom*. This text gives instructions on how to practice the completion stage[29] of a particular Nyingma *sadhana*, which it breaks down into the two foundational types of meditation: *śamatha* and *vipaśyanā*. In the section describing the *vipaśyanā* stage of the practice, he describes what is to be done through the framework of view, meditation, action. He states:

> The main part: four points on generating the wisdom of special insight:
>
> 1. deciding through the view;
>
> 2. adopting it as one's experience through meditation;
>
> 3. experiencing continuously through action; and
>
> 4. bringing the fruition to realization.[30]

Here, Dudjom Rinpoche gives very precise instructions on how to practice *vipaśyanā*. One first conceptually establishes the view, adopts it as one's default perceptual mode by meditating on it, and finally brings that experience into one's daily life until it is fully realized. This is how the framework can enact a moral phenomenology. If moral phenomenology is aimed at reworking an individual's natural mode of conduct by reworking their default perceptual, affective, and conative experience of the world, then Dudjom Rinpoche's framework presents us a clear means for doing so. We first decide what the proper view is for a desired ethical outcome, adopt it into our experience through meditation, and act from that basis in our daily lives.

Similar explanations of the practical use of *lta sgom spyod gsum* can be found in the modern Tibetan tradition as well. In his commentary on Patrul Rinpoche's[31] *Heart Treasure of Sacred Practice* (subtitled *A Discourse Virtuous in the Beginning, Middle and End on View, Meditation, and Action*),[32] contemporary Dzogchen master Dilgo Khyentse Rinpoche[33] gives a succinct presentation of the practice of view, meditation, action. He writes, "The first step in establishing the view is to acquire a proper understanding of the teachings about it. Then, to incorporate the view into our inner experience, we put it into practice over and over again; this is the *meditation*. Maintaining our experience of the view at all times and under all circumstances is the *action*. Through the constant combination of these three—*view, meditation, action*—the *fruit* of the practice of Dharma will fully ripen."[34] More interestingly, he also makes a clear statement regarding the relationships among view, meditation, and action as well as their relationship to ethics in general. He writes: "Once you have recognized the view, as you practice it through meditation, all your actions, words, and thoughts will become naturally more and more wholesome. Eventually, whether resting, working, eating, or sleeping, whether happy or sad, you will constantly have the thought of Chenrezi present in your mind; this is called action."[35] This is not a practical presentation of view, meditation, action per se but is instead an explanation of what happens *during* the practice. Essentially, Dilgo Khyentse Rinpoche is claiming that as one familiarizes oneself with the view, one will naturally act more ethically. In this sense, view has a *direct* consequence on one's action, and this consequence has a somewhat proportional relationship to how fully one familiarizes oneself with that view in meditation. He also states that the culmination of this meditative familiarization is to constantly have "the thought of Chenrezi present in your mind." Since Chenrezi is the *bodhisattva* of compassion, this statement can therefore be read as stating that one will install a compassionate conative mode through a perceptual familiarization with a particular view, in this case that of emptiness.[36] Thus, Dilgo Khyentse Rinpoche gives us great reason to believe that this framework can indeed be employed toward moral phenomenological ends quite effectively.

## Nuancing View, Meditation, Action

With this understanding of how *lta sgom spyod gsum* functions in the Tibetan contemplative tradition, we can begin nuancing this framework in moral phenomenological contexts. To this end, we can say that *view* is almost always prioritized in the practical application of this framework. In his analysis of Madhyamaka philosophy and practice, Sonam Thakchoe states that "the Buddha himself considers the right view as the forerunner of all spiritual practices,"[37] so this priority makes sense. Indeed, many teachers who use view, meditation, action as a practical tool for moral and perceptual transformation have stressed that view is to be privileged over meditation and action. For example, in a text titled *A Brief Presentation of View, Meditation and Action*, Yangthang Rinpoche[38] states,

> Among the view, meditation, and action, view is most important.
> It is extremely important that one realizes the view without any mistakes.
> If the view is not realized, then meditation will be without any basis whatsoever.
> So, after one directly realizes the view without any mistakes,
> Then, when one brings it into one's personal experience through meditation,
> Residing in that state of the view which one has recognized and
> Extending the amount of time in that state through effort is the meditation.
> Therefore, apart from this, there is not a single other object of meditation.[39]

Similarly, Ringu Tulku Rinpoche[40] focuses in on view as the means for changing our perspective and our behavior. He writes, "Human ignorance sees others as a threat to our survival. In fact, we benefit from seeing everyone as a potential partner. 'View' is the most important factor in bringing about this shift."[41] There is a good reason for this. When thinking through view in the practical use of *lta sgom spyod gsum*, both meditation and action relate back to the specific view you have established. Meditation is the cultivation of a particular philosophical position, and action stems directly from this newly established perceptual mode. We might say meditation is a *tool* for establishing a view *experientially* and for bridging the gap between how one thinks of and acts in the world. Thus, when Yangthang Rinpoche says that the view must be established flawlessly, he is really saying that an error in the view will become an error in the resultant default perceptual mode, which will in turn cause one to act in inappropriate ways.

To put this differently, if meditating on a "correct" view has the capacity to bring about positive action and ultimately liberate oneself from *duḥkha*, then meditating on an "incorrect" view will equally have the capacity to do the opposite. Khensur Jampa Tegchok warns against this in his commentary on Nāgārjuna's[42] *Ratnāvalī*. He writes:

> When those who lack proper study and a correct understanding meditate on emptiness, there is danger that they meditate incorrectly and come to the wrong conclusion. Falling to the extreme of nihilism and thinking that karma and its effects do not exist, their behavior becomes reckless, and their destructive actions lead them to ruin. This is similar to a person who grasps a poisonous snake improperly—instead of being able to extract the medicine from the snake, he will be bitten by it.[43]

This is why such importance is placed on correctly establishing the view—it is the direct referent for action once it is perceptually and experientially established through meditation.

Despite this emphasis on view, we should be careful not to regard view *alone* as sufficient for either liberation from *duḥkha* in Buddhist soteriological settings or a moral phenomenological approach to ethics. Action is necessary in both contexts for bringing about the desired result of liberation and ethical behavior. The proper fruition of *lta sgom spyod gsum* is a unity of view and action such that both aspects are always informed by one another. Shabkar writes about this idea in his *Emanated Scripture of Mañjuśrī*, stating,

> Both an authentic view of selflessness and a completely pure conduct are necessary. To give an analogy, to be able to fly in the sky a bird needs two wings—it cannot go

anywhere with one, even if it's an excellent wing. Likewise, having relied on the practice which unites view and action one will attain the level of omniscience. Even if the view or conduct is excellent, if either is missing, one will not be able to continue beyond some point of the ground or path. Now, if one were to wonder what the practice is that unites view and action, it is the practice of the holy ones, the saints of the Kadampa tradition who previously condensed the complete collection of sutras into what one should actually engage in and who saw that the root which produces all the suffering of *saṃsāra* is the ignorance which grasps selflessness as a self. This ignorance is brought down by the awareness which liberates the single and the many and reaches decisive insight into the selflessness of persons and things. Through the emptiness of meditative equipoise like the sky and the emptiness of dream-like post-meditation, one perfects the path by means of the union of view and action.[44]

To liberate oneself from *duḥkha,* both view and action are necessary components. Liberation cannot be accomplished with only one. The same might be said of a moral phenomenological approach to ethics. Action without view would be uninformed and hence potentially inappropriate, while view without action would be entirely ineffectual. Shabkar also gives us an example of what this unity of view and action looks like: a meditative equipoise like the sky and a postmeditation like a dream. Thus, meditation is positioned as the link between view and action, and their unity can be understood as maintaining the view (established in meditative absorption) in one's day-to-day life (postmeditation).

Finally, we might consider the order by which view, meditation, action is practiced. In many of the prior examples, the view, meditation, action was presented according to the sequence of terms. First, one establishes the view philosophically, then one meditates on that view to install it as one's default perceptual mode, and finally one goes about one's life acting in accordance with that acquired perceptual and conative set. This is the fairly standard order of operations we find in most practical uses of *lta sgom spyod gsum.*

However, there are apparent exceptions to this rule. In a recent work by Chöden Rinpoche[45] titled *Mastering Meditation: Instructions on Calm Abiding and Mahāmudrā*, there is an insightful account of a student asking whether it is better "first to settle on the view of emptiness and then to actualize calm abiding, or first to actualize calm abiding and then to settle on the view."[46] Chöden Rinpoche responds, "That depends on your degree of familiarity with these two topics. If you have greater familiarity with emptiness, it is better first to meditate on emptiness and then to actualize calm abiding. If you have greater familiarity with calm abiding, then you should actualize that first."[47] He repeats this twofold approach later in the text, stating, "There are two kinds of people: (1) those who first gain certainty about the view, realize the view, and from within the view, actualize calm abiding, and (2) those who first actualize calm abiding, and having actualized calm abiding, gain certainty about the view."[48] At face value, this seems to somewhat contradict the standard process by which one enacts the framework of view, meditation, action, but if we recall how meditation is understood in the Tibetan Buddhist system, we can easily reconcile these two approaches.

In brief, meditation is typically divided into two categories: *śamatha* and *vipaśyanā*. *Śamatha* meditation involves developing calm and concentration while *vipaśyanā* is involved with developing direct insight into particular philosophical points. In the *lta sgom spyod gsum* framework, *sgom* is typically used to refer to an analytical *vipaśyanā* meditation rather than a calming concentration meditation. For view to be installed as one's default perceptual and conative mode, one cannot simply meditate on the breath or a visual object but must instead conduct a process of familiarization with a given conceptual view. However, one must have a basis in *śamatha* meditation to be able to remain focused on this view. Chöden Rinpoche states this quite clearly when he writes, "With such strong concentration, one can much more easily develop deep insight into these topics and can eventually develop direct perception of them, thereby gaining an antidote that cuts ignorance at the root."[49] This is why Chöden Rinpoche's twofold approach does not contradict the standard order of view, meditation, action. *Vipaśyanā* meditation must always come after one establishes the view intellectually, but *śamatha* meditation, which increases the efficacy of *vipaśyanā*, can occur either before or after establishing the view. Thus, we can conclude that *śamatha* meditation can be practiced either before or after establishing the view in order to strengthen one's *vipaśyanā* meditation and that the standard order of operations for *lta sgom spyod gsum* is as follows: (1) establish the view philosophically/intellectually; (2) practice analytical meditation on that view in order to familiarize oneself with it and install it as one's default perceptual mode; and (3) act in a way that is informed by and naturally emergent from that view. This is the case in the general Tibetan Buddhist religious context and is the case in a moral phenomenological approach to ethics.

## View, Meditation, Action as Moral Phenomenological Praxis

We have thus analyzed the various ways *lta sgom spyod gsum* is used in Tibetan contexts and have unpacked some of the nuances of its practical applications. In doing so, a picture of how view, meditation, action could be posited as a viable candidate for a moral phenomenological praxis should be becoming apparent. To summarize the core points of Buddhist moral phenomenology, it is an ethical theory primarily concerned with the perceptual and affective experience of an individual and is built from the claim that one's action stems from one's experience of the world and that to change one's experience of the world is to change one's behavior. Moral development in this theory therefore entails priming an individual to respond naturally and effortlessly to situations in accordance with the way they recognize their situatedness in myriad relationships, communities, ecosystems, and so forth. It entails adjusting one's *default perceptual mode*, being the lens through which we see the world and involves both our bare sense experience and, more importantly, the way we label and process that sense data through our acquired conceptual frameworks. Moral phenomenology goes directly to the root of *experience* as it happens, in the present, and without reflection, rather than refining one's ability to conduct a moral calculus or developing secondary qualities that themselves emerge from the grounds of experience.

Whether we are talking Buddhist moral phenomenology specifically or some non-Buddhist form of ethical comportment, the Tibetan Buddhist tradition is a useful practical interlocutor by virtue of how it understands the role of "practice." The Tibetan term for practice, *nyams su len pa*, consists of two parts: *nyams su* and *len pa*. The latter term, *len pa*, connotes grasping, accepting, bringing, obtaining, and so forth. The former term, *nyams su*, means "into experience" or "into vision." Thus, practice in the Tibetan Buddhist system means to bring into one's experience. To use familiar language, *nyams su len pa* refers specifically to the process by which a particular philosophical view is integrated into one's default perceptual mode. It thus accords incredibly well with a moral phenomenological approach to ethics. Obviously, different kinds of practice will bring different objects or ideas into one's personal experience and thus have different ethical consequences. Nonetheless, the way in which practice is understood, Tibetan Buddhism makes it a rich tradition for practically engaging moral phenomenology.

The first step in this process is therefore to determine which view will bring about the desired result. In terms of its original Tibetan Buddhist context, Jay Garfield clearly lays out what the desired result is in terms of one's conative state, comportment, and behavior. He writes, "Care, grounded in the awareness of our joint participation in global life, hence, from the Mahāyāna perspective, is the wellspring of the motivation for the development of all perfections, and the most reliable motivation for morally decent actions."[50] He also tells us the view that brings about this result, stating, "Care is also, on this view, the direct result of a genuine appreciation of the emptiness and interdependence of all sentient beings. Once one sees oneself as nonsubstantial and existing only in interdependence, and once one sees that the happiness and suffering of all sentient beings is entirely causally conditioned, the only rational attitude one can adopt to others is a caring and careful one."[51] Of course, there are exemplary figure across the Buddhist and non-Buddhist world who have perfected compassionate activity not through a realization of interdependence but through the development of virtue of compassion itself. Nonetheless, in this moral phenomenological context, we might follow Garfield and assert that determining what it means to be nonsubstantial, existing only in interdependence, and empty of intrinsic existence is the first step in practicing a Buddhist moral phenomenology.

We have seen this step phrased in a number of ways earlier in this chapter. Dudjom Rinpoche's first step for practicing according to *lta sgom spyod gsum* is "to decide through the view."[52] More than just deciding which view is appropriate, we also need have confidence in the particular view we intend to assume. This can be seen when Rangjung Dorje states, "To cut through misconceptions of the ground is to have confidence in the view."[53] Similarly, Dilgo Khyentse Rinpoche writes, "The first step in establishing the view is to acquire a proper understanding of the teachings about it."[54] Thus, the first step to practicing moral phenomenology involves both identifying the view and understanding its philosophical nuances to be confident that it is correctly understood. It therefore involves intellectual study, reflection, and debate to learn and develop confidence in a particular ontological position. Of course, this position may change from tradition to tradition, and various views may be used to effect varying ethical outcomes. Nonetheless, we may claim that intellectually understanding a particular philosophical view of the world is the necessary first step for practicing moral phenomenology.

Once the view that leads to ethical behavior has been properly established, the following step is to meditate on said view. Meditation in this context has the connotation of familiarization, contemplation, and making a living experience of a concept as we saw in the earlier definitions of *sgom pa*. The kind of meditation to be applied here is an analytical *vipaśyanā* meditation wherein one sits with and familiarizes oneself with a particular view until that view is thoroughly integrated into one's experience. While concentration or *śamatha* meditation is useful as a preliminary practice prior to engaging in *vipaśyanā* meditation, it is this latter type that is highlighted in this framework. This is for obvious reasons: While *śamatha* meditation is an integral part of mindfulness stress-relief programs (which may inadvertently lead more ethical action as a consequence of the calming states they can produce), *śamatha* is unable to uproot the fundamental perceptual misapprehension of the world that, on the Buddhist account, leads to unethical behavior. It is only by familiarizing oneself with concepts in a meditative setting that one can reorient oneself to different perceptual, affective, and conative modes. Therefore, the second step to practicing moral phenomenology is to engage in analytical meditation on that previously established view.

Again, we have seen this step articulated quite clearly earlier in this chapter. Erik Pema Kunsang defined meditation as "the act of growing accustomed to that [view]—usually in sitting practice," gesturing to how this familiarization does not exclusively occur in meditation but that it is the predominant method for doing so. Further, Wangchuk Dorje states, "To meditate without distraction on the meaning of that [view] is the meditation."[55] This kind of experiential exploration of the *meaning* of a view is precisely what is referred to by *vipaśyanā* meditation. Similarly, Dudjom Rinpoche describes the second step of *lta sgom spyod gsum* as "adopting [the view] as one's experience through meditation."[56] This adoption is again done via an analytical meditation wherein one familiarizes oneself with the view until it becomes one's default perceptual mode. A further quote by Gampopa shares this sentiment in its claim that "experience is produced in dependence on the meditation."[57] This tells us that it is not meditation *alone* that produces the desired experience but that it is certainly a necessary factor for an experiential understanding of the view.

However, these two examples should not lead us to claim that *śamatha* is not a component in this step whatsoever. Rather, as Rangjung Dorje writes, "To maintain that view without distraction is the crucial point of meditation."[58] Thus, there is an element of *concentration* required in this step as well. To efficiently practice this meditative step, a degree of concentrative ability is useful insofar as it allows one to sustain one's analytical meditation for longer periods of time and increases the efficacy of the analytical meditation's ability to bring the view into one's experience. That said, even if one practices meditation effectively, truly bringing the view fully into one's experience may take a long time even for meditative adepts. As Dilgo Khyentse Rinpoche says, "To incorporate the view into our inner experience, we put it into practice over and over again; this is the *meditation*."[59] Thus, this practice is to be done continuously until the view is fully brought into one's perceptual experience. Taken together, we might describe step 2 in the practice of moral phenomenology to be the concentrated focus on analyzing, thinking through, and becoming familiar with the earlier view such that it becomes adopted as one's default perceptual mode and reorients one's conative and affective modes as a result.

This brings us to the final point of *lta sgom spyod gsum*: action. The way that action is understood in this moral phenomenological context differs slightly from the ways that we have seen it thus far. In a moral phenomenological ethic, action is considered a *result* of experience. Moral phenomenology and contemplative practice are directed at the experience of the individual rather than the action. Proper action is simply the byproduct of this experiential shift. This can be seen in the various ways Tibetan authors describe action in their explanations of *lta sgom spyod gsum*. Dudjom Rinpoche relates the third step as "to experience [the view] continuously through action,"[60] implying that one's day-to-day actions are themselves aspects of the view. Similarly, Wangchuk Dorje instructs one's actions to accord with one's view when he states that to "maintain that view during any of the four actions is the conduct."[61] Finally, Gampopa[62] states that "to continually abide in that [experience of the view] is the action."[63] In each of these statements, we can see how not only *action* is intimately tied to view, but also how action is framed as the continuous *experience* of view. Another way to put this, as Milarepa does, is that "action is the mindfulness of this view in daily activities, meaning that the yogi is able to remember his meditation experience even during all the vicissitudes of [their] daily experience."[64] Thus, once one has meditatively familiarized oneself with the view, one must bring that experience with them into their daily happenings. In doing so, one's actions become informed by that particular view, and, in turn, one practices moral phenomenology.

More poignantly, some of the aforementioned sources refer to action as a specific *mode* of acting. Not only must one maintain the experience of the view during daily life, but one must also act in a way that *accords* with said experience. For example, Erik Pema Kunsang writes that action is "the implementation of that insight during the activities of daily life";[65] Barawa[66] states that "always acting in that way is the action";[67] and Jigten Sumgön writes that "by acting in that state itself, it is the action."[68] In other words, once an individual has meditatively installed a particular view as their *default perceptual mode*, their actions will emerge naturally from that view such that they will spontaneously respond to the situations presented to them from that position. This is precisely the ethical approach of moral phenomenology.

The spontaneity of ethical action that results from establishing and becoming familiar with a specific view (in this case the view of Mahāmudrā, Dzogchen, and the Madhyamaka) accords well with how we have seen moral phenomenology and ethical comportment described in the previous chapter. This natural, spontaneous mode of action is directly articulated when Thubten Jinpa states, "Once you have formed a good habit through internalization and integration, you can move to the third stage: action. The kind of action we are talking about would arise naturally out of transformed states of mind."[69] Phagmodrupa[70] explains this way of acting through metaphor when he states, "Their action needs to arise by itself like an old ox drinking water,"[71] and Tilopa states bluntly that "when one is without deliberate action, that is majestic action."[72] We may therefore conclude that when one puts moral phenomenology into practice by establishing a specific view conceptually and subsequently meditating on that view to bring it into one's nonconceptual experience, one's actions will be informed by this experience such that one can spontaneously, appropriately, and ethically respond to events as they happen.

## The Role of View in View, Meditation, Action

The function of *lta sgom spyod gsum* in a moral phenomenological ethic should therefore be clear. It is a directed way to bring a particular view into one's default perceptual mode. Further, we have seen the outcome of this framework in the previous chapter: Action is formed by *bodhicitta*. Like the kind of spontaneous, contextually appropriate actions we find in feminist care ethics,[73] view, meditation, action primes an individual to act in a way that accords with the specifics of the situation in a compassionate manner. What remains to be seen, therefore, are the specifics of view and meditation in the implementation of a Buddhist moral phenomenological ethic. Since I consider this moral phenomenology a *contemplative* approach to ethics, I will present a full treatment of meditation in the following chapter. Before this, however, we should parse how *view* is understood in this tradition given its aforementioned importance.

At the risk of being overly simplistic, there are three main views that might be considered "ultimate" in the Tibetan tradition: that of the Madhyamaka, the Mahamudra, and Dzogchen. These three approaches have quite different associated practices, theories, and histories, but the *consequences* of their realization are the same. Across each tradition is an emphasis on the realization of emptiness (though how emptiness is understood may vary from lineage to lineage) and an appreciation for how this realization results in *compassionate* behavior. As we saw in the previous chapter, the Tibetan tradition holds that emptiness begets compassion (*śūnyatā-karuṇā-garbham*), and each of the main ultimate views of the Madhyamaka, Mahamudra, and Dzogchen culminate in the desired ethical end of *bodhicitta*.

This emphasis on the shared *consequences* of particular views can help us make sense of how Madhyamaka, Mahāmudrā, and Dzogchen could all be put forward as potential views to be used in a moral phenomenological praxis. Shabkar Tsogdruk Rangdrol, a paragon of the nonsectarian approach to Buddhist practice, equates these three traditions in his *Emanated Scripture of Mañjuśrī* when he quotes Lhaje Chogyal, stating, "The pith instructions of the Madhyamaka, Dzogchen, and Mahāmudrā, reside in the middle of the gracious lama's heart."[74] In this way, he essentially equates these three traditions by suggesting that by putting their respective view into practice, one will be practicing properly according to their lama. Similarly, he writes,

> When your mind is cognizant, look into the essence of
>     cognizance—
> That is Mahāmudrā of cognizant emptiness.
> When your mind is blissful, look into the essence of
>     this bliss—
> That is Dzogchen of blissful emptiness.
> When your mind is empty, look into the natural face
>     of this emptiness—
> That is the great Madhyamaka of empty awareness.[75]

Thus, in this instance, different qualities of the ultimate nature of one's mind are ascribed to different traditions. Mahāmudrā is associated with cognizance, Dzogchen with bliss, and Madhyamaka with emptiness. However, each tradition is put forward as a legitimate view that adequately captures what it means to realize ultimate reality.

Tsele Natsok Rangdrol also makes this comparison in his work *Heart of the Matter*.[76] He writes:

> The Madhyamaka, the union of the two truths beyond
>   all extremes,
> The Mahāmudrā, the pristine awareness of the uncon-
>   trived natural state,
> And the Great Perfection, the primordial Samant-
>   abhadra of original purity,
> Are all of a single intention and agree on their
>   meaning.[77]

In this sense, while they may use different language to describe their notion of the ultimate and may engage in different practices to actualize that state, these three all point to the same conclusion. The *consequences* of practicing according to the Madhyamaka, Mahāmudrā, and Dzogchen traditions are identical. That said, Tsele Natsok Rangdrol does not simply conflate these three traditions but instead acknowledges and nuances their unique features to assert their similarities. He writes:

> There are some who say they are thoroughly different,
>   but
> Regarding the essential, key point,
> The nature of the view itself is in agreement.
>   However,
> The difference is in the fabricating or not fabricating
>   of the mind, or
> In the existence or nonexistence of clinging to one's
>   opinion.[78]

Thus, the difference lies in how the Madhyamaka approaches the view conceptually while Dzogchen and Mahāmudrā do not. In other words, the Madhyamaka position is substantiated through philosophical analysis while the Dzogchen and Mahāmudrā positions are substantiated through meditative experience.

Nonetheless, what links the views of the Madhyamaka, Mahāmudrā, and Dzogchen is the shared conative states that emerge from their perceptual or experiential realization. Scholars in each tradition emphasize compassion as one of the primary consequences of realizing their respective ultimate views. Indeed, this shared conative result may even be said to be *the* qualifying characteristic for a "correct view." In his text titled *The Union of Mahāmudrā and Dzogchen*, Chökyi Nyima Rinpoche states: "The correct view is embraced by the unity of emptiness and compassion."[79] Thus, without these twin aspects, a view would be considered erroneous. Similarly, we might assert that, in the case of moral phenomenology, the same rings true. Seeing how the Madhyamaka, Mahāmudrā, and Dzogchen positions each include a deep understanding of emptiness and are directly related to compassion, the equation of these views by individuals like Shabkar becomes quite understandable. These three views form the ultimate views in both the soteriological tradition of Tibet and a moral phenomenological approach to ethics.

But what of nonultimate views? Emptiness was not the only teaching forwarded as useful in the Buddhist tradition, so surely these other views have ethical import. If one looks at the *lamrim* and *lojong* traditions, one approaches the view of emptiness by first familiarizing oneself with the emptiness of the self (*anātman*), the view of *pratītyasamutpāda*, or a general understanding of causality and impermanence. These are distinct from the ultimate view of the Mahāmudrā, Dzogchen, and Madhyamaka, but are nonetheless steppingstones for eventually arriving at these ultimate views. By familiarizing oneself with these provisional views, one primes oneself to gradually understand emptiness and can thus realize it more easily. However, these views might *themselves* have ethical utility. As the seventeenth Karmapa writes,

> If someone hits us with a stick, are we angry at the stick or at the person hitting us? This question might seem absurd, but breaking it down logically, it is the stick that directly caused us pain. However, we know the stick

is not in control, and so we do not direct our anger at the stick. Like us, the stick is a victim in this scenario. We likewise don't blame the hand wielding the stick. Rather, we look to the person controlling the hand. This seems logical to us. Yet the person himself or herself was overpowered by anger and driven to act by their rage. Following this line of reflection, logic should lead us to recognize that the locus of power is not the person but the emotional forces that have taken control from within. The person attacking us fell under the control of their anger, just as has surely happened to us on occasion.[80]

In this case, having a default perceptual mode that involves *anātman, pratītyasamutpāda, anitya,* or cause and effect would help us react to this situation more ethically than if we do not. Each of these ideas would help us view the situation in a different light. We might understand that there is no "I" to be offended, we might see that there are underlying factors out of the perpetrators control that led to them hitting us, or we might see their behavior as a brief manifestation of a broader material system. Furthermore, through experientially understanding these positions, we may avoid succumbing to anger (or other afflictive emotions) and putting ourselves in the shoes of our assailant. In each of these cases, experientially acclimating to these ideas allows us to not respond immediately with anger, but with compassion. In doing so, these provisional views can also contribute to a moral phenomenological approach to ethics. And, as we will see, the notion that both ultimate and provisional views can have ethical utility is of great importance in the application of a moral phenomenological ethic to the more-than-human world. The remaining piece to explore is thus how contemplative practice can bridge *view* and *action* and bring a view like emptiness into one's default perceptual mode.

4

# From Value to Action

## The Ethics of Contemplative Practice
## and Direct Meditative Experience

For view to fully inform one's action, it needs to be brought into one's default perceptual mode and move from a concept to an *experience*. This is where meditation comes in. Through meditation, one can occasion a direct meditative experience of a particular view and actually come to *see* the world through its lens. This chapter will outline the process of meditation in the context of *lta sgom spyod gsum* and will work to unpack what a direct meditative experience of view entails. This will involve a thorough discussion on how one practices *śamatha*, how this relates to *vipaśyanā* practice, and the way *vipaśyanā* must be practiced in a moral phenomenology. It then discusses how the direct meditative experience toward which this *vipaśyanā* is practiced is distinct from the ways that mystical experience has been understood in religious studies settings. In doing so, it will complete our picture of view, meditation, action and its relationship to a moral phenomenological approach to ethics and allow us to apply this ethical framework to a novel, contemplative approach to environmental ethics.

## Unpacking *Śamatha*

The most prominent text on meditation in the Tibetan tradition is the *Bhāvanākrama*[1] by Kamalaśīla.[2] According to its hagiography,

101

the text was composed after the great Samyé[3] debate where the merits of the gradual Indian approach and the sudden Chinese approach to enlightenment were put against one another. As Sam Van Shaik notes:

> Zen's[4] radical tendencies were disliked by some of the Indian Buddhist teachers in Lhasa. As followers of the Mahāyāna, or "Greater Vehicle" of Buddhism, all were in agreement about basic principles. . . . The dispute concerned how to achieve this. The Indian Buddhists insisted on the need to combine meditation with rational analysis and the basic practices of ethical conduct. For Buddhists of the Greater Vehicle this combination was summarised by the Six Perfections: giving, morality, patience, energy, meditation and wisdom. By contrast, the Zen teachers said that if one recognised the true nature of one's own mind, the Perfections could be dispensed with.[5]

Tempers flared between the two factions, leading to some crushing their own genitals, setting their own heads ablaze, and threatening to kill one another.[6] Thus, to put an end to the unrest, King Trisong Detsen organized a debate to establish which side held the correct view and would be formalized as the Tibetan position.

Kamalaśīla, a student of Śāntarakṣita,[7] came from Nalanda University and represented the Indian position, which proposed a staged approach to enlightenment involving a gradual familiarization with key Buddhist concepts and the development of the *pāramitās*. The Chinese position was represented by Hashang,[8] who argued that "it was only by stopping ordinary thought that the cycle of *saṃsāra* could come to an end. Both virtuous and sinful actions, the very distinction between them belonging to ordinary thought, were part of the problem. They were like black and white clouds; both blocked out the sun. The Buddha's teachings on the practice of virtue were for his duller disciples. The sharpest could get straight to the point by abandoning ordinary thought."[9] According to traditional Tibetan histories, Kamalaśīla successfully defended his position, undermining Hashang's in the process, and Trisong Detsen ultimately sided with the gradual Nalanda approach.[10] That said, Van Shaik notes that "some ancient manuscripts indicate that Hashang Moheyan had a more nuanced view of meditation, and a Chinese version of the debate concludes with the king giving his blessing to the Chinese teachers," while "modern scholars have even questioned whether a debate ever really took place."[11] Further, there is evidence that major Buddhist figures in Tibet's philosophical history, including Longchenpa[12] and Jigmé Lingpa, both accepted and defended the view of Hashang and saw it as commensurate with the Nyingma approach to practice.[13] As Yaroslav Komarovski writes, one scholar, Nubchen Sangye Yeshe,[14] even outlined "four Buddhist approaches to awakening, with each succeeding one being superior to the preceding ones: the gradual approach taught by Kamalaśīla, the instantaneous Chan approach of Heshang Moheyan, the approach of Mahāyoga, and the approach of Dzokchen."[15] Nonetheless, it is within this context that Kamalaśīla wrote his treatise on meditation, and it was the gradualist approach to practice that was advocated therein.

The *Bhāvanākrama* delineates two major forms of meditation that are consistently found across all Buddhist meditative traditions: *śamatha* and *vipaśyanā*. We briefly looked at these categories in the previous chapter as the two components of Gegen Dorje Tharchin's definition of *sgom pa*. Recall, *sgom pa* is "the mind resting single-pointedly . . . [I]t refers to the cultivation of *citta* and so forth."[16] Here, we can find a concise definition of *śamatha* in the first half and of *vipaśyanā* in the second half. However, to further understand how one might implement these two kinds of meditation in the context of moral phenomenology, we must further unpack *śamatha* and *vipaśyanā* with reference to the primary texts of the tradition.

Meditation manuals across Buddhist traditions universally point to *śamatha* as the starting point for an individual's meditation practice. However, this is not the starting point for practice as a *whole*. The *Bhāvanākrama* states, "If one is without consideration for the desire for gain and so forth, is well-established in morality, has come to possess the mode with which one voluntary assumes *duḥkha* and so forth, and begins the practice with diligence, then *śamatha* will be very quickly accomplished. For that reason, the *pāramitās*, dana and so forth, have been repeatedly taught to be themselves its causes in the *Aryasaṃdhinimocana* and so forth."[17]

Tsongkhapa's *Lamrim Chenmo* quotes this passage directly and comments on how the first four of the *pāramitās* (generosity, morality, patience, diligence) are here directed toward the cultivation of the fifth, meditation, and its culmination in the sixth, wisdom.

We can make good sense of these instructions when we consider the goal of *śamatha* meditation. The Tibetan word *zhi gnas* consists of two words, *zhi* and *gnas*. *Zhi* means "peace, calm, stillness, and quiescence," while *gnas* means "to abide, to dwell, and to establish oneself in a particular place." Thus, while *zhi gnas* and its Sanskrit equivalent, *śamatha*, are typically used to refer to a particular *method* of meditation, they can just as easily describe the *resultant state* of the practice. In *zhi gnas*, one abides in calm, establishes one's mind in peace, or dwells in quiescence. This "peace," "calm," and "quiescence" are qualities of mind and thus directly relate to the way the practitioner thinks and feels. Pursuant to this goal, generosity, morality, patience, and diligence are incredibly useful by virtue of how their opposites can create ruminating thoughts and a turbulence of emotions. Should one steal, lie, lash out in anger at someone, or have a lazy attitude, a peaceful state of mind will be more difficult to achieve because of the feelings of guilt, anger, greed, and so forth that they cause.

A good way to think of *pāramitās* in this context is that they are the internal supports for practice. They establish a mental set for a practitioner to effectively calm the mind and develop *śamatha*. They can be seen as the mental equivalent of another necessary component for establishing *śamatha*: the external prerequisites for *samādhi*.[18] While Kamalaśīla does not speak to these external supports directly, Tsongkhapa parses these them alongside the aforementioned mental supports in his *Lamrim Chenmo*. He writes that "the yogin should at the outset take recourse to the equipment for calm abiding, which is the foundation for speedily and pleasantly accomplishing calm"[19] of which he gives six parts: residence in a favorable place, meager desire, contentment, elimination of multiple activities, purity of morality, and the elimination of discursive thinking of craving and so on.[20] Each of these factors relates to how an individual mediates their relationship with the world, and each constitutes a reduction or elimination of external stimuli. With less external stimuli comes less mental fluctuation, and the meditator can therefore more effectively practice and come to experience *śamatha*.

In terms of the actual practice of *śamatha*, these two texts agree as to the method for developing calm and concentration. Kamalaśīla writes that "in the beginning, one must fix the mind for a short while all aspects of the object of analysis so that it will come together in its entirety" and states that the object of meditation can be either with form or without form.[21] Thus, we have two components to *śamatha* meditation: the act of concentration and the object of concentration. With respect to the former, Kamalaśīla gives a brief account of *śamatha* practice in the second book of the *Bhāvanākrama*. He writes, "Initially, calm abiding must be accomplished. Having calmed the distraction of outer objects, one naturally and continuously engages in focusing inward and abides in mind itself which is endowed joy and is thoroughly purified. This is why it is named calm abiding."[22] We therefore have a three-pronged approach to developing *śamatha*. First, we quell the constant chatter of our discursive thought; then we practice returning our attention to our chosen meditative object; and finally, by doing so for longer and longer periods, we develop contentment and concentration in the mind.

Classical texts on *śamatha* also give a nine-step progression for developing a strong *śamatha* practice. While these simple meditation instructions remain the same, an individual can gauge the quality of their meditation by referencing these nine steps. These steps can be found in the *Bhāvanākrama* and a detailed explanation of them can be found in Tsongkhapa's *Lamrim Chenmo*.[23] For our purposes, Shabkar's *Emanated Scripture of Mañjuśrī* is a useful place for explaining these points as it works from Tsongkhapa's text but explains them in concise manner. It gives the nine steps to achieving calm abiding as follows:

1. Placement: collect the mind which is distracted by external phenomena and place it on the meditative object.

2. Continuous Placement: continuously place one's focus with the designated mediative object, otherwise one will remain distracted.

3. Re-setting: if one becomes distracted by outer object due to forgetfulness, having realized that, one again re-sets the mind on that very meditative object.

4. Close Placement: again and again one collects the naturally expansive mind and closely places the mind which has become subtle.

5. Controlling: having contemplated the good qualities resulting from meditative stabilization, through the joy of meditative stabilization mind becomes controlled.

6. Making Peaceful: having perceived the disadvantages of distraction, one's dislike for meditative stabilization is made peaceful.

7. Making Fully Peaceful: that which arises from a mind of attachment, unhappiness, drowsiness and torpor, and so forth are made fully peaceful.

8. Single-Pointed Placement: having thoroughly exerted oneself, the obstacles of drowsiness and agitation will no longer exist. Therefore, one is now continuously settled in meditative stabilization.

9. Settling in Equipoise: having thoroughly freed oneself from all distractions of drowsiness and agitation, one spontaneously and effortlessly achieves meditative stabilization, and having relaxed into nondiscursive, effortless equanimity at the time of this natural placement, one settles in equipoise.[24]

Through these nine steps, we have a clear picture not only of how to meditate but of how our meditation will progress. Shabkar (along with Kamalaśīla and Tsongkhapa) gives us a direct roadmap for what our experience will be with *samatha* meditation and thus gives practitioners confidence by letting them know where they are and where they are headed.

With its method and path established, the final aspect of *śamatha* we must address is the *object* of meditation. Tsongkhapa dedicates a large portion of his chapter "Calming the Mind" to explaining how one concentrates on a meditative object and agrees with Kamalaśīla's approach to calm abiding. However, he seeks to develop *śamatha* beyond the instructions given in the *Bhāvanākrama*. For example, Kamalaśīla states that "in order to clear away the faults of distraction of a beginner, a collection of concepts is temporarily a suitable meditative object. When one has reached the point of mental concentration, one can further engage only a particular meditative object such as the aggregates, the dhātus, and so forth."[25] As Tsongkhapa notes, Kamalaśīla is vague about the specificities of what the parameters are for considering something a meditative object,[26] and the *Lamrim Chenmo* states that "many meditative objects are set forth in the great texts about accomplishing *samādhi*."[27] Thus, we may ask, "What are these meditative objects?" Tsongkhapa spends a great deal of time going over each of these and the reasons each may be used by different kinds of practitioners. Some of these objects include unpleasant things for those with too much lust, *maitrī* or lovingkindness meditation for those with too much hate, and fixing the mind on dependent origination for those with too mistaken a view of reality.

For those familiar with contemporary mindfulness meditation, these may seem a little odd. As Tsongkhapa notes, these are meditative objects "both for cultivating understanding with discernment and for cultivating the fixation with calming. Hence they are not meditative objects for calming alone."[28] However, Tsongkhapa also includes a familiar object in his list: the breath. He writes, "The meditative object while inhaling and exhaling is the one by way of counting and observing the inward and outward passage of the breath, so that the mind does not stray elsewhere."[29] We might say that this is the most direct approach to cultivating *śamatha* since it does not involve extraneous concepts, but outside of this brief mention, Tsongkhapa says little about focusing on the breath. Thankfully, we can find his reason for this later in the chapter. He writes, "There is the requirement that the diversity of persons perform in the diverse meditative objects; and, in particular, if one who has not gone to the limit of calming that reaches certainty and is among those with a predominance of lust, and so on, he has the requirement to perform with a definite meditative object, because if he does not (so) perform, although he may attain a *samādhi* favorable to calming he will not actually achieve calming."[30] This is to say that those with too much desire will not actually achieve *śamatha* without working to lessen that desire *alongside* their concentration practice. Thus, for this person, there is a specific kind of meditation they must do: meditation on unpleasant things. Doing so cultivates concentration while also quelling desire.

Tsongkhapa was writing at the turn of the fifteenth century, so one may wonder if this approach to meditative objects still stands today. Simply put, are contemporary people in our globalized world to be categorized in the same way as Tibetans six hundred years ago? On the one hand, it may be argued that humans have neither changed physiologically nor psychologically and are still to be categorized according to their dominant afflictions (desire, anger, ignorance, pride, and jealousy). However, it may also be argued that the barriers to achieving *śamatha* are altogether different. In a recent discussion with Daniel Aitken, Jetsunma Tenzin Palmo explained how the order of operations in Dzogchen practice has changed in contemporary times. Typically, students would begin their practice by completing the preliminaries practices[31] before moving on to *śamatha*, *vipaśyanā*, and so forth. However, in contemporary times, she instructs students to practice *śamatha* first. She states, "Our minds are just jam packed with stuff already, most of it trash . . . and to build a *buddha* palace on top of a trash heap doesn't make sense. First, we need to clean out, get some space in there, open the windows, throw out all this junk. And that is where *śamatha* and *vipaśyanā* come in."[32] Daniel Aitken concurs and replies, "In the modern world, *śamatha* is more foundational than even the preliminaries."[33] The reason for this is that modern people are inundated with sensory experience and information in a way that historical Buddhists were not. As a result of the proliferation of television, billboard advertisements, social media, and so forth, the most important step to meditative practice has become *śamatha* so that an individual can make space in their mind to practice more conceptual meditations that ultimately progress them down the path. To this end, we can return to Tsongkhapa for some instruction on an object of meditation. He writes, "One with predominance of discursive speculation definitely has the requirement to cultivate the breath."[34] Certainly it is this kind of discursive speculation that Tenzin Palmo and Daniel Aitken are identifying. Thus, I argue that among the meditation objects given by Tsongkhapa, the breath would be preferred for cultivating *śamatha* for most people today.

To return briefly to moral phenomenology, this might seem like an odd approach to solving social issues that require immediate and drastic *action* to solve. At first glance, to sit and watch one's breath to establish some sort of calm abiding might seem futile for developing a clear perception of reality and for recalibrating one's behavior. However, to effectively establish a particular view as one's default perceptual mode, calm abiding is incredibly important. As Chöden Rinpoche writes, "If you want to cut down a tree, you need a sharp axe that will cut it directly, but it is not sufficient just to have the axe. You also need a strong, steady shoulder to swing the axe. Likewise, special insight is like the axe that directly cuts the root of *saṃsāra*, and calm abiding is like the steady shoulder that swings it."[35] Thus, to effectively implement meditation in the framework of view, meditation, action, we need the ability to focus on a given view. To this end, *śamatha* is absolutely necessary. It affords practitioners the ability to develop concentration and calm such that when they introduce concepts to their meditation, they may remain with them without distraction. In doing so, they are poised to more quickly have the experiential realization necessary for making a conceptual view into one's default perceptual mode. As Atiśa states in his *Lamp for the Path*:[36]

> Since one has not attained calm abiding,
> Extraordinary knowledge will not arise.
> Therefore, in order to attain calm abiding,
> One must exert themselves again and again.
> If the branch of calm abiding is weak,
> Even if one fully strives to meditate
> For a thousand years correctly,
> One will not establish meditative stabilization.[37]

Thankfully the Tibetan tradition has given us a detailed program for practicing *śamatha* including a clear method, roadmap, means of problem solving, and object of meditation.[38] Kamalaśīla's *Bhāvanākrama* and its development in the works of Tsongkhapa and Shabkar provide us with the means to develop concentration and calm that we can then apply to more specific meditations for enacting the moral phenomenological project in general and, as we will see, in a more specific ecological context.

## Directly Perceiving through *Vipaśyanā*

Having established a calm mind and an ability to concentrate, Buddhist texts direct practitioners to practice *vipaśyanā* meditation next. So, we might ask, what does the term *vipaśyanā* mean in the context of *lta sgom spyod gsum*? Simply put, it is the practice that bridges view and conduct. *Vipaśyanā* meditation involves directing one's calm mind to particular conceptual views and concentrating on them until they are directly perceived. Buddhist texts are consistent in their conviction that *śamatha* alone is insufficient for either liberation or simply overcoming afflictive emotions. For example, Kamalaśīla writes, "Through the arising of the experience of wisdom, the seed of delusion is absolutely eliminated. If it is not like that, there would be no elimination of the afflictive emotions through meditative concentration alone as is the case with non-Buddhists."[39] This sentiment is shared by Tsongkhapa, who echoes Kamalaśīla and states,

> One should not be satisfied with merely that calming attended with the rapture and pleasure that are of special benefit. It is necessary to cultivate discerning for generating the conclusive, errorless insight into the meaning of reality. Because, if this is not done, and one merely has that (sort of) *samādhi*, it would mean his [*sic*] being in common with the outsiders, so that although one meditates in that mere (*samādhi*) in the same way as the path of those persons, he does not eliminate the seed of defilement and so does not free himself from phenomenal existence.[40]

Thus, while some benefit may come from establishing calm and concentration through a *śamatha* practice, it is not able to address negative emotions or behaviors alone. In both the Tibetan Buddhist tradition and a moral phenomenological approach to ethics, one must therefore engage in *vipaśyanā* meditation.

This relationship between calming and insight meditation is most bluntly stated in the second book of the *Bhāvanākrama*, which Tsongkhapa uses to ground his own thought. He quotes Kamalaśīla thusly:

> Then should he [*sic*] think, "Having accomplished calming, I shall contemplate by discerning." All the pronouncements of the Lord are well stated, and either directly or gradually clarify reality to incline one toward it. When the light cognizing reality arises, one becomes free from all the net of views in the manner of dispelling darkness. By calming alone, knowledge does not become pure, nor does one dispel the darkness of obscuration. When one well contemplates reality with insight, knowledge becomes pure, and one comprehends reality. One insight rightly eliminates the obscuration. Hence, one thinks, "Now that I am stationed in calming, I shall search the reality with insight. I shall not rest content with calming alone." What is that reality? In the absolute sense, all entities, whether personality (*pudgala*) or natures (*dharma*), are the voidness of self.[41]

It is clear that, in this tradition, *śamatha* is insufficient for achieving the desired ends, and this quotation tells us why. Calming the mind by developing concentration does not address the afflictive emotions (greed, hatred, delusion, and so forth) that give rise to *duḥkha* and does not create the necessary perceptual set for moving through the world in a way that benefits oneself and others.

Ultimately, it is only through the union of *śamatha* and *vipaśyanā* that afflictive emotions are quelled, and this perceptual set is established. Without *vipaśyanā*, the afflictive emotions do not subside, but without *śamatha*, one will have greater difficulty incorporating views into their default perceptual mode. Thus, the practice of both *śamatha* and *vipaśyanā* are absolutely necessary for both the soteriological aims of Tibetan Buddhism and the ethical aims of moral phenomenology.

With respect to the object of meditation in *vipaśyanā* practice, a useful place to turn is Longchenpa's chapter "Meditation on the Meaning of the View," in his text *Shingta Chenpo*.[42] Longchenpa presents meditation along three distinct lines that accord with the three kinds of practitioners: those of high capacity, those of middling capacity, and those of lesser capacity, characterized according to the ease with which an individual realizes the ultimate view of emptiness. For those with high capacity, their path is brief and involves little to no meditation. This is because of their ability to "remain naturally in the state of the yoga of the stream of the Mind, all the time, with no need of meditation with effort."[43] In doing so, they attain liberation "due to the circumstances [of the blessings] of the lama,"[44] rather than their own meditative effort. Later in the chapter, Longchenpa gives a reason for this. He writes, "For people of high intellect, just as on a golden island, even if you search, you won't find earth or stone, whatever arises is liberated into the ultimate nature (*chos nyid*). So the antidotes have been purified into the ultimate sphere (*dbyings*), and there is no longer a need for contemplative periods."[45] Perhaps there are certain individuals outside of the Buddhist tradition who might have a similar proclivity to these highest views and would therefore require no meditation for establishing a given ethical view as their default perceptual mode. However, just as in the Buddhist tradition, these cases would be incredibly rare. It is incredibly difficult to overcome years of conditioning simply by being introduced to a particular view, be that view emptiness, no-self, or interdependence.

Most Buddhists would fall into one of the latter two categories of practitioners and must practice meditation to experientially realize the view. To differentiate these two, Longchenpa details them as follows:

> For people of mediocre intellect, after having realized the view, by contemplating without moving in the state of birthlessness and clarity which is free from torpor and elation, like an unpolluted pond, [one] unites tranquility and insight and dissolves the concepts into the ultimate sphere, and space-like realization arises. For people of

lesser intellect, one should meditate and tame the monkey-like wild mind, which does not abide even for a while, by means of one-pointed tranquility. When one becomes able to concentrate, then by meditating, as the antidote, upon the discriminative insight such as emptiness, the absence of inherent existence in phenomenal existence, and by meditating that all appearances are illusions, one realizes the meaning of birthlessness.[46]

Regarding those of middling capacity, they are able to achieve liberation through the contemplation of the mind itself. Seeing as Longchenpa is writing in the context of Dzogchen, this is an unsurprising path of action. Those of middling capacity can meditate directly on the ultimate view, in this case "ultimate nature of phenomena, the unborn nature" and the mind as "the play of nonduality of *saṃsāra* and *nirvāṇa*, the primordial wisdom of transcending existence and nonexistence, and the changelessness of clarity."[47] This can be regarded as the object of meditation, and to the end of its realization, Longchenpa provides eight methods of contemplation. One of these methods is the "contemplation in the state of unwaveringness and nonconceptualization," which he describes thus: "In the sky-like Mind, by letting the thoughts of the mental events remain naturally (*rang sor bzhag*), they dissolve (*dengs pa*) like clouds disappearing [in the sky]. One should contemplate in the state of that view, the nature of the example [the sky], without wavering."[48] The other examples follow similar lines and include the "contemplation without partiality, like space," "contemplating naturally and effortlessly," and "contemplation in effortlessness and spontaneity."[49] Each of these contemplations provides a method for directly approaching the aforementioned ultimate view and allows the practitioner to bridge view and action directly through meditation.

But most important for the present discussion is the meditation for those of lesser capacity. Longchenpa begins this section by asserting the necessity of *śamatha* meditation as the principal means of quelling a turbulent mind. He then instructs practitioners to train in the Four Immeasurables (compassion, lovingkindness, sympathetic joy, equanimity) and quotes the *Bodhicaryāvatāra*'s statement: "Having pacified the thoughts, meditate on the Mind of

Enlightenment."[50] This is to be done until "there is no projection of thoughts as long as one doesn't abandon the contemplation of concentrating on the object," and "mind and body are at ease, speech is lessened, words become gentle, and the complexion becomes rich."[51] These are the markers Longchenpa gives for knowing one has established one-pointed tranquility (*śamatha*), and indicate the practitioner's ability to begin meditating on emptiness by means of the "eight illusory examples."[52] These examples are found in a separate text by Longchenpa, *Finding Comfort and Ease in Illusion*,[53] which provides eight similes for emptiness: a dream, magical illusion, hallucination, mirage, echo, city of *gandharvas*,[54] reflection, and apparition.[55] Finally, one is to meditate on "[seeing all] as space without having any conceptualization even of the perception [of things] as illusions,"[56] meaning that one meditates on the emptiness of emptiness itself.

So, it seems that we are given a succession of objects with which we are to practice. Each of these is given to the practitioner in a particular order such that they may progressively gain insight into the ultimate view that those of the highest and middling intellect begin with. In this progression, one inches toward the ultimate view through a series of provisional realizations. As one does so, one slowly tunes into the ultimate view of the world and, in a moral phenomenological context, acts ethically accordingly. Understanding the relationship between view and meditation in this way helps us understand the utility of what we may call "provisional views." In both the Buddhist soteriological context and the broader moral phenomenological context, simply meditating on the Four Immeasurables is insufficient. This alone will not liberate the individual from *duḥkha* and will not put them in a position to properly respond to ethical situations as they present themselves. These ends can only be achieved in this context through a full understanding of emptiness. However, these provisional realizations are not without value. Each is a meaningful step toward the soteriological goal, and each primes the practitioner to act in a way that is *more* attuned to the ultimate reality than before.

Thus, it is here that we find perhaps the best approach to meditation for the purposes of moral phenomenology. This is not because most people are of a lesser capacity (though, meditatively speaking, this may be the case) but rather because this approach to insight meditation is straightforward and gradual. It shows how the object of meditation should remain accessible and should be built upon in stages. Just as one should not try to solve calculus equations before they've fully grasped multiplication, exponents, and so forth, so too one should not try to experientially realize interdependence or emptiness prior to realizing more introductory positions like impermanence. This is not because it is impossible to jump right into calculus or interdependence, but rather that these are built upon other ideas that should first be understood to make these more difficult points easier to grasp. Thus, Longchenpa gives us a useful way of understanding meditative objects and the use of provisional views to experience the ultimate.

## *Listen, Reflect, Meditate:* The Method of *Vipaśyanā*

When it comes to bringing these conceptual meditative objects into one's perceptual experience, the Tibetan tradition provides a clear path for making intellectual knowledge into experiential knowledge: *listen, reflect, meditate.* This framework is primarily concerned with how a view is ascertained prior to meditation and frames meditation as but a single step in the experiential realization of view. A classical presentation of this framework can be found in Vasubandhu's[57] *Abhidharmakośabhaṣyam,*[58] which states, "One listens to that which is in accordance with the truth, or hears its meaning. Having listened to it, one gives unmistaken thought to it, and having thought about it, one engages in single-pointed concentration. Hence, the wisdom born from thought arises based on the wisdom born from listening and the wisdom born from meditation arises on the wisdom born from thought."[59] Thus, the path to experientially understanding Buddhist views is sequential and graded. Far from being some far-out mystical practice, meditation builds upon the philosophical exploration of a particular idea and functions to integrate a particular philosophical position into one's experience.

We can also find this framework for insight in many Tibetan contexts where it is consistently used as a progressive method for realizing view. For example, Khensur Jampa Tegchok writes, "This wisdom develops gradually, first by hearing and studying the teachings, then by contemplating and reflecting on them to ensure we understand them correctly, and finally by integrating them in our mind through meditation."[60] If we are to understand meditation as a reifying procedure wherein the concepts one focuses on are installed as one's default perceptual mode, then this approach makes great sense. Of course, the first step to installing a particular view would be to hear it or encounter it in a text, but this first step also involves *studying* the view by referencing the variety of materials that explain it. In the Tibetan tradition, this would often mean consulting root texts and commentaries to obtain a cursory understanding of the position. The second step involves a more thorough reading of the commentaries and debate and oral interviews with one's teacher to arrive at a more comprehensive intellectual understanding of a particular idea. Finally, one brings this view into their meditation to cultivate a direct experience of the position and incorporate it into their default perceptual mode.

Thus, meditation only comes *after* one has engaged in a thorough intellectual study of a particular subject. Far from being a nondiscursive spiritual practice, meditation in this framework is used in tandem with an academic study of philosophical material to fully develop critical acumen of the view. Tsongkhapa used this framework himself in his religious training. In his autobiography, he writes:

> First, one should seek in abundance extensive listening
> In the middle, one should consult the scriptural tradition such that it appears as direct instruction
> In the end, one should put them into practice in every way, day and night,
> And this should be dedicated to the spread of the teachings everywhere.[61]

However, this framework is seen not only in the scholastic traditions of Tibetan Buddhism but also in the more yogically oriented traditions. Take, for example, Shabkar's instructions in his autobiography:

> When studying, hearing and reflecting, don't fall under the sway of distraction by day, or of sleep by night: Be

diligent, son of my heart. After thoroughly listening to and reflecting on the meaning of the teachings, as your home take a cave blessed by the great sages, as friends, take the birds and wild animals; As for food, rely on begging. Meditate one-pointedly without distraction. Don't meditate for just a little while: Practice for as long as you live, and in mountain solitudes quit your illusory body.[62]

Whether the given view is the lucid, compassionate, nonclinging nature of mind or is more of a scholastic Prasaṅgika-Madhyamaka view, the process is the same. Meditation must always be preceded by listening and reflecting so that the view reified during the meditative process is without error and leads to the desired outcomes of the practitioner.

Alongside this listen, reflect, meditate framework is a parallel gradient of understanding wherein one develops critical acumen in progressive stages. In his book on scholastic education in Tibetan Buddhism titled *The Sound of Two Hands Clapping*, Georges Dreyfus explores this gradient, which he separates into three consonant categories: "acumen arising from listening," "acumen arising from thinking," and "acumen arising from meditation."[63] He calls the first of these a superficial, preliminary understanding that comes from reading a text or listening to someone's explanation. He contrasts this acumen[64] with the later stages and states that "this superficial grasp helps orient one's investigation but differs from the mature comprehension that inquiry brings. It does not yet enable us to penetrate the text, comprehending its consequences and the questions that it raises."[65]

This kind of comprehension begins to emerge in the second kind of acumen, that arising from thinking. The Tibetan term Dreyfus translates as thinking is *bsam* which also has the connotation of contemplating, considering, and imagining. Thus, this acumen arises from exploring the logical consequences of a particular position to arrive at a more nuanced understanding of the idea. Dreyfus states that this acumen arising from thinking is the "proximate goal of scholastic education" and can be understood on three levels. First, he writes that this "implies a greater textual comprehension derived from the sustained practices of commentary and debate,"[66] though he concedes that this outcome is sometimes included under the acumen arising from listening. Second, Dreyfus notes how this acumen allows an individual to "take the text into oneself" and "internalize one's comprehension" such that "one realizes the religious relevance of the great texts of the tradition—how its ideas can be used to lessen one's defilements and eventually eliminate them."[67] Third, this kind of contemplation can "also lead to an understanding of the view of emptiness, offering insight into the Madhyamaka view and the realization of how that insight can disrupt ordinary ego-centered subjectivity."[68] He also importantly notes how this comprehension is still only conceptual but is nonetheless a necessary step toward internalizing the concepts of the tradition and coming to directly realize them.

This ultimate internalization or direct experience gets termed the "acumen arising from meditation" and is described by Dreyfus as the "last phase in the program of soteriological transformation sought by the tradition."[69] He writes that meditation "can lead to a more direct insight into the nature of persons and other phenomena, which gradually frees an individual from the bondage of negative emotions."[70] Thus, Dreyfus is implying that the acumen arising from listening and thinking does not actually address negative emotion or negative behavior. It is only through the meditative understanding of the view that one can overcome greed, hatred, and delusion and reorient ethically. Moreover, he writes that the meditative process "culminates in the full internalization of the content of the tradition."[71]

Thus, for the purposes of both the soteriological goal of Buddhism and the ethical transformation of moral phenomenology, it is clear that meditation is necessary. However, for *vipaśyanā* meditation to be effective, it must be practiced in concert with philosophical study and intellectual contemplation. *Śamatha* practice can be done without recourse to philosophical study and is certainly a necessary step toward effective *vipaśyanā* practice. However, when it comes to actually developing insight and experientially realizing the view during *vipaśyanā* meditation, the subframework of listen, reflect, meditate is crucial. It provides a step-by-step approach to realization that begins with a conceptual encounter, proceeds into a deep conceptual understanding, and culminates in an experiential or direct perceptual realization of the view. John Dunne echoes this method in his analysis of Dharmakīrti[72] and links it directly to an extraordinary experience: "Dharmakīrti does not choose to present yogic perception as a mystical gnosis that encounters or uncovers real things in the world; instead he presents it as a process that is designed to inculcate transformative concepts into the mind through an intense, vivid and nonconceptual experience that arises from learning, contemplating and meditating on those concepts."[73] Thus, to further make sense of meditation's role in bridging view and action we must also analyze the particular direct meditative experience occasioned by listening, reflecting, and meditating on the view.

## Understanding the Mechanism of Direct Meditative Experience

The listen, reflect, meditate method for developing an experiential understanding of the view makes clear how to bridge an intellectual view and spontaneous ethical action. Prior to practicing *vipaśyanā* meditation, one must both come to a nuanced intellectual or conceptual understanding of the view and develop calm and concentration during *śamatha* meditation. Then, when *vipaśyanā* is practiced, and this view is meditated upon, it becomes integrated into one's default perceptual mode, and one is able to bridge the gap between value and action. This is how a moral phenomenological praxis is applied. Despite this clear path, the actual *mechanism of action* is still somewhat blurry. It is clear that at the heart of this transformation lies a particular *experience* that bridges the gap between the conceptual and the experiential, but none of the above meditation manuals actually details what this experience is. Thankfully, we have writing both in the Tibetan Buddhist tradition and in the broader field of religious studies that can help us make sense of this experience.

The first problematic that arises is this gap between the conceptual view and nonconceptual experience. The core of a moral phenomenological approach to ethics is a reflexive, spontaneous mode of action that does not rely upon conceptual deliberation. In this system, the perceptual or experiential set of an individual is paramount. However, as we have seen before, *vipaśyanā* meditation bridges the gap between view and action, and concepts are integral to this process. Anne Klein frames this relationship thusly: "Before one can develop a yogic direct perception of mind and body as devoid of a substantially existent self-sufficient self, the absence of such must be understood conceptually. The philosopher-practitioner develops a mental image of selflessness until finally, through increased familiarity with that image, direct perception becomes possible."[74] Thus, we may ask: How does one go from having a conceptual understanding of a particular view to a nonconceptual experience of it?

Klein has dealt with this problem directly in several of her scholarly works and dedicates a lengthy monograph to resolving this question from a Tibetan Buddhist perspective. Her book *Knowledge and Liberation* details a Gelugpa approach to transforming dualistic conceptuality into nondual (i.e. experiential) wisdom. Klein uses a good deal of technical terminology derived from the Gelugpa tradition and presents a more nuanced approach to the topic than we are able to address here. However, there are certain elements of her work that can greatly inform the direct meditative experience required for enacting moral transformation.

One such element is her distinction between term and meaning generalities and the play of these concepts in the process of directly realizing concepts such as impermanence and emptiness. She presents a threefold typology for the kinds of thoughts that appear in our mind: (1) only a term-generality; (2) only a meaning-generality; and (3) a mixture of both.[75] To demonstrate the differences among these three kinds of thoughts, Klein uses an example of a magnolia, about which she writes:

> When a person who has never seen a magnolia hears the term "magnolia," that person's thought has only a term-generality as its appearing object. In other words, an image corresponding merely to the sound of the term appears to the thought consciousness, but no sense of its meaning. On the other hand, when someone who does not know what a magnolia is—and who thus cannot identify it by name—happens to remember a magnolia blossom seen previously, that person does not remember it as a magnolia, but only recalls its shape, color and

other features. The image of the flower that appears to such a person's thought consciousness is only the meaning-generality. Finally, when a person who knows what a magnolia is remembers one seen previously, that person's thought consciousness has a mixture of term and meaning generalities as its appearing object.[76]

Thus, with respect to physical phenomena, there are multiple ways of approaching conceptual understanding.

While this may be a useful typology for understanding our thought's relation to the material world, it also allows us to understand how immaterial concepts such as no-self or emptiness come to be understood. Klein uses the idea of subtle impermanence to demonstrate this operation. She writes,

> In the Buddhist perspective, it is possible to begin with the mere internal reverberation of sound like "subtle impermanence" and then, through reasoning and contemplation, cultivate a sense of its meaning until the appearing object of thought is no longer a mere term-generality but a mixture of term and meaning generalities. As one cultivates an increasingly profound and deeply felt understanding of the meaning, reliance on words gradually decreases. Once one is truly well accustomed to the meaning of subtle impermanence it is possible for only the meaning-generality of subtle impermanence to appear, without depending on the term or word "impermanence" at all.[77]

This movement from term generality to a mixture of term and meaning generality to purely meaning generality pairs well with the listen, reflect, meditate framework. One first hears about a concept through its term generality; then one comes to intellectually grasp the concept through contemplation to ascertain a mixture of term and meaning generality; and finally through meditation one is able to ascertain the meaning generality without recourse to the term. With a view like impermanence that does not have a physical corollary, the meaning generality is an *experience*, just as viewing the form of a magnolia is an experience, and Klein notes how "this experience is far removed from mere mental rattling of the words 'subtle impermanence.' Deeply cultivated, it can prove a life-changing experience."[78]

With respect to the highest views that purport to be beyond all conceptual construction, this operation remains the same. One might think that in the Prasaṅgika-Madhyamaka system or in the Dzogchen tradition that one would systematically eradicate thought to arrive at some empty no-thing-ness. However, this is not the case. Emptiness (alongside the views in Mahāmudrā and Dzogchen) is arrived at in the same way as a provisional view like impermanence. Klein writes, "Emphatically, in this system, an understanding of emptiness is not seen as merely a matter of divorcing oneself from conceptuality. It requires patient cultivation of a specific understanding which is then brought to the level of direct experience. As in the case of realizing impermanence, one progresses from a mere term-generality—dry words—to an apprehension of term and meaning-generalities as mixed, to an apprehension of only the meaning-generality of emptiness itself."[79] Thus, the movement from term generality to a mixture of term and meaning generality to meaning generality alone persists even when it comes to so-called nonconceptual views. While the ultimate view of the Madhyamaka, Mahāmudrā, and Dzogchen systems may be beyond concepts, conceptuality is still an integral component of arriving at the final view. The movement described by Klein does well to show us how these views can be approximated by using concepts. To borrow a common Buddhist trope, concepts are the raft that takes one across the river to the opposite shore of ultimate view, but once one is at their destination, the raft is no longer necessary. We may therefore claim that this operation functions in every meditative tradition of Tibet and serves as the principal means for making a conceptual view into a perceptual mode.

Despite the experiential aspect of meaning generalities for immaterial objects of thought, Klein also notes how the meaning generality of something like subtle impermanence is still considered conceptual in the Gelugpa tradition. True direct perception of an idea only happens when all generalities fall away, and the practitioner is left only with the thing itself. In her words, "Direct perception occurs when even the meaning-generality fades away and one is left with the actual, specifically characterized impermanence."[80] Nonetheless, both term and meaning generalities are required to reach this end. Rather than contradict each other, conceptual and nonconceptual experience are in fact related. Earlier in the text, Klein notes how conceptual understanding and direct perception are compatible with one another since the former is "required for development into the latter."[81] Here, she gives more insight into how these function and writes, "It is possible for conceptuality to yield to direct perception because the actual impermanence appears through the medium of an image at the time of conceptuality. When the image fades away, the actual impermanence remains as an appearing object of direct perception."[82] Thus, meditation allows one to move from a mixture of term and meaning-generality to purely a meaning generality and finally to the thing itself. In other words, "through cultivating a mental image of subtle impermanence or emptiness, through making it more and more vivid, one can eventually realize the actual fact of impermanence or (in the higher systems) of emptiness in direct experience, no longer needing the medium of the conceptual image."[83]

It is this final direct perception of an object of thought that ultimately transforms one's default perceptual mode and can have a prolonged effect on an individual's day-to-day behavior. Klein writes, "Only such a vivid and direct cognition of impermanence and selflessness is capable of destroying the ignorance which Buddhists see as the source of cyclic existence and all its sufferings."[84] Of course, she is speaking in the context of the soteriological goal of Buddhism, but this sentiment can also be extended to a moral phenomenological approach to ethics. Only a vivid and direct cognition of a view like emptiness can overcome conceited modes of behavior and installing a conative mode of compassion in an individual. In fact, there is a term for this in Tibetan: *sgom pas nyams su myong bya'i nges don*.[85] This phrase translates to "definitive meaning which is experienced in meditation" and is used by scholars such as Shakya Chokden to emphasize the bare experiential aspect of the realization of view.

In Klein's formulation, direct perception is an *experience* that can directly overcome the afflictive emotions and lead to liberation. Similarly, in the purview of moral phenomenology, this experience can directly change our default perceptual mode and reorient our normative affective and conative states. Early in her book, Klein writes that "such cognitions, ineffable and profoundly reorienting of the human psyche, are certainly forms of mystical experience."[86] Clearly, her description of this experience resembles William James's classical definition of mystical experience as ineffable and noetic,[87] but I would nonetheless hesitate to use that terminology. Instead, I prefer the term *direct meditative experience* to *mystical experience* for two reasons.

First, the other two qualities of mystical experience in James's classical definition are transiency and passivity. In *Varieties of Religious Experience*, James has this to say about transiency: "Mystical states cannot be sustained for long. Except in rare instances, half an hour, or at most an hour or two, seems to be the limit beyond which they fade into the light of common day. Often, when faded, their quality can but imperfectly be reproduced in memory; but when they recur it is recognized; and from one recurrence to another it is susceptible of continuous development in what is felt as inner richness and importance."[88]

In contrast with this sort of mystical experience, *direct meditative experience* is aimed at the integration of a view into one's everyday experience. Far from being transient, direct meditative experience is meant to allow one to sustain the direct perception of a view throughout one's day-to-day life. We see this emphasis on sustaining the experience of the view many times in the in the literature on view, meditation, action, such as when Yangthang Rinpoche states,

> After directly realizing the view without confusion,
> Then, when making an experience of it through
>   meditation,
> To remain in that ongoing state of that realized view,
> Through diligence for prolonged periods of time—this
>   is meditation.[89]

The transient factor of mystical experience therefore does not apply to the experience of direct perception. Instead, direct meditative experience causes one to continually abide in that direct perception and assume it as an aspect of one's default perceptual mode.

Furthermore, James gives the following explanation for characterizing mystical experience as passive: "Although the oncoming of mystical states may be facilitated by preliminary voluntary operations, as by fixing the attention, or going through certain bodily performances, or in other ways which manuals of mysticism prescribe; yet when the characteristic sort of consciousness once has set in, the mystic feels as if his own will were in abeyance, and indeed sometimes as if he were grasped and held by a superior power."[90] Certainly, we may say that the experience of direct perception is precipitated by voluntary operations, but can we say that once one attains direct perception that their will is suspended, and they are grasped by a superior power? I think not. We have been describing the experience and consequences of direct perception as a shift in one's perceptive, affective, and conative modes, none of which requires a suspension of will. Instead, in descriptions of both the initial experience and the sustenance of direct perception, we are told to develop diligence and to continually return to this experience in our daily life. Thus, the characterization of mystical experience as passive also does not apply to the kind of direct meditative experience present in the Buddhist tradition.

Second, *mystical* is popularly contrasted with *rational* and derided as a superficial, uncritical religious experience outside the realm of rationality. Klein herself makes this distinction in the first line of her book and writes, "In Western religious and philosophical discourse, mystical experience is commonly seen as antithetical to reflective thought."[91] Similarly, in its contemporary usage, the mystical is often associated with new age spirituality, pseudoscientific health modalities, and associated forms of uncritical practices. However, we have seen how direct meditative experience is not only compatible with intellectual analysis but requires it. Direct meditative experience is the consequence of combining rigorous philosophical study and reflection with meditative practice. Thus, to term it "mystical" would be to obfuscate the great amount of intellectual rigor required for bringing about this experience.

## Theories of Mystical Experience

It is for these reasons that I prefer the term *direct meditative experience* over *mystical experience*. Nonetheless, many religious scholars have used the frameworks and lenses of analysis from the study of mysticism to investigate how these kinds of experiences map onto the Buddhist tradition. As Komarovski writes, "Despite the fact that the terms 'mysticism' and 'mystical experience' are not 'native' Buddhist terms, they can justifiably be used when exploring diverse Buddhist experiences and realizations characterized by ineffability, nonconceptuality, etc., that are not foreign to Buddhism at all."[92] Despite Komarovski's contention, there is little written on mystical experience in Tibetan Buddhism, with only a handful of articles and a single monograph that take up the subject.[93] While I may be skeptical of characterizing the experience of direct perception as mystical, we can nonetheless better understand the phenomenological contours of this meditative experience by comparing it to how mystical states have been categorized in Western academic contexts. After all, there is a reason Klein so bluntly connects scholastic meditative experience with mysticism when she states, "A scholastic tradition, source of the meditative dialectic, may be considered an essential formulator of a certain type of mystical experience."[94]

*Perennial and Constructive Mysticisms*

Before diving into these connections, it would be worthwhile to review two major divisions in the scholarship on mysticism to help situate direct meditative experience: the perennialist-constructivist debate and the introvertive-extrovertive distinction.[95] The perennialist-constructivist debate centers around the nature of the mystical experience itself. Those on the perennialist side have sought to identify the commonalities of mystical experience across traditions to assert the universal nature of these experiences. This approach to the study of mystical experience is typically traced back to Aldous Huxley and his eponymous work *The Perennial Philosophy*,[96] but the most notable proponent of perennialism was Walter T. Stace. In his work *Mysticism and Philosophy*, Stace advances two possible mystical states that have universal characteristics. First, he argues that there is a universal extrovertive experience that is characterized by a joyful "unifying vision, expressed abstractly by the formula 'All is One.'"[97] This vision is marked by a "concrete apprehension of the One as being and inner subjectivity in all things" and is said to have a sense of objectivity, sacredness, and paradoxicality.[98] Second, he argues that there is a universal introvertive experience in which individuals attain a "state of *pure* consciousness" that he calls "a complete vacuum of particular mental contents."[99] He writes that this state is sometimes called "the Void," "nothingness," "the One," and "the Infinite" and that each of these terms refers to the same thing because "that there are in [this state] no particular existences is the same as saying that there are no distinctions in it, or that it is an undifferentiated unity."[100] Recently, this universal introvertive state has garnered significant attention by scholars such as Robert K. C. Forman who advocate for the existence of a *pure consciousness event* (PCE) that ignores religious distinctions and can be found across time and culture.[101]

Those on the constructivist side of the debate push back against this universal claim and instead forward the argument that mystical experiences are intimately tied to the cultural and religious conditioning of the individual. Within this camp, there are two positions taken up by scholars: hard constructivism and soft constructivism. Hard constructivism is the position that "the experience itself as well as the form in which it is reported is shaped by concepts which the mystic brings to, and which shape, [their] experience."[102] This contrasts with the soft constructivist position, which concedes that there may be similarities across traditions but that individual experiences nonetheless have some conceptual substance and are hence culturally mediated. Thus, we may see these two differing simply in degree. The hard-constructivism position credits the religious context with complete influence over the mystical experience, and the soft-constructivist position leaves open the possibility of shared aspects of the mystical experience but maintains that experiences of pure consciousness are impossible since all experience is conceptually mediated. In both instances, the constructivist position pushes back against the perennialist claim that all mystical experiences are the same but are simply described as different based on the religious and cultural circumstances of the mystic and assert that "this process of differentiation of mystical experience into the patterns and symbols of established religious communities is *experiential* and does not only take place in the post-experiential process of reporting and interpretating the experience itself: it is at work *before, during, and after the experience*."[103]

*Introvertive and Extrovertive Mysticisms*

The other major division in the scholarship on mysticism is the introvertive-extrovertive distinction. Introvertive mystical experience is conducted by turning one's attention inside of oneself in meditation or contemplation. It is a mystical experience that happens primarily in the mind, without recourse to or interaction with the external world. Extrovertive mystical experience is the opposite, wherein an individual's mystical experience involves connecting with the outside world, seeing it in new ways, and relating to it in an altered state. It is important to note that these are not mutually exclusive categories in the way that perennialism and constructivism may be. Instead, these two may be thought of as opposite ends of a spectrum of conscious states. In his article "A Cartography of the Ecstatic and Meditative States," Roland Fischer maps out this spectrum, which has ergotropic experience on the left and trophotropic experience on the right. In terms of ecstatic experience, one begins with ordinary perception before becoming aroused and feeling anxiety, creativity, and sensitivity. Then one becomes hyperaroused and experiences acute schizophrenic states and catatonia before achieving the mystical rapture of the ecstatic state.[104] With respect to meditative experience, one begins with ordinary perception before becoming tranquil and experiencing *zazen*. Then one becomes hypoaroused and finally achieves what he calls "yogic *samādhi*."[105]

It is unclear if Fischer clearly understands meditative traditions given his unorthodox use of *zazen* and *samādhi*. However, even if his presentation of these terms is problematic, this kind of spectrum is useful for understanding introvertive and extrovertive experience as the two bookends of human experience. This spectrum affords us the ability to imagine both PCEs and constructivist content-full experiences as equally viable kinds of mystical experience.[106] A fully developed *śamatha* practice will culminate in the formless meditative states marked successively by an infinity of space, infinity of consciousness, no-thingness, and neither perception nor nonperception. However, there are certainly content-filled meditative experiences in both yogic practice and more straightforward *vipaśyanā* practice that can result in bliss, rapture, and so forth. Thus, leaving open the ability to term each of these as legitimate mystical experience is useful for understanding the nuances of direct meditative experience through this Western hermeneutic.

That said, Fischer's cartography, like a great deal of scholarship on mystical states, is hampered by his attention to extremes. Mystical rapture and yogic *samādhi* are highlighted as the final mystical states with anything less being considered provisional and hence less important. I think this is a major mistake. Focusing exclusively on peak experiences (either ecstatic or quiescent) ignores the experiences that lie just outside of ordinary conscious states but are nonetheless significant for the individual. Thankfully, Paul Marshall has dedicated a book to exploring these experiences. Titled *Mystical Encounters with the Natural World*, Marshall explores the ways in which individuals have experienced extrovertive mystical states outside of traditional religious settings. Rather than commune with God or achieve a yogic *samādhi*, the individuals surveyed described their experiences as a transformed relationship with the world using naturalized, secular language. Marshall uses these to construct a typology of extrovertive experience that eschews the axiological bracketing of religious traditions and instead presents these experiences as extraordinary yet human. Marshall writes that to qualify an experience as an extrovertive mystical experience one or more of the following are required:

> —*unity* with the world or some of its contents
> —incorporation of the world into the *self*
> —an intuitive *comprehension* of the world
> —a *love* that encompasses all things
> —expansive *vision* of the world
> —extraordinary *beauty* of the world
> —*luminous* transfiguration of the environment
> —an altered *temporality* that includes all times and place[107]

Marshall provides a broad swathe of characteristics that we can use to identify mystical experience. His theorization allows us to understand love and beauty as kinds of mystical experience alongside the more classical visions and raptures that conservative religious scholars denote as mystical.

This can help us make sense of some of the provisional states of a moral phenomenological approach to ethics. On the way to a full experiential realization of emptiness, an individual may first come to a nonconceptual understanding of impermanence or practice the *brahmavihārās* and have a direct meditative experience of lovingkindness. In most typologies of mysticism, these would not be regarded as "mystical" because they do not go far enough into the ineffable or the noetic. Nonetheless, these relatively minor direct meditative experiences can have significant impacts on an individual's comportment and can be important steps to take in a moral phenomenological approach to ethics. Opening up the understanding of mystical states to include these kinds of experiences can help us better understand the breadth and diversity of nonconceptual experience.

*Dualistic Mystical States*

On top of these two divisions, there is another recent development in the theorization of mystical experience that can help us better understand the Buddhist direct meditative experience: Robert K. C. Forman's notion of the "dualistic mystical state." In short, Forman defines the dualistic mystical state as "an unchanging interior silence that is maintained concurrently with intentional experience in a long-term or permanent way."[108] In other words, one can maintain the mystical experience (in this case a pure consciousness event) *after* one returns to ordinary waking consciousness and goes about their life. Forman writes, "The subject is directly aware of consciousness itself, knows itself reflexively in a pure and direct way. And, simultaneously, it is intentionally aware of its content, sensory objects, feelings, thoughts, etc. That means that in the DMS one can be aware of the *nature* of the self and think about it at the same time."[109] In order to unpack this kind of state, Forman turns to both the work of Jean Paul Sartre and the Chan epistemology of Huineng and frames his discussion around the Roman god Janus and concludes that "both sides exist simultaneously, Janus-like, with their faces pointing in opposite directions, one within and one without. And yet each illuminates the nature of the other."[110] Thus, Forman draws an eclectic picture of a mystical state far from being transient. With reference to the experiences of former nun Bernadette Roberts, the narrative of Huineng in the *Platform Sūtra*, and an autobiographical account, Forman lays the groundwork for the possibility of a long-term, permanent mystical state that is maintained in tandem with one's ordinary consciousness.

Forman relates this state explicitly to the kinds of pure consciousness events on which his scholarship is primarily focused (hence "interior silence"), and there is perhaps a good reason for this. Pure consciousness events, being without content, do not interfere with the content-filled experience of ordinary life in the way that a constant mystical rapture filled with visions and auditions of a divine being might. This kind of dualistic mystical state is therefore simpler to understand phenomenologically and less likely to be immediately dismissed as mental illness. However, we might be able to broaden this understanding of dualistic mystical states to include more than simply pure consciousness events. I am thinking in particular of the kinds of extrovertive mystical experiences described by Marshall. Many of the characteristics described in his formulation of extrovertive mystical experience could certainly become permanent states including the love that encompasses all things, the incorporation of the world into the self, the extraordinary beauty of the world, bliss, joy connection, and so forth. In either case, the idea that mystical experience can persist long-term alongside one's ordinary day-to-day consciousness is important and can help inform our understanding of direct meditative experience and view, meditation, action in a moral phenomenological setting.

## Past Scholarship on Tibetan Buddhist Mysticism

With this brief foray into the scholarship on mysticism complete, we can now turn to how mystical experience has been used as a lens for analyzing Tibetan Buddhist practice. As stated earlier, there has not been a lot written on this intersection, and some of these articles are of dubious quality.[111] Nonetheless, there is at least one major work on this subject worth considering. Yaroslav Komarovski's *Tibetan Buddhism and Mystical Experience* sets out the following goals: "To analyze some of the key Buddhist experiences and realizations in the context of Tibetan Buddhist views and practices, link that analysis with the issue of (un)mediated mystical experience debated by contemporary scholars of religion, and explore the issue with the help of the interpretative theories and polemical tools used by Tibetan thinkers in their discussion of the seminal "mystical experience"—the realization of ultimate reality."[112] The first of these can greatly help us elucidate how mystical experience functions in Tibetan Buddhism.

The major claim that Komarovski makes with respect to mystical experience is how the Tibetan tradition eludes the strict boundaries of Western modes of classification. In short, he proposes a hybrid classification of mystical experience wherein these experiences are conditioned by philosophical study and meditative practice before their occurrence but are themselves beyond concepts. Komarovski puts it thusly:

> We know already that according to Tibetan thinkers, no realizations on the Mahāyāna path are possible unless one has first developed the mind of awakening. Likewise, no substantial progress on the path is possible unless one first generates renunciation of worldly existence. Nor is it possible to directly realize the emptiness of all phenomena unless one uses specific techniques to do so. Likewise, it is believed to be impossible to acquire genuine realizations on tantric paths without receiving tantric empowerments and instructions. In a word, no matter what Buddhist system or tradition dealt with by Tibetan thinkers we look at, it is virtually impossible to find mystical experiences that are not seen as being mediated by specific causes, conditions, and practices.[113]

However, Komarovski also notes that "although those experiences are linked with, and conditioned by, the paths, they are not necessarily mediated at the time when they actually occur."[114] In other words, direct meditative experiences of emptiness (in the Madhyamaka) or luminous, nonclinging awareness (in the Dzogchen and Mahāmudrā) are necessarily brought about through cause and condition like any other experience, but they are experienced as though they are unmediated and outside of this initial process of cause and condition.

There are two more important aspects to mystical experience in Tibetan Buddhism posited by Komarovski. First, he notes how the conditioning prior to a mystical experience does not need to *immediately* precede the experience but "can occur at some earlier time."[115] Moreover, he asserts that condition "usually consists of a long—often a lifelong—process that eventually results in a certain mystical experience."[116] This is significant for two reasons. First, it helps us understand the tradition's impetus on consistent practice. Meditation is not a one-and-done kind of practice with which an individual will have immediate results. Rather, it is a subtle process of gradually conditioning the mind to a desired experience.

Second, this understanding helps us explain accounts of individuals spontaneously experiencing mystical experiences or states of *samādhi* as Daido Sensei Loori once did. Robert Forman recounts Loori's experience where, after setting up his camera to photograph a tree, several hours went by, yet "he had no recollection of anything from that entire period."[117] Through the Buddhist understanding of mystical experience, we can see this not as a random occurrence but a consequence of prior conditioning. Understanding how practice must not *immediately* precede mystical experience can help us make sense of both the *how* and the *why* mystical experiences occur.

Furthermore, Komarovski notes how certain experiences rely on more than a single condition for their fruition. For example, emptiness cannot be experientially realized by meditating on emptiness alone. Instead, "the direct realization of emptiness within the Mahāyāna context is believed to be brought about not solely by contemplation of reality, but by that contemplation in tandem with the great compassion and other Mahāyāna practices and states of mind."[118] The one-to-one kind of cause and effect we might typically think is present in occasioning mystical experience is hence complicated in the Tibetan tradition. Komarovski focuses primarily on compassion's role in bringing about the realization of emptiness. He states that "the development of compassion as it is understood in Mahāyāna is indispensable for producing such mental states as realization of emptiness" and that "compassion in its turn is the main cause of developing the mind of awakening and the nondual mind."[119] Such an understanding of direct meditative experience can help us make sense of the emphasis on "path"[120] in Tibetan Buddhism. Full liberation from *duḥkha* requires various factors[121] that must be present for it to occur. Similarly, direct meditative experience requires various factors for it to occur. By being mindful of this point, we can account for those who meditate for years without grand meditative experiences as not having the requisite conditions for that experience to occur.

In sum, Komarovski splits the difference between emic and etic interpretations of Buddhist mystical experience. He shows that "like mystical experience in other traditions, Buddhist mystical experiences come as a part of a package which is bound together with unique worldview, objectives, and problems" and makes a solid case for how "any attempts to extract those experiences from that bundle will necessarily result in losing the very means of their adequate understanding."[122] By approaching the subject in this way, he moves beyond the "interpretive models used by 'constructivists' and 'perennialists' in their debates regarding unmediated mystical experience"[123] by presenting a hybrid Tibetan interpretive model. In this model, "the direct realization of ultimate reality is not mediated by any concepts or mental constructs at the time of its actual occurrence, but it is necessarily mediated by conditioning contemplative processes leading to it."[124]

## Situating Direct Meditative Experience

To recap, *direct meditative experience* is the term that I have used for the direct, nonconceptual perception of a particular view in meditative practice. It is the experiential culmination of the process of listening, contemplating, and meditating on a view until the term generality of the view becomes a mixture of both term and meaning generality, develops into a meaning generality alone, and finally yields to direct nonconceptual perception of the view. Furthermore, this experience is considered the principal mechanism for turning an intellectual understanding of a particular view into the default perceptual mode of an individual. It is therefore indispensable to the project of moral phenomenology and is the key to understanding the view, meditation, action framework.

In comparing this experience to the Western academic understanding of mystical experience, we can see some clear similarities and differences. First, regarding the perennialist-constructivist debate, this experience eludes strict placement in either camp. The kind of direct meditative experience brought about through listening, reflecting, and meditating on a view is absolutely conditioned. In the direct meditative experience, the practitioner realizes the particular view with which they were intellectually familiarizing themselves. However, Klein's explanation of conceptuality in the meditative process shows how this experience is also beyond concept or conditioning while it is occurring. Thus, just as Komarovski writes about general mystical experience in Tibetan Buddhism, the direct meditative experience that functions as the primary mechanism of view, meditation, action lies between the categories of constructivism and perennialism.

With respect to the introvertive-extrovertive distinction, direct meditative experience again fits neatly into neither side. Given its name, one would imagine that direct meditative experience is an internal experience. Meditation is typically seen as a method for turning one's attention inside oneself and for quieting the fluctuations of the mind. Perhaps this is the case for the kinds of *śamatha* meditation in the Buddhist tradition and this classification of the experience occasioned by this practice, but direct meditative experience as I have been using it goes beyond this introvertive classification for two reasons. First, we saw how Komarovski claimed that mystical experiences do not need to be immediately preceded by practice but can arise spontaneously from a lifetime of meditative conditioning. I would assert that this understanding applies to direct meditative experience as well. While cultivating this experience necessarily involves meditation, it does not necessarily have to occur *during* meditation. Instead, direct meditative experience must be conditioned by meditation but can be precipitated by other factors outside of a meditation session. The conditioning of one's study and meditation on the view can come to fruition at any time and can just as easily be extrovertive as it can be introvertive. Thus, direct meditative experience eschews this dichotomy and fits neatly into neither category.

Second, while direct meditative experience may be considered beyond concepts, it is nonetheless associated with specific qualities. As we have seen in earlier chapters, a realization of emptiness is typically associated with compassion in the Madhyamaka tradition, and the realization of primordial awareness is typically associated with bliss in the Dzogchen tradition. These associated qualities elude the typical classification of introvertive mystical experience and are instead more reminiscent of the kinds of experiences described by Paul Marshall. In fact, many of Marshall's characteristics of extrovertive experience could be easily conditioned with earlier practice while also being considered beyond conditioning or conceptuality in the actual experience. An intuitive understanding of the world or a transformed beauty of the world are nonconceptual experiences that can happen without meditation. Thus, there could easily be a line drawn between direct meditative experience and extrovertive mystical experience. We may therefore assert that while *śamatha* meditation may lead to introvertive kinds of experience, the *vipaśyanā* meditation involved in view, meditation, action leads to a direct meditative experience of the view more akin to the extrovertive kinds of experience described by Marshall.

Finally, and most important, I have been describing direct meditative experiences as the mechanism by which one integrates the view into one's default perceptual mode. In other words, it is through a direct meditative experience of the view that the view becomes incorporated into the perceptual, affective, and conative set of the individual in their day-to-day life. In this way, direct meditative experience seems to give way to a kind of dualistic mystical state as described by Forman. Direct meditative experience does not supplant ordinary consciousness but is incorporated *into* it. For example, if one were to come to a direct meditative realization of beyond-conceptual emptiness, one would still be able to use concepts. This individual would simply not be fooled by the appearance of these concepts. Thus, they would be able to go about their daily life while maintaining that experience of emptiness or whatever other view has been experienced. This kind of permanent incorporation of the view into one's default perceptual mode can therefore be seen to be akin to Forman's dualistic mystical state, which can be a helpful foil for understanding how direct meditative experience becomes maintained in daily life.

## A Picture of Tibetan Buddhism's Contemplative Ethic

Understanding meditation and direct meditative experience in this way completes our understanding of *lta sgom spyod gsum* and its relevance to the moral phenomenological project. In the preceding chapters, we saw how a moral phenomenological approach to Buddhist ethic is distinct from other interpretations of Buddhist ethics along Western ethical standards and how this approach preserves some of the unique characteristics of Buddhist ethics. We saw how the Tibetan tradition offers substantial evidence for this interpretation and parsed some of the possible issues present in a moral phenomenological approach to ethics. However, one major gap was identified in the literature on moral phenomenology: praxis.

Thus, we turned to the framework of view, meditation, action and argued that this framework is the best way to implement a moral phenomenology. We surveyed the use of this framework in Tibetan literature and identified two major ways this framework is used: as a descriptive framework and as a practical framework. Within this latter category, we found examples of *lta sgom spyod gsum* being used in a moral phenomenological sense and found evidence that it has the ability to put moral phenomenology directly into practice. We therefore detailed how view, meditation, action would function in the specific context of a moral phenomenological approach to Buddhist ethics and began nuancing this relationship between theory and praxis. However, what remained to be seen was how these views became integrated into one's default perceptual mode and how meditation linked view with action.

Filling this theoretical gap was the purpose of this chapter. For a view to fully inform one's action, it needs to be brought into one's default perceptual mode and move from a concept to an experience, and meditation is able to do just this. Having intellectually established a conceptual view, one first develops concentration through *śamatha* practice before directing this concentrated mind to the view. With sufficient practice, one will come to experience the view directly in this meditative state and integrate it into their default perceptual mode. This resultant nonconceptual understanding of the view is that which is brought into daily life and can inform one's action. By referring to the literature on mystical experience, we were able to better understand this nonconceptual meditative experience and see how *vipaśyanā* meditation can bring about such an experience.

Thus, we have a clear picture of both the theory behind moral phenomenology and the practical aspects of *lta sgom spyod gsum*. Ultimately, it is through the framework of view, meditation, action that moral phenomenology can be put into practice, and it is in this framework that we find a novel, contemplative approach to ethical practice. This discussion has remained squarely within the bounds of the Tibetan Buddhist tradition, but of course neither the theory of moral phenomenology nor the framework of *view, meditation, action* is inherently Buddhist. Both this theory and its praxis can have great utility outside of the Buddhist tradition if brought into dialogue with other ethical traditions or applied to contemporary situations. To demonstrate this utility and how a Buddhist moral phenomenology can bring a novel perspective to discussions on ethics, the remainder of this book will apply this ethical approach to issues facing the more-than-human world. Hopefully, we will come to see how moral phenomenology and view, meditation, action can present us new ways for thinking about and addressing ethical problems and how this approach to Buddhist ethics can serve as the foundation for a novel contemplative approach to environmental ethics.

5

# Seeing Climate Change Directly

## Moral Phenomenology in Ecological Contexts

Up to this point, we have conducted a close reading of normative Buddhist ethics with a particular attention to the theory and praxis of moral phenomenology and have surveyed previous approaches to Buddhist environmental ethics. However, these two areas have thus far overlapped very little. Outside of some parallel ideas in the eco-Buddhist literature, moral phenomenology has not been mobilized toward environmental ends, and there is (understandably) very little in the metaethical literature that deals with the environment. Nonetheless, I contend that, as with Buddhist ethics in general, the best approach to a Buddhist environmentalism lies in the application of its moral phenomenological framework to environmental questions. This chapter will therefore concern itself with applying the theory of Buddhist moral phenomenology and the contemplative framework of view, meditation, action to the more-than-human world.

To caveat this discussion, we must note how Buddhism is limited in its ability to propose direct solutions to the climate crisis and the ongoing degradation of global ecological systems. In terms of material praxis, Buddhism has little new to offer in terms of direct ecological practices beyond perhaps some ritual *puja* and *sadhana* practices that have ecological implications.[1] In many ways, the managerial approach to land and nature found in much of the early Buddhist canon is what has caused the Earth to be in the

139

position it is today.[2] With respect to ameliorating climate change, the *what* of the situation must be determined by the sociopolitical and economic structures we find ourselves in, and action must be informed by a keen attention to climate science, ecological science, and biological science. However, Buddhism can play a major role in the *why*. As we have seen, Buddhists around the world have engaged questions of environmental degradation largely through the lenses of value and virtue. Moral phenomenology deals with the fundamentals of human experience and hence can reorient the conative and affective modes of an individual profoundly. It can therefore play a significant role in supporting environmental behavior by rewiring the motivation, determination, and consistency of environmental behaviors.

This chapter will show how moral phenomenology can be used to this ecological end by first looking at how phenomenology has been understood in environmental contexts in the Western philosophical milieu. Then, it will investigate what an applied moral phenomenology looks like and how it might operate outside of Tibetan Buddhist contexts. The framework of view, meditation, action will then be applied to the environment by asking the following questions: What is the view of environmentalism? What is the role of meditation in the context of environmental ethics? and What might action look in this scenario? This chapter will look at moral phenomenology, view, meditation, action as a whole, and the specific role of view, while the next will take up the precise function of contemplative practice in this ecological milieu. Together, these two chapters will form a cohesive picture of a contemplative approach to an eco-Buddhist moral phenomenology.

## Eco-Phenomenology

Since I will be articulating an ecological, phenomenological ethic, it is worth first looking at how Western philosophy has approached the intersection of ecology and phenomenology. While there are numerous articles and monographs exploring the topic of eco-phenomenology, very few deal with the *moral* implications of an ecologically oriented phenomenology. That said, there are still ideas in this field important to consider, and there are texts that *do* deal with the morality of phenomenology that can shed light on what a moral phenomenological approach to environmental ethics might look like.

Eco-phenomenology is a discipline concerned with the experience of nature, the environment, and the more-than-human world. It begins its inquiry by going to the things themselves as they are presented to the individual, rather than philosophical ideals or abstractions. In other words, eco-phenomenology begins with an immediate experience of the more-than-human world and builds this into philosophical analysis and speculation. A formal definition of eco-phenomenology can be found in the eponymous volume *Eco-Phenomenology: Back to the Earth Itself,* coedited by Charles S. Brown and Ted Toadvine. In their introduction, they write, "Eco-phenomenology is based on a double claim: first, that an adequate account of our ecological situation requires the methods and insights of phenomenology; and, second, that phenomenology, led by its own momentum, becomes a philosophical ecology, that is, a study of the interrelationship between organism and world in its metaphysical and axiological dimensions."[3] It therefore stands to correct the scientific naturalism that pervades contemporary environmental discourse and articulates how our direct experience of the world can lead to both ontological claims and certain sets of value.

This phenomenological approach to nature avoids a major issue identified by Neil Evernden, that "those approaches to nature that strip it of all experienced qualities leave us with an unrecognizable abstraction, and certainly not with any version of nature that could have inspired our initial appreciation."[4] In this way, eco-phenomenology tends to reassert the importance of the environmentalist over the ecologist insofar as the ecologist deals purely with the quantitative (though perhaps in service of their own environmentalist motivations), and the environmentalist deals with the qualitative, aesthetic, and ontological. Evernden 's definition of an environmentalist is "one who bears a concern for a world in which he [*sic*] experiences a sense of value."[5] And, as we have seen, this value often serves as the foundation for an environmental ethic.

That said, explicit mentions of ethics are largely absent in the literature on eco-phenomenology. For example, David Wood's exploratory article "What Is Ecophenomenology?" never uses *ethic* or *morality*.[6] At face value, this may seem curious for a tradition that purports to provide a philosophical basis for axiological claims. Given the intimacy of experience, value, and Dasein in eco-phenomenological literature, one would expect eco-phenomenologists to also have something to say about *how* one should engage with the more-than-human world. However, this is not the case, and there is perhaps a good reason for this. If we recall an earlier statement by Joanna Macy about Buddhist ethics, then we can understand this absence: "A full recognition of the true nature of the self as interconnected with all life . . . is essential because it can serve *in lieu of* ethics and morality."[7] Macy's notion of the relationship between recognition and morality is phenomenological in nature and makes clear why ethics are not commonly found in eco-phenomenological literature: the kinds of being and experiencing called for by eco-phenomenologists can serve in lieu of an abstract ethic. Nonetheless, there are indeed instances of ethics and morality being explicitly implicated in eco-phenomenology that can shed some light on what a moral phenomenological approach to the environment can look like.

One of the most foundational works in eco-phenomenology (and environmental philosophy in general) is David Abram's *The Spell of the Sensuous: Perception and Language in a More-Than-Human World*. In its introduction, Abram makes a brief comment about ethics, stating:

> It may be that the new "environmental ethic" toward which so many environmental philosophers aspire—an ethic that would lead us to respect and heed not only the lives of our fellow humans but also the life and well-being of the rest of nature—will come into existence not primarily through the logical elucidation of new philosophical principles and legislative strictures, but through a renewed attentiveness to this perceptual dimension that underlies all our logics, through a rejuvenation of our carnal, sensorial empathy with the living land that sustains us.[8]

Abram therefore sees phenomenology as playing an important role in the formulation of novel environmental ethics, but he does not pursue this line of inquiry himself. Instead, his work uncovers and articulates this "carnal, sensorial empathy with the living land," which may in turn lead to kinds of ethical thought and practice.

Others, however, do take initial steps towards a phenomenologically based environmental ethic. For example, Charles S. Brown's contribution to the volume *Eco-Phenomenology*, titled "The Real and the Good: Phenomenology and the Possibility of an Axiological Rationality," contends that moral experience is "one of the irreducible domains of lifeworldly experience"[9] and argues that environmental values are built into the foundational act of perception. He writes:

> Our everyday life is filled with moral sentiments that appear from a phenomenological perspective as instances of a prereflective axiological consciousness—that is, as an intentional and evaluative aiming at objects and states of affairs. Value experiences may be analyzed as a form of intentional consciousness in which the phenomenon of valuing and something valued are given together. As phenomenology is a "return to the things themselves," it does not wish to break apart the primal unity of the act of valuing and thing valued, as theory often does, but rather to simply describe that primal unity.[10]

Thus, Brown describes a kind of eco-phenomenological methodology for crafting an environmentalism that involves addressing the "form of naturalism that separates the Real from the Good."[11] He writes that "such a phenomenology can be used in the service of an experiential grounding of ecological ethics" that "recognizes that embodied existence is primordially and unavoidably experientially embedded within the planetary biotic web."[12] He concedes that the "current configuration of technocentrism and consumerism" may impede our ability to experience nature "as infused with goodness and from within an attitude of concern and empathy"[13] but nonetheless offers hope by recognizing that the experience of planetary destruction and the ecological crisis "is increasingly a morally charged experience for many people."[14] Moreover, he sees this kind of experience as being informed by and articulated in the writings of Thoreau, Muir, Leopold, and today's radical ecologists who attempt "to establish a new mode of moral and aesthetic discourse in which experiences of the intrinsic goodness of nature can be registered, expressed, and rationally developed."[15] Thus, while Brown does not provide concrete actions to take or practices to directly evoke an experience of "nature as infused with goodness," he nonetheless sees the kinds of value-embedded experiences found in eco-phenomenological writings to possess the kind of morality required for positive environmental behavior and suggests that environmental writings can act as a way for cultivating this experience in others.

Another chapter in *Eco-Phenomenology* deals with the ethical implications of an environmental phenomenology. Don E. Marietta Jr.'s "Back to the Earth with Reflection and Ecology," begins by stating that "environmental ethics requires an ontological commitment"[16] and goes on to identify this requisite ontological position and its ethical implications. After addressing some of the issues in in prior attempts to ground environmental ethics in the metaphysics of Spinoza, Leopold, and Naess, Marietta comes to articulate what he calls a "critical holism." This critical holism is holistic in how it "acknowledges that humans are a part of the system of nature" without going so far as to assert a kind of "biospherical egalitarianism" and is critical in how "new developments in biology do not threaten it."[17] This kind of ontological speculation is standard fare for the field, but Marietta brings some novelty to the conversation by how he relates ontology and ethics. He states, "Mere intellectual assent to an ontological doctrine is not the commitment I believe necessary. An environmental ethic will not be adequate if it is an abstraction that does not engage a person's thought and feeling and result in the adoption of a way of living."[18] In other words, the kind of ontological commitment that is required for establishing an environmental ethic is one that is adopted not only intellectually but perceptually, affectively, and so forth. This adoption is of the very kind found in Buddhist approaches to moral phenomenology and of the kind that I also see as foundational for a phenomenological approach to environmental ethics. However, while Marietta is right to recognize the necessity of an experientially realized ontological view, he does not provide any means for enacting this realization. Further, his direction for moving from ontological commitment to ethics simply involves reflection on one's experience and nothing more. Thus, while Marrietta does indeed take significant steps to link phenomenology to ethics, he still leaves this connection wanting to be developed further.

By grounding ethics in a particular experience (tied to a specific ontology), we can respond to the issues concerning humans and the more-than-human world in a consistent yet flexible way, not bound by particular rules or consequentialist calculations. Arne Naess, the seminal thinker in the deep ecology movement, has said in various places that it is necessary for "the philosophy of environmentalism to move from ethics to ontology and back."[19] In many ways, what those in the eco-phenomenologist movement have done is to move beyond initial formulations of environmental ethics based on contested views of nature and reinvigorate the discourse with an attention to one's immediate experience of the more-than-human world. They have made the move from ethics to ontology. Therefore, the remaining step is to go back. Articulating an environmental ethic from the position of moral phenomenology can help environmental ethics come full circle and complete Naess's required movement from ethics to ontology and back. We have seen earlier what a moral phenomenological approach to ethics looks like, but this discussion remained largely in the confines of normative Buddhist ethics. What we must therefore develop is the means by which moral phenomenology can respond to the specific problems and situations facing the more-than-human world today. We must develop an *applied* moral phenomenology and direct it toward the more-than-human world.

## What Is an Applied Moral Phenomenology?

What I am proposing, and what Tibetan Buddhism encourages practitioners to do, is a reworking of our phenomenological experience of the world through a specific contemplative process to effectively change our moral behavior. The kinds of moral theory found in eco-phenomenological literature gesture to the connections between the phenomenological and the ethical but provide no means for working with the former in the service of the latter. If one wishes to develop and promote an environmental ethic from a phenomenological point of view, one needs to provide a roadmap for enacting the desired experiential change. Eco-phenomenology, as it has been articulated by scholars thus far, lacks this roadmap for transforming an individual's experience of and relation to the environment. However, Tibetan Buddhism can work to fill this gap and articulate not only a theory of eco-phenomenological morality but also an *applied* moral phenomenology of the environment.

As we have seen, the way to work with the default perceptual mode is through the framework of view, meditation, action. View, meditation, action provides a distinct path for bridging the gap between one's conceptual understanding of the world and one's direct perceptual experience of it and has the ability to direct this perceptual and conative transformation toward desired ethical ends. Recall that moral phenomenology is the installment of a *particular ontological view* as one's *default perceptual mode* through *meditation* and *contemplative practice* resulting in compassionate *action* or *conduct* that accords with said view. In many ways, this idea has much in common with how eco-phenomenologists understand the relationship between experience and ethics. However, this understanding allows us to work directly with concepts, affect, and perception to direct our experience to specific ends and address ethical blind spots we may have.

An applied moral phenomenology would therefore first articulate the ethical problem at hand, identify a philosophical view that would address this problem, and integrate this philosophical view into one's default perceptual mode through contemplative practice. If the antidotal view is correctly identified, then this would reorient an individual's conative mode such that their actions would naturally and spontaneously address the issue at hand without any kind of abstract moral reflection. In other words, one would change the experience to change the comportment to change the action, and the contemplative framework of view, meditation, action provides a direct means for enacting precisely this kind of ethical transformation. Thus, if we are to articulate a moral phenomenological approach to environmental ethics, we must begin by identifying the ethical problems we collectively face.

## Material Harm Facing the More-Than-Human World

There is no dearth of issues facing nonhuman animals and the environment today. To name a few, we are contending with climate change and its effects on extreme weather, ocean acidification, biodiversity loss and species extinction, mass deforestation, microplastics polluting our water, chemicals such as Roundup polluting our air, the systematic exploitation and butchering of nonhuman animals, and so on. Some of these issues have been quantified by climate scientists whose findings portray an even bleaker picture of our ecological future. As we saw in our introductory chapter, Johan Rockstrom and colleagues' "A Safe Operating Space for Humanity" outlines nine "planetary boundaries." If these boundaries are crossed, "important subsystems, such as a monsoon system, could shift into a new state, often with deleterious or potentially even disastrous consequences for humans."[20] We have already crossed three of these boundaries and are nearing two others. Likewise, the Paris Agreement's goal of limiting global warming by 1.5°C to abate the most deleterious effects of climate change is decidedly out of reach.[21]

A great deal of environmental concern is directed exclusively toward how *humans* will be negatively impacted to the detriment of nonhuman sentient beings. Such an exclusive concern is predicated on an unstable anthropocentrism and speciesism that place humans over and above all other animals (and flora for that matter).[22] This anthropocentrism is explicit in Rockstram and colleagues' article and is likewise found throughout mainstream environmentalist literature. However, nonhuman animals are in an equally dire state as the environment when it comes to their treatment by humans and, in many ways, are more directly impacted by the effects of climate change than humans as well. The animal liberation movement has made little headway in the forty-five years since Peter Singer first published the eponymous work *Animal Liberation*. Nonhuman animal experimentation, the use of animals for entertainment, and the consumption of animals as food are still massively problematic practices that, despite efforts (and some successes) by some activists to end certain captivity practices, problematize medical and cosmetic animal trials, and promote plant-based alternatives, are still relatively normalized in the general population.

Taking the environment and nonhuman animals together, the more-than-human world is at the precipice (if not already beyond the precipice) of annihilation. We have already begun to see the impact of climate change in the form of heat waves, droughts, wildfires, extreme hurricanes, and so forth, and the negative consequences of these extreme weather events are shared by human and nonhuman alike. Further, the goals for abating even *some* of the disastrous ramifications of climate change outlined by the international community in the Paris Agreement are not being met or even taken seriously by a great deal of oligarchic, conservative, and neoliberal governments around the world. This list of the material issues concerning the more-than-human world could go on for pages more, but I will stop here and make two conclusions: the more-than-human world, inclusive of sentient beings and non-sentient phenomena, is under threat of significant devastation, and human action is the cause of this threat.

## The Underlying Views That Support This Harm

In a Buddhist moral phenomenological analysis of our present situation, this human destruction of the more-than-human world has roots in particular *views* that humans hold and that direct their action in particular ways. These views are ontological in the sense that they are claims about the nature of certain modes of existence and our individual relationships to them. Given our prior discussion around the influence of views on behavior, the claim that negative human intervention in the more-than-human world is conceptually mediated is perhaps a given. Nonetheless, it is worth considering the *kinds* of views or ontological positions that scholars have identified as leading to our contemporary environmental situation.

One of the simplest ways of explaining the human intervention into the more-than-human world is with recourse to the belief that man (specifically gendered here in the masculine) has the right to dominate, manipulate, and extract value and pleasure from that which it deems "other" (often construed as female, animal, nature, and so forth). Jim Mason calls this belief "dominionism" and sees it as the root cause of misogyny, misothery, and the exploitation of the environment. As Mason writes, misothery is "hatred and contempt for animals. And since animals are so representative of nature in general, it can mean hatred and contempt for nature."[23] This is the same idea captured in Peter Singer's *Animal Liberation* under the label *speciesism* that he defined as "a prejudice or attitude of bias toward the interests of members of one's own species and against those of members of other species."[24] Moreover, Mason claims that not only was misogyny necessary to make the shift from a female-centric foraging culture to a male-centric hunter-agricultural society,[25] but, according to ecofeminist philosophy, is also an important factor in the ongoing subjugation of human and nonhuman others who are "excluded, marginalized, exploited, devalued, or naturalized . . . in systems of unjustified domination-subordination relationships."[26] Thus, Mason pins the blame for both our contemporary environmental crisis and the ongoing suffering of human and nonhuman animals on the pernicious view of dominionism, which, on his account, must be addressed and overcome. This, however, is perhaps too simplistic a reduction. I would assert that it is not a single perennial view shared by all of humanity (i.e., dominionism) that is responsible for all problems. Instead, I follow scholars such as David Naguib Pellow who have made the argument that our contemporary ecological situation and the oppression of the more-than-human world is intimately related to other forms of oppression, both human and nonhuman. He writes that "one cannot fully grasp the foundations of racism, classism, ableism, heterosexism, and patriarchy without also understanding speciesism and dominionism because they are all ideologies and practices rooted in hierarchy and the creation of oppositional superior and inferior subjects."[27] As a result, he identifies a total liberation approach to earth, animal, and human liberation that addresses all forms of oppression wherever they arise. We may therefore say that there are myriad views that intertwine to produce our contemporary ecological situation. This approach acknowledges that "all oppression is linked" and that the lesser ontological status of that which is designated as "other," such as nature, is reinforced by the othering of the queer, feminine, racialized, lower-class, and animal. Thus, in Pellow's total liberation analysis, these views are *together* responsible, and must all be identified, challenged, and replaced.

Furthermore, if we are to take a step back and conduct a somewhat Buddhist meta-analysis of these views, we might conclude that each of these emerges through an overidentification with a (mis)perceived Self that is set against and distanced from the other. In other words, anthropocentrism, dominionism, speciesism, and misogyny all stem from a chauvinistic attachment to one's sense of Self. They are each a kind of egocentrism that results from an inability to take into account the perspective of others or to consider the fallibility of one's own perspective. If seen through a Buddhist lens, this egocentrism also arises from a fundamental misapprehension of the self as independent from all other phenomena. In contradiction with the Buddhist understanding of *pratītyasamutpāda* and *anātman*, individuals mistakenly view themselves as having a separate essence that stands apart from that which they deem the other, and this mistaken identification leads to the belief that they have license to subjugate, exploit, and so forth.

Thus, we may say that the material problems presented to us have roots in the ontological views that individuals around the world hold. These views inform action that has historically justified and continues to justify not only the human intervention into the more-than-human world but also the outright exploitation of the environment, nonhuman animals, and human beings. Whether the root of this crisis is seen as dominionism, egocentrism, or a confluence of various negative ideological positions, it is clear that view plays a major role in the human relationship with the more-than-human world, and that addressing these views that are not only harmful but philosophically untenable is an important means to address our environmental crisis.

## Epistemic Issues That Support This Harm

Relatedly, there are epistemic issues that contribute to the degradation of the environment that must be considered. For example, Timothy Morton presents this issue of negative habitual action as fundamentally a problem of this kind. In their presentation of global warming as a "hyperobject," they gesture to the inability for us humans to fully understand or conceptualize the urgency and scope of our ecological situation. Hyperobjects are concepts or phenomena that are "so massively distributed we can't directly grasp them empirically" (despite attempts like Rockstrom and colleagues to do so).[28] More importantly, since they are epistemologically slippery, these hyperobjects are not confronted in our everyday experience. They write: "When you feel raindrops, you are experiencing climate, in some sense. In particular you are experiencing the climate change known as global warming. But you are never directly experiencing global warming as such. Nowhere in the long list of catastrophic weather events—which will increase as global warming takes off—will you find global warming. But global warming is as real as this sentence."[29] Because of this epistemic gap, we have conservative senators bringing snowballs into the US Congress to refute climate change and catastrophic wildfires blamed on Californians not raking their forest floors. These *are* tangible things to those who, for whatever political or financial reason, wish to publicly refute the reality of climate change and, because they are tangible, become a part of the public discourse. But, as Morton says, the intangible yet "viscous" object we call "climate change" remains concealed even as its "very nearness is what menaces."[30] Thus, the sheer scale of environmental degradation (not to mention the systemic violence done to nonhuman animals) and its conceptually elusive nature is a massive problem that must be addressed alongside its causes and its consequences. If we wish to abate climate change, we must first *see* climate change and experience it in its entirety. Given how a Buddhist moral phenomenological approach to ethics involves conceptually and experientially realizing subtle phenomena such as impermanence and selflessness,[31] I hold that it presents a particularly useful way for addressing this epistemic problem.

That said, this is not the only epistemic problem found in environmental literature. Morton's analysis of climate change as a hyperobject might be considered a somewhat abstract, philosophical presentation of the epistemic gap in understanding climate change, but other scholars have looked at how ordinary people fail to recognize or respond to information regarding the climate. Kari Marie Norgaard's *Living in Denial* summarizes the research on this epistemic gap and outlines several of what she calls "psychological blocks" to understanding climate change. First, she identifies the *information deficit model*, which assumes that "if people only knew" about climate change, they would change their behavior.[32] Addressing this block is a common tactic of mainstream political actors and direct-action groups such as Extinction Rebellion alike, but perhaps to questionable effect—people *know* the climate is changing, but they just don't recognize why that matters to *them* (and perhaps choose *not* to seek out that information to remain apathetic). Second, she observes the role that cognitive dissonance plays in climate denial by complicating how people receive information in situations where the prior knowledge deficit is overcome. One study she cites noted that "respondents with higher levels of information about global warming show less concern"[33] because "unless they feel able to do something about the problem, an awareness of concern or sense of responsibility would be a conflicting cognition [that creates an unpleasant feeling]."[34] Thus, they ignore the information to maintain their pleasant state. Finally, on top of this "psychological cost of acting,"[35] there are emotional blocks to accepting the reality of climate change and hence to acting to address it. Norgaard identifies guilt, helplessness, and fear as emotions that can "prevent people from thinking about serious issues"[36] and shows that "individuals may block out or distance themselves from certain information in order to maintain coherent meaning systems, desirable emotional states, or a sense of self-efficacy."[37] Each of these psychological blocks that Norgaard identifies can thus be seen as more individualized epistemic gaps that contribute to our inaction on issues concerning the environment. Altogether, we can see that there are clear material issues facing the more-than-human world but that these material issues are supported by certain views we hold, the epistemic difficulty of fully grasping a hyperobject such as climate change, and psychological blocks that prevent individuals from acting.

## Solving These Issues

An applied Buddhist moral phenomenology is obviously more relevant to some of these issues than others. With respect to material issues such as our planetary boundaries, Buddhism and its system of ethics can contribute little. Neither the Buddha nor those who practiced his teachings were particularly concerned with the state of the climate or the environment at large. Even the positive treatment of nonhuman animals and the adoption of vegetarianism[38] were relatively late developments in the tradition that originally regarded animal life as an unfortunate birth—a status that justified their exploitation at the hands of humans.[39] Nonetheless, these material issues are caused by human intervention in the more-than-human world and therefore have roots in the ontological views that mediate this intervention.

In a moral phenomenological approach to environmental ethics, identifying, challenging, and replacing these views is the target of practice. If our behavior stems from our direct experience of the world, and if this experience is conditioned by and mediated through the views we hold, then our behavior can change by changing our experience and the views that inform it. To this end, both Buddhist philosophy and its practical framework *of view, meditation, action* can be of great use. Not only can they address some of the philosophically flawed, self-centered ontological positions by showing how many of them are untenable under philosophical analysis, but they can also work to install a default perceptual mode that is more in line with the reality of the radical interconnectivity of the self and phenomena—a perceptual mode that leads to compassionate conduct.

Similarly, with respect to the epistemological problems related to the environmental crisis, Buddhist philosophy and practice can work toward alleviating some of the fundamental issues with how we acquire and hold on to knowledge about the environmental crisis. Morton's presentation of hyperobjects such as climate change as thoroughly immanent yet imperceptible is precisely the kind of presentation that we find in Buddhist settings concerning subtle phenomena such as impermanence and emptiness. These latter qualities are ever-present and yet are difficult to actually perceive *outside of meditative settings*. We might therefore infer that this epistemic gap can be overcome by turning the *vipaśyanā* meditation one would typically do on emptiness to the idea of climate change. This kind of meditative approach to overcoming epistemic gaps is also applicable to the issues presented by Norgaard where indifference, hesitation, and lack of confidence in the effects of one's actions lead individuals to do nothing about the climate crisis. A meditative approach to digesting information about climate change can help alleviate some of the conceptual difficulty and emotional distress associated with facing its reality and can work to reorient individuals to address the material problems present today.

Thus, while Tibetan Buddhism may have little to do with *directly* reducing excess nitrogen in the air or mitigating biodiversity loss, it can absolutely have an indirect positive effect on the material issues facing the more-than-human world through its ability to address the views that support and maintain the negative human intervention into the environment and the lives of non-human animals. The material issues facing the more-than-human world directly stem from the actions of humans, and these actions are rooted in a specific set of egocentric views. To address these mistaken views and replace them with an experientially understood, realistic view of the self and the world would therefore be to reorder one's behavior and reorient one's action. This kind of project is what constitutes a Buddhist moral phenomenological approach to environmental ethics, and this approach can be implemented through the framework of view, meditation, action. To see what this kind of approach would actually look like, we should first look specifically at what views are relevant to this kind of contemplative Buddhist environmental ethic.

## The Role of View in an Ecological Moral Phenomenology

We have already seen the kinds of views that do *not* support this behavior: dominionism, misothery, misogyny, and egocentrism to name a few. We might therefore think that the opposite views to these would be what a Buddhist moral phenomenological approach to ethics would consist of, being reciprocity, love of animals and nature, equality and respect for all human beings, and nonegocentrism. However, this line of argumentation runs into an issue quite quickly: If we are constructing a *Buddhist* moral phenomenological approach to environmental ethics, where are these to be found in the Buddhist tradition?

As we can see in the great amount of eco-Buddhist literature in the past several decades, there is a tendency to treat the

Buddhist tradition as inherently green, animal friendly, and so forth by Western Buddhists. To simply cherry-pick a couple of lines from a text that supports a love of animals and nature would, in my opinion, be an insufficient ground for establishing a truly Buddhist environmental ethic. It may demonstrate that there is precedent for a certain orientation to the more-than-human world in the tradition, but if our goal is to articulate a fully Buddhist environmental ethic, then the view we use to this end should be more ubiquitous than those found in a single text or tradition.

However, this isn't to discount these views—far from it. Plugging in a view like lovingkindness or equality and respect for all living beings into a moral phenomenological framework may very well lead to positive ecological behavior. These may thus be provisionally useful but are not what I would consider an ultimate eco-Buddhist view in a moral phenomenological context. This distinction, between provisional and ultimate views, is one found in the Tibetan Buddhist tradition itself. As Nāgārjuna says in his *Mūlamadhyamakakārikā*, "The Dharma taught by all of the *buddhas* completely relies upon the two truths: the relative worldly truth, and the ultimate truth."[40] A Madhyamaka explanation of the two-truths theory would contend that all things indeed appear as a result of cause and condition yet they are found to be empty of any kind of independent designation or intrinsic essence upon the final analysis. In other words, there is a conventional theory of how things *appear* and an ultimate theory of how things *are*, and both of these are *true*. Tsongkhapa restates and expands upon this statement in his *Praise of Dependent Relativity*:

> The Dharma taught by all of the Buddhas
> Completely relies on the two truths:
> The relative worldly truth and
> The ultimate truth.
> "All of this is empty of essence" and
> "From this arises this effect"
> These two determinations mutually
> Do not obstruct but assist one another.[41]

Thus, that which conventionally appears only does so as a result of its emptiness (of independent existence), and phenomena are empty as a result of how they appear in dependent origination. We can find similar sentiments in the yogic traditions of Tibet, which utilize this appearance-emptiness distinction as a foundation for their philosophical expositions and approach to practice.[42]

All of this is to say that we might take a similar approach when determining the view in a Buddhist environmental ethic. I suggest that the ultimate view in a moral phenomenological approach to environmental ethics would remain the same as the Tibetan Buddhist tradition: emptiness. The kind of action that results from a deep phenomenological understanding of emptiness is utterly compassionate, and this disposition would necessarily remain when approaching actions in and on the more-than-human world. In this sense, I might (perhaps controversially) argue that the Buddhist tradition *is* inherently eco-friendly if we understand all aspects of the tradition pointing to and cultivating this final view. That said, on the way to that ultimate adoption of emptiness as one's default perceptual mode, there is no promise of eco-friendly action. The experiential realization of emptiness and its resultant compassionate conative mode would lead to spontaneous, compassionate action on the various actors in the more-than-human world, but the mere intellectual understanding of emptiness (and the broader tradition that teaches this view) may not.

However, Buddhism also holds this notion of conventional or provisional views. In the literature on eco-Buddhism, there are a great number of scholars who point to and mobilize some of the conventional truths of the Buddhist tradition for environmental ends. Understanding impermanence, *duḥkha*, rebirth, the overcoming of avarice, and so forth have all been gestured to as having positive environmental implications. However, unlike the view of *śūnyatā*, they do not result in the pure compassionate conative mode that a moral phenomenology calls for. Simply coming to an experiential realization of the classical Tibetan view that all sentient beings have been our mothers would not *necessarily* result in eco-friendly behavior. It certainly *could*, but it just as well may not (as evidenced in the conflicting positions on eating nonhuman animals in Tibet). Likewise, a view originating from outside of the Buddhist tradition (deep ecology, the reality of climate change, etc.) may establish the necessary phenomenological lens for an individual to naturally and spontaneously act positively toward the environment and its nonhuman inhabitants when plugged into the framework of view, meditation, action.

In a personal correspondence, Lama Chökyi Gyaltsen[43] told me, "If it doesn't lead to liberation, it's not Dharma," and indeed some of these provisional views will not lead to either the liberation of the self or of others from *duḥkha*. In the Tibetan Buddhist tradition, only the ultimate view of emptiness and the conventional views that point one toward that realization can do this. Similarly, I might make the claim that in a Buddhist moral phenomenological approach to environmental ethics, only an experiential understanding of emptiness that is fully integrated into an individual's default perceptual mode can prime an individual to respond to *all* issues that they may be confronted with in their relationships with the more-than-human world. However, even a cursory reading of the Buddhist tradition would show that this kind of realization is quite rare. Thus, in lieu of a full realization of emptiness (or, better yet, on the way to this full realization), we might also look for provisional views that, when brought into our default perceptual mode, will allow us to naturally respond to the needs of the environment and its nonhuman inhabitants in an appropriate manner. But before we look at some of these provisional views, we will first turn to the ultimate view that can be mobilized toward a moral phenomenological approach to environmental ethics.

## The Ultimate Ecological View

The ultimate view that could foster a moral phenomenological environmental ethic is, of course, emptiness. While there are myriad interpretations of emptiness in the Tibetan tradition, scholars and yogis are united in the recognition that a complete understanding of emptiness on an experiential level creates a compassionate conative mode in the practitioner. Thus, in both a general Buddhist moral phenomenology and an applied moral phenomenology of the more-than-human world, adopting emptiness as our default perceptual mode will give us the ability to compassionately and spontaneously respond to the ethical issues presented to us in daily life, ecological or otherwise. I am not the first to make the claim that emptiness is a profound source of Buddhist environmentalism. In 1995,[44] Gary Snyder wrote about "our ethical obligations to the nonhuman world" and stated, "Buddhist teachings go on to say that the true source of compassion and ethical behavior is paradoxically none other than one's own realization of the insubstantial and ephemeral nature of everything."[45] Similarly, I argue that since compassion naturally emerges from an awareness of emptiness (i.e., *śūnyatā-karuṇā-garbham*), a compassionate concern for the more-than-human world will likewise emerge from an experiential realization of this ultimate view.

It is important to note that this is different from relying on compassion alone as a basis for an environmental ethic as many scholars have done before. Martine Batchelor, for example, has argued that Buddhism has a clear respect and concern for nature that emerges from its emphasis on lovingkindness, compassion, morality, and so forth.[46] Similarly, David E. Cooper and Simon P. James have argued that Buddhist ethics emerges from a set of virtues that the tradition promotes that notably includes solicitude (their term for the collection of lovingkindness, compassion, and sympathetic joy).[47] They claim that the Buddhist notion of solicitude is "founded upon a sense of kinship with all sentient beings"[48] and place it as a core source of how we should approach decisions, both in our personal life and in our political policy, related to the environment.[49]

In both cases, the scholars come to their conclusions about compassion and environmental ethics through a great deal of textual analysis and solid interpretation. However, I share the concern of Lambert Schmithausen when he critiques the overemphasis of certain eco-Buddhists on nonviolence, lovingkindness, and compassion. He writes, "Stating the traditional Buddhist attitudes of not injuring (*ahimsa*), benevolence (*mettā/ maitrī*) and compassion (*karuṇā*) to entail an 'ecological' behaviour is surely justified in so far as these attitudes are not limited to human beings as their object but include also other living beings, especially animals. Still, it should be clear that neither of these attitudes has, primarily, an 'ecological' purport."[50] In other words, the environmental outcomes of these attitudes are not grounded in an ecological view of the world but are a by-product of a certain disposition. As such, the full force of this compassion is left untapped, and a fully developed concern for the more-than-human world is left unrealized. However, when this compassionate mode emerges *from* an ecological view, it assumes this ecological purport by virtue of the ontology it is supported by.

I claim that emptiness *is* this ecological view. Recall that emptiness is commensurate with dependent origination and the Buddhist truth that all phenomena are intimately linked in a vast matrix of cause and effect. Phenomena are empty of self-essence or independence precisely because their being relies on myriad other phenomena, without which they would simply not exist. This view is inherently ecological if we are to understand ecology as the relationships between living beings and the systems that support them. John Clark makes this point in his analysis of Nāgārjuna's Madhyamaka, stating, "For Nāgārjuna, a being can only be understood adequately as part of a system of relations. On the basis of such a philosophical position, there are good reasons to hold that our compassion for sentient beings must extend outward to the communities of life and the greater ecological wholes of which they are a part."[51] Thus, Clark agrees that the experiential recognition of emptiness and dependent origination results in a compassionate conative mode aimed not only at individual sentient beings and the communities they make up but also the ecological systems that support them. In contrast to the compassion forwarded by Batchelor, Cooper, and James, this compassion grounded in the ecological view of emptiness *is* of ecological purport. While Nāgārjuna (along with all Buddhist philosophers) was concerned primarily with the alleviation of *duḥkha* and was compelled in his philosophy and practice by this goal, we can nonetheless see how his articulation of emptiness is ecological in its presentation of the interdependence of all phenomena.

As I argued earlier in this book, a Buddhist environmental ethics emerges quite naturally from the combination of a concern for the *duḥkha* of all sentient beings, a recognition of this *duḥkha* being interdependently mediated, and a novel recognition of ecological systems as a key factor in the alleviation and exacerbation of this *duḥkha*. When one has an experiential recognition of the emptiness and/or interdependence in our contemporary scientific world, all three of these preconditions for a Buddhist environmental ethic are met; genuine compassion for the *duḥkha* of sentient beings is produced, the interdependence of *duḥkha* is seen, and the role of ecology in this *duḥkha* is appreciated. The conative mode that emerges from the realization of this ecological emptiness is therefore a compassion inclusive of all sentient beings and the systems that support them.

## Contemporary Examples of the Ultimate Ecological View

This is precisely the kind of ecological compassion that His Holiness the Karmapa talks about in his article "Walking the Path of Environmental Buddhism through Compassion and Emptiness." In this piece, he first gives his explanation of emptiness before writing that "to experience this freedom from the conviction of a self and the self-importance it creates means that we can dispense with the artificial distinction between self and other and can be part of all phenomena everywhere."[52] He sees this view as a corrective to a fundamental ignorance that lies at the heart of human-nonhuman relations. In his words, "Perceiving the diversity of the world through the limited lens of self means we can impose grave harm upon Earth without concern, because Earth has become 'other.' "[53] He then links this view to compassionate environmental activity through Śantideva's *Bodhicaryāvatarā* and uses the following quotation to unpack the relationship between emptiness and compassion:

> May all beings everywhere
> Plagued by sufferings of body and mind,
> Obtain an ocean of happiness and joy
> By virtue of my merits.[54]

He writes that "in this verse, Śantideva chooses to dedicate his life to alleviate the suffering of others because of his insight into the interdependent nature of life" and that "with this understanding, generating compassion for all living beings and turning that motivation into action is the most ecologically aware thing we can do."[55] His commentary on the verse makes clear the link between emptiness and compassion and their relevance to environmental issues, and his article acknowledges the kind of compassion that emerges from a deep experiential understanding of emptiness as having great environmental merit.

We can find other instances of this link between emptiness and compassion and their relevance to environmental discourse in the writing of Thich Nhat Hanh. While outside the Tibetan focus of this present work, Thich Nhat Hanh forwards an interesting presentation of emptiness and interdependence through his term *interbeing*, which adapts these ideas for a Western audience. He sources his understanding of emptiness from Nāgārjuna's *Mahaprajnapāramitāsastra*, which states that "all phenomena that arise interdependently, I say that they are empty,"[56] and he uses this to give weight to an earlier statement in the chapter: "In early Buddhism, we speak of Interdependent Co-Arising. In later Buddhism, we use the words interbeing and interpenetration. The terminology is different, but the meaning is the same."[57] Elsewhere in this text, he links the direct experiential awareness of interbeing to compassion and states, "to obtain fearlessness and great compassion, practice the contemplations on interdependence" which he goes on to explicate.[58] Finally, he links both of these, the view of interbeing and the great compassion that emerges from its experiential awareness, to the more-than-human world in his mindfulness trainings. The first mindfulness training he calls "Reverence for Life" and explains it thusly:

> Aware of the suffering caused by the destruction of life, I am committed to cultivating the insight of interbeing and compassion and learning ways to protect the lives of people, animals, plants, and minerals. . . . Seeing that harmful actions arise from anger, fear, greed, and intolerance, which in turn come from dualistic and discriminative thinking, I will cultivate openness, non-discrimination, and non-attachment to views in order to transform violence, fanaticism, and dogmatism in myself and in the world.[59]

Thus, in Thich Nhat Hanh's experience and in his teachings on the subject, an ethic inclusive of all aspects of the more-than-human world arises from an awareness of emptiness (or interbeing) and the compassion that emerges therefrom. It is *this* kind of compassion that is of ecological purport and this kind of great compassion cultivated through an awareness of emptiness that is of relevance to a moral phenomenological approach to Buddhist environmental ethics.

A final point to note is how the ultimate view of emptiness that I am advocating for as a powerful view for enacting a Buddhist moral phenomenological approach to environmental ethics is distinct from notions of being "one with nature." Christopher Ives has pointed out how certain eco-Buddhist claims about nonduality and insight into dependent arising "often lead to arguments that we are metaphysically 'one with nature' and hence it is in our self-interest to preserve and protect the natural world."[60] This is emphatically *not* what emptiness means in the Tibetan tradition, but this notion of "being one with nature" is often found in Buddhist approaches to the environment. There are two ways this is problematic from a Madhyamaka perspective. First, to claim to be one with all of nature is to imply that there *is* a self that is ultimately distinct from all other phenomena before making the assertion that they are intimately related to one another. Despite alleging that we are nondual and "one with nature," this kind of rhetoric reinforces this self-other divide and therefore strays from the interpretation of emptiness that we find in the Tibetan tradition. Second, even if we were to grant that the self and nature are *not* distinct from one another but are indeed "one," there would be an attribution of this "one" with some sort of essence. This kind of monistic approach to reality is best refuted in the Madhyamaka's own claims that emptiness is itself empty, leaving no room for a fundamental substance or essence that permeates all things. To realize emptiness is therefore a distinct goal from becoming "one with nature" since emptiness is a separate view from a monistic holism where self and nature are one.

Thus, I argue that the emptiness I see as functioning as the ultimate view with regard to a moral phenomenological approach to Buddhist environmental ethics is distinct not only from certain provisional views like impermanence or nonself in Buddhist approaches to environmental ethics, but also certain kinds of eco-Buddhist presentations of interbeing and one's unity with nature. Consequently, the conative modes that emerge from a phenomenological or experiential understanding of emptiness are distinct from the kinds that emerge from these other views. Compassion is forwarded by many eco-Buddhist scholars as a key factor for engaging the Buddhist tradition with environmental ethics, but the kind of great compassion engendered by an experiential knowledge of emptiness is distinct from the kind forwarded by certain eco-Buddhist scholars. Compassion must be grounded in an ecological view to find its full expression in an environmental ethic, and this kind of ecological compassion will emerge by installing emptiness as one's default perceptual mode through the contemplative framework of view, meditation, action.

## Provisional Ecological Views

Of course, until we have this full experiential realization of emptiness, we must support our ecological practice by looking to provisional views. If we look to the Buddhist tradition for these provisional views, we can find many that could lead to positive outcomes. Some of these views are quite broad ontological views, and others are more specific views about the nature of our current environmental situation. What's important is that these views address one of the fundamental ideological pitfalls that contribute to exploitative relationships between humans and the more-than-human world. My contention is that short of a full realization of emptiness, the direct perceptual understanding of these views will lead to individuals acting more in a way that alleviates the *duḥkha* of both human and nonhuman sentient beings and leads to the flourishing of the ecological systems that support them. The remainder of this chapter will identify these views and outline their behavioral consequences in a moral phenomenological approach to environmental ethics.

### Cause and Effect

The most important provisional view one could establish is a deep confidence and recognition of cause and effect. Without this, all ethical practice is completely moot. Both an intellectual and an experiential recognition of the reality of cause and effect are necessary for enacting any applied moral phenomenology, including one directed toward the more-than-human world. If one does not believe that their actions have consequences, that their actions are motivated by their views, and that these views can be changed through a set of causes and conditions and then the entire apparatus of moral phenomenology falls apart, then why would one bother to establish an ecological view and meditate on it? Conversely, understanding cause and effect allows us to engage with material problems facing the more-than-human world through the recognition that these problems have causes, their solutions have causes, and every action of our body, speech, and mind has either a positive, neutral, or negative effect on each.

This kind of understanding of cause and effect is fundamental to the Tibetan Buddhist tradition and underpins the entire path to liberation. Again, should cause and effect not (conventionally)[61] exist, then the entire premise of Buddhism falls apart. If our actions don't have consequences, then there is no point in working to actually liberate ourselves and all other sentient beings from *duḥkha*. It is for this reason that one of the necessities for engaging in Buddhist practice posited in Gampopa's *Jewel Ornament of Liberation* is confidence in cause and effect. He writes, "Regarding trusting confidence, it is dependently produced from the objects of action and effect, the truth of *duḥkha,* and the truth of its origination. Furthermore, have confidence that the virtue of the desire realm arises due to the causes of virtuous action. Have confidence that the *duḥkha* of the desire realm arises due to the effects of nonvirtuous action."[62] In other words, we need to be confident that our actions have effects, that wholesome actions have wholesome outcomes, and that negative actions have negative outcomes. Similarly, with respect to climate change, this confidence in cause and effect is absolutely necessary. Climate change and other aspects of the contemporary environmental catastrophe are simply effects of a specific set of causes and conditions. Likewise, the solution to the climate crisis will only come about through the confluence of a particular set of causes and conditions. Without this understanding of cause and effect, the entire project of solving climate change or abating some of its consequences would be pointless. These things aren't fated or destined to be—they have only come about and will cease to be through cause and condition. Therefore, coming to an experiential recognition of cause and effect can reorient ourselves not only to the reality that the climate crisis is causal and can therefore be solved through the right causes and conditions, but to the reality that we as individuals can actually affect the state of the environment through our actions (however minute these effects may be).

Outside of understanding the role of causation in the broader scheme of climate change, we can also see the importance of its recognition on a personal level. One of the barriers to climate action that Norgaard identified was that "unless [people] feel able to do something about the problem, an awareness of concern or sense of responsibility would be a conflicting cognition [that creates an unpleasant feeling]."[63] If we are able to come to an experiential recognition of cause and effect, then this notion of "not being able to do something" becomes a nonissue. One's actions *always* have effects, and these effects can be good or bad. Everything we do in our daily lives, from the meals we eat to the way we commute to the information we share, has a positive or negative effect on the more-than-human world. These effects may be incredibly small compared to those taken by nation-states, corporations, and other industrial actors, but they create effects nonetheless. Thus, if we bring a deep understanding of causation into our default perceptual mode then we will be able to resist nihilistic views about the inevitability of ecological catastrophe and our inability to do anything about it. Instead, we'll recognize that our actions do in fact have an effect on the greater environment and will naturally come to a more intentional, refined way of acting. Or, to use Buddhist terms, we will develop a discriminating kind of awareness that is able to determine what actions lead to wholesome outcomes (i.e., conducive to the flourishing of the more-than-human world) and what actions lead to unwholesome outcomes. This will allow us to sow better and better causal seeds as we go about our daily lives.

*The Suffering of Nonhuman Animals*

A second obvious view that could lead to positive action on the more-than-human world is the recognition that nonhuman animals experience *duḥkha*. Just like us, they want happy states, and just like us, they avoid painful and unhappy states. This is perhaps an obvious statement to most people, but the degree to which individuals actually *see* the suffering of nonhuman animals varies greatly. To really see other beings as sentient and to clearly see the effects of our actions on them would reorient our conative mode to one that cares for the well-being of all sentient beings in a dramatic way. Thus, meditating on this view and actually *seeing* the *duḥkha* of nonhuman animals at an experiential level can be important steps toward acting in ecologically beneficial ways.

The term *sentient being* is used in English to denote an entity that can experience pain and pleasure. In the Buddhist tradition, this definition is slightly different, and what qualifies as "sentient being" has historically been clear. The Tibetan term for sentient beings is *sems can*, which directly translates to "mind-having" and is inclusive of gods, demigods, humans, animals, ghosts, and hell beings. In his dictionary, Gegen Tharchin provides the following definition: "Transmigrator, living being, that which possesses a mind, that which possesses a birth, that which has had the opportunity to be born, that which has a mind, living creatures, that which possesses knowledge, that which possesses a body, and beings, these are all synonyms of *sems can*."[64] I say that the category of sentient being has *historically* been clear because of the shifting nature of the category in modernity. For example, the Canadian teacher Lama Chökyi Gyaltsen[65] includes single-celled creatures, amoebas, bacteria, diatoms, paramecium, moss, lichen, shrubs, bushes, flowers, grass, and trees in his aspiration prayer and makes the wish that each of these kinds of beings "be well and happy and move towards transcendent growth."[66] We can also find instances of plants exhibiting thought and practicing the Dharma in historical sources such as Shabkar's autobiography,[67] and pioneering eco-Buddhist scholar Lambert Schmithausen has scrutinized early Buddhist *vinaya* sources to complicate Buddhist ideas of plant sentience.[68] While these examples are outliers, and the category of sentient being has historically been quite rigid, we can nonetheless see how sentience can be opened up to include living entities outside of the traditional six realms of rebirth. Outside of the Buddhist tradition, the sentient capacity of nonhuman animals, including mammals, amphibians, fish, reptiles, insects, and so forth, is not contested. These are biological facts. We even have an increasing amount of evidence suggesting the sentient capacity of flora such as trees[69] and pea plants[70] in their ability to seek out positive conditions and avoid negative states based on sensory inputs (and I have thought through some of the implications of these recent findings for Buddhist ethics elsewhere).[71] For our purposes, the most basic definition of *sentience* as the capacity to feel pleasure and pain will suffice, and directly seeing this sentient capacity can be an ecologically efficient view.

In the Tibetan Buddhist tradition, there's a common saying that all sentient beings have once been our mothers and have taken great care of us, prioritizing our happiness over their own and safeguarding us from pain. This contemplation is used to compel an individual to act compassionately toward every being they encounter in order to repay their kindness in that past life. Imperative to this saying and its ethical outcome is *seeing* other sentient beings in a certain way. Most people in the global north do not believe in rebirth, but this kind of contemplation can nonetheless still function outside of Buddhist contexts. If one truly sees the ability for other beings to experience pleasure and pain like humans, then, I argue, they will similarly be compelled to act in a way that promotes the mutual flourishing of self and other. Bringing such a view into one's default perceptual mode would bring a natural concern for all sentient beings, human and nonhuman, into one's experience of the world and would reorient one's actions accordingly.

Another way that this Tibetan adage could be mobilized toward an ethic of the more-than-human world lies in how other sentient beings do in fact contribute to our wellness. Even if we reject the idea that all sentient beings have been our mothers in past lives, we can nonetheless acknowledge the important role that all kinds of flora and fauna contribute to the ecosystems that support us. In other words, just as our ecosystems support us, we have an obligation to in turn support the actors therein. Simply directly seeing this reciprocity and the harm done to all when it is not respected can compel an individual to act in a way that benefits the greater system. This can in turn help combat the delusion that we are independent entities who should only act in our own self-interest. Especially when this is taken to heart through contemplation and meditation, this kind of view will install a compassionate conative mode in us that naturally cares for the beings and the systems that support us.

There is evidence both inside and outside of the Buddhist tradition that an experiential recognition of the suffering of non-human animals, especially at the hands of humans, can have a profound shift in one's own behavior. This was the case with perhaps the most famous vegetarian of the Tibetan tradition, Shabkar Tsodruk Rangdrol, who as a young boy saw the slaughter of sheep and felt a strong reorientation in his relationship with nonhuman animals and the consumption of meat. In his autobiography, he writes, "One autumn, the harvest was excellent. Both rich and poor families said this was something to celebrate, and thus many scores of sheep were slaughtered. This grim spectacle horrified me and filled me with compassion."[72] Later in his life, Shabkar finds himself confronted with a similar scene and ultimately makes a formal commitment as a result. Again, in his autobiography he writes,

> One day, I remained in the presence of the Jowo for a long, long time, and I was praying so intensely that I entered a state of profound absorption. Later, as I was walking along on the outer circumambulation path around the city, I came upon the bodies of many sheep and goats that had been slaughtered. At that moment, the compassion that flooded into me for all the animals in the world that are killed for food was so strong that I could not stand it. I returned to the Jowo Rinpoche, and with prostrations made this vow: "From today onward, I will abandon the negative act of eating the flesh of beings, each one of whom was once my parent."[73]

Shabkar is not an isolated case. We can see that others in Tibetan history make similar commitments and change their actions on the more-than-human world as a result of their experiential recognition of the suffering of other sentient beings.

Another striking example of this can be found in the autobiography of eighteenth-century yogi and *tertön* Jigmé Lingpa, where he writes,

> The killing of these beings reminded me of the actions of great dogs. Seeing and hearing it caused me great

suffering. I wanted to immediately liberate these beings from their suffering and wished that I had a safe house to protect them. Horrific activities such as these occurred here, merely because it was the season for slaughtering animals. Thinking like this, uncontrived compassion arose. Until that day, even though I had recited the words of the mind-training of the four immeasurables hundreds of thousands of times, I had never had true, uncontrived compassion of that strength. This experience was the most important event of my life.[74]

This passage is particularly interesting in its juxtaposition of the rote repetition of phrases on lovingkindness and compassion and the direct experiential awareness of the suffering of nonhuman animals that naturally brought rise to great compassion. As Geoffrey Barstow comments, "Jigmé Lingpa describes his experience here as one of uncontrived compassion, the spontaneous compassion that is a hallmark of the enlightenment experience. Further, this experience was more profound than any he had experienced previously, despite hundreds of thousands of repetitions of more conventional practices. . . . All based on the sight of lambs awaiting slaughter."[75] In many ways, it parallels the story of Asaṅga and Maitreya, where the former only came to the fruition of his practice and met the buddha-to-come through seeing a diseased dog on the road.[76] There is no doubt in both cases that the lovingkindness and compassion meditations he had done hundreds of thousands of times had primed them for this experience, but it was only at the direct perceptual experience of seeing the suffering of nonhuman animals that Jigmé Lingpa and Asaṅga ultimately gave rise to the great compassion of bodhicitta.

In contemporary times, very few people see the suffering of nonhuman animals directly but instead do so through descriptions in books, presentations in documentaries, clips on social media, and so forth. These literary and visual accounts allow individuals to encounter the suffering of nonhuman animals in a visceral way despite how slaughterhouses, vivisection labs, and so forth are often hidden behind closed doors. In a study of vegan motivations, Barbara McDonald identified the "experience that introduced the [individual] to some aspect of animal cruelty"[77] as being absolutely integral to the transition from one who neglects the welfare of nonhuman animals in their daily life to one who places this concern at the center of their daily practices. In fact, His Holiness the Karmapa came to his advocacy for vegetarianism and a better treatment of the more-than-human world through this very kind of exposure to the suffering of nonhuman animals. He wrote,

> Although I had considered giving up eating meat for many years, I became a complete vegetarian only a few years ago. Somebody presented a short documentary that showed how animals suffer before and during the act of killing. Watching it, I could feel the fear felt by the animals. Like a thunderclap, I became aware that these living beings were suffering so greatly simply to satisfy my habitual preferences. Eating meat became intolerable for me at that moment, and so I stopped.[78]

While of course this kind of seeing can lead quite directly to a vegetarian position, I contend that the consequences of this experience have a broader scope. Should we come to an experiential recognition of suffering of nonhuman animals and the relationship between this suffering and our daily actions, we will not only naturally act in a way that avoids harming nonhuman animals but also in a way that preserves the environment that supports them. In other words, there are ways our actions both directly and indirectly affect nonhuman animals, and seeing this will reorient our conative mode accordingly. Thus, the experiential understanding of the suffering of nonhuman animals and the ways that our actions affect them and their environment can certainly be used as a provisional view for promoting a moral phenomenological approach to environmental ethics.

### The Reality of Ecological Collapse

Another quite obvious view that could be mobilized toward a moral phenomenological approach to environmental ethics is the reality of climate change and ecological collapse. Outside of reactionary political organizations and conservative petrostates, the reality of climate change is largely acknowledged as a real and imminent threat. Further, the scientific consensus on has grown to be over 99 percent certain that climate change is caused by human activity as reported by recent metanalyses of the scientific literature.[79] However, despite this near universal recognition, there is very little that has been done to address the well-known causes of climate change by either individuals or institutions.

If we look at how the neoliberal governments around the world responded to the COVID-19 pandemic, it is unsurprising that little has been done on their part to meet even the minimum requirements for avoiding absolute catastrophe. The COVID-19 pandemic was an immediate threat to the economic, social, and political system, and yet provincial and federal governments alike failed to adequately mobilize and fund the requisite healthcare and social/financial initiatives to maintain the health, well-being, and life of their citizens in my home country of Canada. How then are we to expect they will take the requisite steps to confront an issue like climate change, whose consequences will ultimately be felt years if not decades from now?

Unfortunately, many view institutional change as the *only* way to abate climate disaster. They (rightly) see animal agriculture, transportation, the military, and other industries as the primary emitters of greenhouse gasses and therefore place the solution for climate change in their hands alone. Again, this plays into one of the barriers Norgaard identified that prevents people from engaging in environmental behavior. By solely attributing the cause of climate change to industrial actors, they feel as though they cannot do anything as individuals and hence don't. This tension between institutional and individual approaches to addressing environmental degradation has been a consistent theme in the history of environmentalism and mirrors tensions found in other kinds of political movements.[80] However, in many ways, this is a false dichotomy. In a talk to the New York Public Library, political scientist Katharine Hayhoe presented this issue thusly: "Is it up to individuals to change their lifestyles and through sacrifice to fix climate change? Or is it up to system-wide solutions at the level of governments, states, companies, large organizations? This debate will never end but I have an answer to it. My answer is: yes."[81] I entirely agree with her conclusion. Institutions are only given legitimacy through individual actors, and barring a shift to the kind of eco-socialism necessary for navigating climate change in a way that maximally protects human and nonhuman beings from its harmful consequences, the neoliberal states and corporations will only act under pressure from individuals. In other words, the only way institutions will change is if our individual actions, be it our consumption patterns, advocacy, or what have you, put pressure on capital and the political system that supports it.

It is for this reason that the view of the reality of climate change is an important input into a moral phenomenological approach to environmental ethics. If we as individual actors are to internalize this view and adopt it into our default perceptual mode through contemplative practice, then our actions will naturally orient themselves to ecologically friendly behavior, and we will be able to navigate both personal and political situations from this foundation. That said, this particular view needs to be supplemented by a second view: that the consequences of climate change are dire. Some conservative podcast hosts have made the nationalist argument that climate change will benefit countries such as Canada and Russia by providing them with a longer growing season for crops and so forth. If this is the case, then seeing the reality of climate change would do little to shift one's behavior. However, this claim is obviously absurd. While in grad school, I was living in British Columbia, where 595 people dropped dead from the heat alone, and large swathes of the province's forests went up in flames, disproportionately affecting the indigenous people of this land.[82] These kinds of catastrophes are a direct consequence of climate change, and acknowledging these terrible outcomes is necessary for this view to have an impact.

## Deep Ecology

We might also turn to Western environmental philosophy as a source for potential views. However, in doing so, we must grapple with the diversity of views therein. One of the main splinters in environmental philosophy is between shallow and deep ecologies that respectively represent anthropocentric and biocentric approaches to environmentalism. In other words, shallow ecologies see only the instrumental value in nature *for human ends*, whereas deep ecologies view the flourishing of the natural world as a legitimate end unto itself. In this latter category, there is the eponymic deep-ecology movement developed by Arne Naess, George Sessions, Bill Devall, and others, which was largely responsible for staking out the boundaries of this divide in the first place.

At its core, deep ecology is built from the premise that all life on earth has intrinsic value. Arne Naess's formulation of this premise is as follows: "The well-being and flourishing of human and non-human life on earth have value in themselves (synonyms: intrinsic value, inherent worth). These values are independent of the usefulness of the non-human world for human purposes."[83] This is, of course, an ontological position[84] rather than purely an ethical view, which allows it to function quite neatly in a moral phenomenological approach to environmental ethics. From this basis, several actionable items are articulated by deep ecologists, such as lessening the encroachment of human activity into the more-than-human world and (voluntarily) reducing the human population to lessen humanity's burden on nature. In fact, the deep-ecology platform and Naess's approach to deep ecology which he calls Ecosophy T are themselves a good example of a moral phenomenological approach to environmental ethics (without calling it such a name). The prescriptions of deep ecology's platform stem directly from the direct experience of Naess and Sessions with the more-than-human world through the lens of its intrinsic valuation, linking ontology and ethics in the same intimate way that we find in moral phenomenology.

Further, in *Ecology, Community, Lifestyle*, Naess argues that our engagement with the more-than-human world should stem from the Self-realization of ourselves and should preserve the capacity for Self-realization in others. He draws from Spinoza for his understanding of Self-realization, whom he quotes as stating, "To persevere in one's own (way of) being, no mere keeping alive."[85] Naess gives a specific definition of what the human Self is, writing, "We are not outside the rest of nature and therefore cannot do with it as we please without changing ourselves. . . . We are a part of the ecosphere just as intimately as we are a part of our own society."[86] From this Self-realization and from the view that all living beings have a right to their own Self-realization (and hence have intrinsic value outside of human activity), Naess claims that individuals should craft their own ecosophy and inform their own environmental activism according to their specific ecological context. This is why he calls his philosophy "ecosophy T," where the T is a stand-in for his local Tvergastein Mountain and is to be replaced by the local bioregion of the individual. His main goal is "to emphasize the responsibility of any integrated person to work out his or her reaction to contemporary environmental problems *on the basis of a total view*."[87] Thus, the ontological commitment and the *realization* of Naess's stated position prime an individual for naturally arriving at ecological modes of being depending on their particular environments. In effect, Naess and other deep ecologists indirectly argue for a moral phenomenological environmental ethic derived from the intrinsic valuation of nature and the preservation of all beings to engage in their own Self-realization.

Of course, this position is not without critique. As we saw in my earlier critique of Capper, from a Tibetan Buddhist position, any kind of intrinsic claim is likely to be challenged given how it contradicts the Madhyamaka position of the emptiness of independent existence and the intrinsic essence of phenomena. Perhaps simply reframing this intrinsic valuation as the more-than-human world having (conventional) value outside of instrumental human ends would avoid this issue. A more poignant critique is whether this kind of valuation outside of human interests is philosophically tenable at all. In his book *Heaven in Disorder*, Slovenian philosopher Slavoj Žižek is quite critical of this deep ecological position. In a short chapter titled "Radical Change, Not Sympathy," he writes:

> The falsity of humanitarianism is the same falsity found in the rejection of anthropocentrism advocated by deep ecology—there is a deep hypocrisy in it. All the talk about how we, humanity, pose a threat to all life on Earth really just amounts to a concern about our own fate. Earth in itself is indifferent. Even if we destroy all life on Earth, this will just be one—not even the greatest—of the catastrophes that befall it. When we worry about the environment, we worry about our own environment.[88]

Ironically, the simple counter to Žižek's argument is that his idea is itself deeply anthropocentric, not only in its reasons for promoting environmentalism but also in its basic understanding of the world. For him to claim that "Earth in itself is indifferent" is to claim that the suffering and flourishing of nonhuman animals and the broader biosphere is inconsequential at a fundamental level. Any deep ecological position, as well as any Mahāyāna Buddhist position, would reject this claim and assert that the suffering of nonhuman sentient beings should be minimized, and the flourishing of the more-than-human world should be supported, simply because of our understanding of how these beings have the capacity to experience and respond to pleasure and pain like humans. Thus, any other position like the one Žižek presents here rests on an arbitrary speciesism and anthropocentrism that is simply untenable.

That digression aside, we can nonetheless see how a deep ecological view can lead to positive environmental action when brought into one's default perceptual mode. This kind of perceptual or experiential recognition was the basis of Naess's philosophy, and the way he talks about Self-realization and ecosophy T allows us to consider the outcomes of bringing the deep ecology ontological position into our experience. Of course, as I said before, other nonanthropocentric environmental philosophies might be slotted into this deep ecological view as well.[89] These may include the ecofeminism of writers such as Vandana Shiva[90] and Ariel Salleh,[91] who identify womanhood with the natural world and call for the liberation (and, therefore, flourishing) of both; the land ethic of Aldo Leopold[92] and J. Baird Callicott,[93] which places value on the integrity of ecological communities; or the total liberation ethic articulated by David Naguib Pellow, which aims for the complete liberation of human and nonhuman beings from coercive and oppressive structures.[94] Regardless of which deep or nonanthropocentric environmental ontology one inputs into the framework of *lta sgom spyod gsum*, the outcome is a moral phenomenological environmental ethic that places a concern for the more-than-human world at the center of one's experiences and one's actions.

*New Materialisms*

The final provisional view that I will touch on can be found in the realm of new materialism. New materialism is a movement in contemporary philosophy that seeks to correct the *"neglect* or *diminishment* of matter in the dominant Euro-Western tradition as a passive substance intrinsically devoid of meaning" by attempting to show how matter is "alive, lively, vibrant, dynamic, agentive, and thus *active*."[95] In doing so, new materialists seek to "problematize anthropocentric binaries" such as meaning and matter, nature and culture, and so forth that inevitably contribute to the degradation of the more-than-human world. Gamble, Hanan, and Nail's paper "What Is New Materialism?" identifies three major trajectories in the field that share these general principles yet articulate this attention to matter in distinct ways. These are as follows: (1) vital materialism; (2) negative new materialism; and (3) performative new materialism. Without going too deep into the weeds of each of these subfields, it is worth looking at the ontological claims of each of these new materialisms and unpacking some of the consequences of these views in terms of a moral phenomenological approach to environmental ethics.

With respect to the first category, vital materialism, Gamble, Hanan, and Nail look to its inception in the thought of Gilles Deleuze and his interpretation of Spinoza and Leibniz's theory of *conatus*. Deleuze's brand of vital materialism is built from these thinkers in general and more specifically from Leibniz's claim that "whatever there is in corporeal nature besides the object of geometry, or extension, must be reduced to this force [of striving towards change]."[96] This emphasis on relations of force informs the work of the most prominent contemporary vital materialist Jane Bennet and her work *Vibrant Matter: A Political Ecology of Things*. In the introduction to this text, she describes her project thusly: "My aspiration is to articulate a vibrant materiality that runs alongside and inside humans to see how analyses of political events might change if we gave the force of things more due. How, for example, would patterns of consumption change if we faced not litter, rubbish, trash, or "the recycling," but an accumulating pile of lively and potentially dangerous matter?"[97] Her list of examples goes on, but the core of her project is clear. If we are to regard matter as *vibrant* or *vital*, then our way of acting would need to change accordingly, and Bennett makes clear that this change would have positive ecological consequences. Thus, what does "vitality" mean in this case? She writes: "By 'vitality' I mean the capacity of things—edibles, commodities, storms, metals—not only to impede or block the will and designs of humans but also to act as quasi agents or forces with trajectories, propensities, or tendencies of their own."[98] Her monograph gives a nuanced presentation of both the details and implications of this ontological position, but for our purposes here, we can simply note how this approach to vital materialism can have broad implications if brought into our default perceptual mode, and we act from this position. If all phenomena are considered actors, then our actions must attune to this web of action in a way not unlike *pratītyasamutpāda.*

Second, Gamble, Hanan, and Nail present what they call "negative new materialism," under which we can find various articulations of speculative realism and object-oriented ontology. The authors of the paper call it "negative" because of its denial of "the relation between thought and matter."[99] They trace the roots of speculative materialism to the French philosopher Quintin Meillassoux and his challenge to post-Kantian *correlationism*, being the idea that humans could not live without the world, and the world could not exist without humans, which Graham Harman says was the "default metaphysics" of the West for over two centuries.[100] Thus, Meillassoux seeks to articulate what matter is outside of human thought and comes to the following conclusion about materialism:

> Materialism holds in two key statements: 1. Being is separate and independent of thought (understood in the broad sense of subjectivity), 2. Thought can think Being. Thesis number 1 is opposed to any anthropomorphism which seeks to extend subjective attributes to Being: materialism is not a form of animism, spiritualism, vitalism, etcetera. It asserts that non-thinking actually precedes, or at least may in right precede thought, and exists outside of it, following the example of Epicurean atoms, devoid of any subjectivity, and independent of our relationship to the world. Thesis number 2 affirms that materialism is rationalism.[101]

Of course, his is not the only speculative materialism. Steven Shaviro has reached a similar conclusion about materialism by way of his study of Alfred North Whitehead. In his book *The Universe of Things*, he writes,

> The basic speculative realist thesis is the diametrical opposite of the "naïve" assertion that things in themselves are directly accessible to us; the key point, rather, is that the world in itself—the world as it exists apart from us—cannot in any way be contained or constrained by the question of our access to it. "Man" is not the measure of all things. We habitually grasp the world in terms of our own preimposed concepts. We need to break this habit in order to get at the strangeness of things in the world—that is, at the ways that they exist without being "posited" by us and without being "given" to or "manifested" by us. Even the things that we have made ourselves possess their own bizarre and independent existence. If philosophy begins in wonder—and ends in wonder, too, as Whitehead insists—then its aim should be not to deduce and impose cognitive norms, or concepts of understanding, but rather to make us more fully aware of how reality escapes and upsets these norms.[102]

This makes clear the speculative dimension of negative materialism/speculative realism. Negative materialists aim to conceive of matter outside the realm of human projection which is a task that is *necessarily* speculative.

The other major strand of negative materialism is that of object-oriented ontology or OOO. Like speculative realism, OOO seeks to articulate a theory of matter outside of human experience and, in doing so, project a kind of essence onto phenomena that is necessarily withdrawn and hidden from human experience. As Harman writes, "What is real in the cosmos are forms wrapped inside forms, not durable specks of material that reduce everything else to derivative status."[103] Gamble, Hanan, and Nail explain this position thusly: "For Harman, the essence of beings is to withdraw from all the objects that compose it and think it. As such, being is never something anthropocentric, experienced, or relational but is something absolutely and non-relationally 'withdrawn' from everything else, as though it were completely 'vacuum sealed.'"[104] Timothy Morton is the philosopher who has most enthusiastically taken up this position and has extended it to new areas of thought. It is also in their work that we see a clearer essentialization of objects. In an article titled "Here Comes Everything: The Promise of Object-Oriented Ontology," they speculate, "How far 'down things' does OOO really go? Are these things made of some kind of substrate, some kind of unformed matter? Does 'withdrawal' mean that objects are impenetrable in some nonfigurative, nonhuman sense? Do objects have a spatial 'inside'? Surely they might. But the principle of irreducibility must mean that this inside is radically unavailable."[105] Elsewhere in the text, they write that "things have an irreducible dark side," that "an object is profoundly withdrawn," and that "objects encounter each other as operationally closed systems that can only (mis) translate one another" making "causation . . . vicarious in some sense, never direct."[106] Thus, both speculative materialism and OOO assert some essence to matter that eludes human experience and that exists "withdrawn from" and hence independent of other phenomena altogether. This challenge to the normative position of human domination in the material world can lead to a renewed carefulness in our interactions with other phenomena and can work against some of the instrumental, technocentric views that have led to our present climate catastrophe.

Finally, the third new materialism that Gamble, Hanan, and Nail identify, and the one they forward in their own work, is that of performative materialism. They locate the origins of performative new materialism in the work of Karen Barad and Vicky Kirby and contrast it with other new materialisms through its view that "ontology and epistemology are inherently co-implicated and mutually constituting."[107] As Gamble, Hanan, and Nail write, this notion that knowing and being are coconstituted is largely informed through the "measurement problem" in quantum physics as found in the "famous double-slit experiments in which, depending on the experimental arrangement, light (or atoms etc.) appears either as a wave or particle, despite their mutually exclusive properties."[108] From this experiment, performative new materialists conclude that "entities simply do not determinately exist apart from the particular, physical measuring apparatuses that constitute them one way to the exclusion of others," and therefore "light, like all matter, is *indeterminate*" and "not fully separable from the physical, material apparatus used to observe it."[109] This coconstitution of the observer and the observed provides the foundation for performative new materialism, which recognizes the interpenetrating nature of all phenomena through their knowing and their being. In other words, all matter, human beings, and nonhuman beings "always constitute and are partly constituted by that which they observe."[110]

This kind of coconstitution applies not only to the physical properties of phenomena (as in the slit experiment), but also the meaning of phenomena as they relate to one another. In *Meeting the Universe Halfway*, Barad writes, "Meaning is not a property of individual words or groups of words but an ongoing performance of the world in its differential dance of intelligibility and unintelligibility. In its causal intra-activity, part of the world becomes determinately bounded and propertied in its emergent intelligibility to another part of the world, while lively matterings, possibilities, and impossibilities are reconfigured."[111] Hence, we arrive at a *performative* materialism where meaning is not essential but is an emergent property of material assemblages. We find a similar process occurring in the philosophical thought of Kirby as well. She extends this idea of performance and materiality to broader questions of nature and humanity and contends that "if we humans are performances of matter as much as anything else, then anything allegedly exceptional about us must be but a particular inflection of a fully generalizable behavior of nature."[112] In other words, if we're simply matter, then our intelligence, language, and so forth are simply emergent properties of matter itself. This leads her to claim that "nature is literate"[113] and draws her to the conclusion that like Derrida's statement *"il n'y a pas de hors texte,"* "there is no outside of Nature."[114] This idea of coconstitution of matter, meaning, and existence approaches a similar conclusion as some of the Tibetan interpretations of Madhyamaka and could therefore install a similar conative mode in the individual that would result in positive ecological action.

Of course, space limits my ability to unpack each of these approaches to new materialism in detail, but what they all share is a challenge to normative understanding of the human being, nonhuman being, and matter at large. Each of these novel approaches to ontology, metaphysics, and epistemology decenters the human in a way that opens up the ability to think of new ways of relating to the world and addressing issues like our environmental crisis. Still, one may wonder how these ontological positions about the nature of matter relate to an environmental ethic. Simply put, many of these authors link their ontological positions to particular ethical stances not unlike that which is found in Nāgārjuna's phrase "*śūnyatā-karuṇā-garbham*." In other words, these ontological positions undergird a particular disposition in the individual and political orientation that can be seen as constituting a form of environmental ethics—one that moves the individual away from an anthropocentric domination of matter and toward an active caring attention to the nonhuman material world.

Take, for example, Jane Bennet's claim that "this same-stuff claim, this insinuation that deep down everything is connected and irreducible to a simple substrate, resonates with an *ecological sensibility*" and that "there remains a natural tendency to the way things are—and that human decency and a decent politics are fostered if we tune in to the strange logic of turbulence."[115] Later in *Vibrant Matter*, she unpacks this relationship between vital materialism and environmental ethics in more explicit terms, writing,

> Vital materialism would thus set up a kind of safety net for those humans who are now, in a world where Kantian morality is the standard, routinely made to suffer because they do not conform to a particular (Euro-American, bourgeois, theocentric, or other) model of personhood. The ethical aim becomes to distribute value more generously, to bodies as such. Such a newfound attentiveness to matter and its powers will not solve the problem of human exploitation or oppression, but it can inspire a greater sense of the extent to which all bodies are kin in the sense of inextricably enmeshed in a dense network of relations. And in a knotted world of vibrant matter, to harm one section of the web may very well be to harm oneself. Such an enlightened or expanded notion of self-interest is good for humans.[116]

Of interest to this current moral phenomenological project, she also provides a direct link between the ontological and the ethical via perception and writes, "We are vital materiality and we are surrounded by it, though we do not always see it that way.

The ethical task at hand here is to cultivate the ability to discern nonhuman vitality, to become perceptually open to it."[117] Thus, it is clear that Bennett's presentation of matter as vibrant has environmental ethical implications when brought into one's default perceptual mode.

Similarly, negative new materialisms like speculative materialism and OOO are often directly related to climate change, ecology, and ethics by the authors of these theories themselves. For example, Levi Bryant, Nick Srnicek, and Graham Harman see speculative materialism as an attempt to rethink the novelty of our era of environmental emergency and write, "In the face of the ecological crisis, the forward march of neuroscience, the increasingly splintered interpretations of basic physics, and the ongoing breach of the divide between human and machine, there is a growing sense that previous philosophies are incapable of confronting these events."[118] Thus, they in turn assert that a new metaphysic such as speculative materialism *can* help us confront these events and think through their implications. However, rarely do speculative materialists engage with broader ecological conversations or environmental ethics broadly construed.

Instead, we find this conversation primarily happening in OOO and the work of Timothy Morton. Throughout their body of work, Morton relates their OOO approach to ecology, the environment, and climate change. In "Here Comes Everything," Morton begins their train of thought by calling the move to OOO as a reaction to the current ecological crisis[119] and consistently refers to OOO as an ecological metaphysic. In several of their works, they make explicit connections between seeing the world through the lens of OOO and a particular mode of being and acting in the world. For example, in *Hyperobjects*, Morton states that "ethics and politics in a post-modern age after Hume and Kant must be based in attunement to directives coming from entities."[120] Similarly, they extend the logic of OOO to nonhuman agents in *Dark Ecology* and argue that

> there are layers of attunement to ecological reality more accurate than what is habitual in the media, in the academy, and in society at large. These attunement structures are necessarily *weird*, a precise term that we

shall explore in depth. Weirdness involves the herme-neutical knowingness belonging to the practices that the humanities maintain. The attunement, which I call *ecognosis*, implies a practical yet highly nonstandard vision of what ecological politics could be. In part, ecognosis involves realizing that nonhumans are installed at profound levels of the human—not just biologically and socially but in the very structure of thought and logic. Coexisting with these nonhumans is ecological thought, art, ethics, and politics.[121]

Thus, Morton contends that ecological awareness (informed by OOO) brings forth a politics unique to our present ecological situation that confronts and addresses some of the problematic "agrilogistics" that have led to our present catastrophe. Similarly, in *Humankind* they argue for a recognition of nonhuman matter, both what we would conventionally consider animate and what we would conventionally consider inanimate, as a basis for a particular orientation to the world: kindness. They write,

> What we are talking about is acknowledging this always-already quality of nonhuman impingement, and bringing that awareness, which is not the opposite of action but rather a quantum of action, into actions at other scales. . . . Acknowledgement includes the deliberate forging of links between humans and nonhumans, based on our acknowledgment that we share their worlds, and they share ours. This is also a matter of modality, not of all or nothing. Let us now define kindness as acknowledgment of nonhumans in the terms I just described, whether acknowledgment is in its quantum or ground state (what is conventionally called "aesthetic experience"), or whether acknowledgment is in its more classical state (what is conventionally called "ethical or political action").[122]

Thus, for Morton, an awareness of the nonhuman (here construed in terms of object-oriented ontology) and an attunement to the mutual worlding of the human and nonhuman brings forth a quality of kindness that informs both our immediate actions and our political projects.

Finally, Barad notes how her approach to agential realism (read: performative new materialism) has broader implications on our ethics. She writes that "the world's radical aliveness comes to light in an entirely nontraditional way that reworks the nature of both relationality and aliveness (vitality, dynamism, agency). This shift in ontology also entails a reconceptualization of other core philosophical concepts such as space, time, matter, dynamics, agency, structure, subjectivity, objectivity, knowing, intentionality, discursivity, performativity, entanglement, and ethical engagement."[123] Kirby comes to a near identical position regarding her own intraology, writing: "An intra-ontology . . . reframes questions of ontology, epistemology, ethics, and science by radically recasting the anthropological."[124] In both cases, an attention to the radical relativity of self and other decenters ethics from a purely humanist position and extends ethical consideration to all phenomena that are involved in constructing our selves materially and conceptually. As Barad writes:

> Responsibility—the ability to respond to the other—cannot be restricted to human-human encounters when the very boundaries and constitution of the "human" are continually being reconfigured and "our" role in these and other reconfigurings is precisely what "we" have to face. A humanist ethics won't suffice when the "face" of the other that is "looking" back at me is all eyes, or has no eyes, or is otherwise unrecognizable in human terms. What is needed is a posthumanist ethics, an ethics of worlding.[125]

This ethics of worlding is imminently ecological. Following the above quotation, Barad writes that "ethics is therefore not about right response to a radically exterior/ized other, but about responsibility and accountability for the lively relationalities of becoming of which we are a part."[126] This attention to relationalities entails "an ongoing responsiveness to the entanglements of self and other"[127] and therefore entails a maintenance of these entanglements such that the self and other are mutually supported in a way that promotes the flourishing of both.

While each of these new materialisms approaches ontology in different ways, they all point to a similar ethical outcome. Through a deep attention to matter and a decentering of the human, each of these new materialisms forms a foundation for novel ethics that takes the more-than-human world as a serious partner for thinking and living. Thus, if these new materialist views are contemplated and brought into one's default perceptual mode through meditation, then we will see a marked change in one's orientation to the more-than-human world that results in positive environmental action. This is the case in both vital and negative new materialisms that attribute novel characteristics to what is conventionally seen as dead matter, but it is even more the case in performative new materialisms that approximate the views of certain Tibetan interpretations of Madhyamaka in their understanding of relativity and interbeing. Thus, these new materialisms can act as provisional views in a framework of view, meditation, action to work toward a moral phenomenological approach to environmental ethics.

We can therefore begin to see how a Buddhist moral phenomenology can translate into a contemplative environmental ethic. To restate how an applied moral phenomenology would work in ecological contexts, it would first articulate the ethical problem at hand, identify a philosophical view that would address this problem, and integrate this philosophical view into one's default perceptual mode through contemplative practice. We have accomplished the first two of these tasks by identifying some of the erroneous views that lead to a negative treatment of the more-than-human world and have explored some of the views that, when plugged into the framework of view, meditation, action, lead to positive ethical outcomes. I claim that, like a general Buddhist moral phenomenology, emptiness functions as the view par excellence in a moral phenomenological approach to the environment, but on the way to its full experiential recognition, a variety of views, from causation to the suffering of nonhuman animals to the reality of climate change to new materialism, can provisionally address some of the erroneous views and epistemological barriers to climate action. What remains to be seen is how contemplative practice functions in this ecological context and how action might emerge from these contemplative foundations. It is to this final task we now turn.

6

# Ecological Meditation, Ecological Action

## Contemplative Practice in a Buddhist
Environmental Ethic

In the previous chapter, we considered what views may be conducive to an environmental ethic and found that there are several views, both Buddhist and non-Buddhist, that can lead to positive environmental action when brought into one's default perceptual mode. But to actually make this shift and turn these views from being simply intellectually understood to being experienced requires *sgom pa* (meditation). In Buddhist moral phenomenology, the role of meditation is quite straightforward. However, one might ask how meditation would function in an applied moral phenomenological response to the more-than-human world. Perhaps anticlimactically, the answer is this: Meditation functions the same way in an applied moral phenomenology as it does in a general Buddhist moral phenomenology. This is because meditation is not partial to any particular view or any specific belief system but is instead a tool for bridging intellect and affect and for bringing philosophical ideas into our experience of the world. Thus, should one wish to implement a moral phenomenological approach to environmental ethics, one must establish a *vipaśyanā* practice grounded in a stable *śamatha* practice in order to have a deep meditative experience of one of the aforementioned views. This chapter will outline this process before searching for other ways view can be brought into one's default perceptual mode in ecological contexts. It will then discuss what the action that emerges from this experiential understanding looks like and address some potential problems therein.

## *Śamatha* and *Vipaśyanā* in Ecological Contexts

I have argued that the first step of meditation in a moral phenomenological approach to ethics is the cultivation of calm abiding or concentration. Given how Jetsunma Tenzin Palmo and Daniel Aitken have characterized *śamatha* meditation as "more foundational than even the preliminaries"[1] in our age of TikTok and the attention economy,[2] *śamatha* would similarly be the starting place for bringing a view into one's default perceptual mode. Without a firm foundation of our capacity to fix our attention to a single object, either physical or conceptual, we will not be able to sufficiently focus on a view such that we can come to fully experience it in our meditation. In a moral phenomenological approach to ethics, this meditative experience of the view is the goal of meditative practice. Therefore, establishing the ability to fix our mind to an object of meditation with relative ease would be the first step in the moral phenomenological meditative process.

The foundational meditation texts in the Tibetan tradition begin with a discussion concerning the prerequisites for successful meditation. Tsongkhapa states that "the yogin should at the outset take recourse to the [supports] for calm abiding, which [are] the foundation for speedily and pleasantly accomplishing calm"[3] and gives six such supports: residence in a favorable place, meager desire, contentment, elimination of multiple activities, purity of morality, and the elimination of discursive thinking of craving and so on.[4] Should an individual who already practices meditation wish to engage in a moral phenomenological approach to environmental ethics, these supports are likely not far from them. They likely already have a *śamatha* practice or are engaged in the cultivation of morality, the lessening of discursive thinking, and so forth. However, if one wishes to engage in a moral phenomenological approach to environmental ethics from outside the Buddhist tradition, these prerequisites might appear quite intimidating. It is for this reason that a particular point in Tsongkhapa's statement should be emphasized: the *speedily* and *pleasant* accomplishing of *śamatha*. Contemporary meditation teachers (especially in the mindfulness tradition) teach *śamatha* to the general public without emphasizing these supports and practitioners can indeed establish a level of calm-abiding without them. However, it may take longer for them to do so and they may have a greater degree of difficulty establishing calm-abiding without first working on moral discipline and so forth. Regardless, whether a Buddhist or non-Buddhist wants to start down the path toward an environmental moral phenomenology, the six meditative supports outlined by Tsongkhapa are helpful for establishing a solid *śamatha* practice.

With these prerequisites addressed, we can now turn to the object of meditation. In chapter 5 we saw how several Tibetan meditation texts offered many different objects with which to cultivate *śamatha*. Tsongkhapa makes this observation himself in his *Lamrim Chenmo*, writing that "many meditative objects are set forth in the great texts about accomplishing *samādhi*."[5] However, after parsing these objects, I came to conclude that breath is the optimal object of meditation for human beings today. My reasoning was twofold. First, as I just alluded to, Jetsunma Tenzin Palmo notes how today's minds are "just jam packed with stuff already, most of it trash," and that we need to "clean out, get some space in there, open the windows, throw out all this junk. And that is where *śamatha* and *vipaśyanā* comes in."[6] Of course, in this quote, we do not find breath being emphasized, but we *do* see Tenzin Palmo identify a major hindrance in modern meditators: a mind full of junk. If we turn to the *Lamrim Chenmo*, we can find a prescription for precisely this kind of person. Tsongkhapa writes, "One with predominance of discursive speculation definitely has the requirement to cultivate the breath."[7] This junk that Tenzin Palmo is identifying can more technically be described as "discursive speculation," which makes the breath an ideal object of meditation for most individuals today.

The second reason for using breath to cultivate *śamatha* meditation in a moral phenomenological approach to ethics is its popularity. If we are to promote an applied moral phenomenology outside of Buddhist contexts, we should turn to the tools available in the broader cultural discourse surrounding contemplative practice to allow for this kind of ethical practice to be accessible. Mindfulness practice in the tradition of the Insight Meditation Society, Thich Nhat Hanh, or even Kabat-Zinn's mindfulness-based stress reduction[8] all use breath as the primary objects of their practice. As we have seen, breath is not the *only* possible object for the cultivation of calm abiding that we find in Tibetan texts, and contemporary teachers will sometimes use other objects such as an image of Shakyamuni Buddha as the basis for cultivating calm abiding.[9] Regardless, given the cultural availability of breath as an object of meditation and its utility for overcoming discursive thought, most contemporary practitioners wishing to establish *śamatha* to effectively incorporate a view into their default perceptual mode should use the breath as the primary object of their *śamatha* practice.

To reiterate, this cultivation of *śamatha* or calm abiding is definitively *not* the goal of meditative practice in either the broader Buddhist tradition or a moral phenomenological approach to environmental ethics. In both cases, *śamatha* is simply a state conducive to the development of *vipaśyanā* (meditative insight). It allows individuals to more fully immerse themselves in a conceptual object of meditation to bring that intellectually established concept into their default perceptual mode. In both the broader soteriology of the Tibetan Buddhist tradition and the narrower goal of a moral phenomenological approach to environmental ethics, *śamatha* is therefore simply a useful tool for engaging the more fruitful *vipaśyanā* meditation. *Vipaśyanā* meditation involves directing one's calm mind to particular conceptual views and concentrating on them until they are directly perceived. And it is in this direct perception that a moral phenomenological ethic emerges.

In chapter 4, we outlined a specific methodology for bringing conceptual views into one's default perceptual mode: *listen, reflect, meditate*. Khensur Jampa Tegchok provides instruction on this process in a very clear way when he writes, "This wisdom develops gradually, first by hearing and studying the teachings, then by contemplating and reflecting on them to ensure we understand them correctly, and finally by integrating them in our mind through meditation."[10] In other words, we initially encounter particular views through listening (or reading) about them, then we critically reflect on them to discern whether they are valid or not, and finally we bring them into our meditation practice to directly experience them. We find this approach to integrating knowledge into one's default perceptual mode and for bridging the gap between purely intellectual knowledge and embodied, experienced wisdom in both the more scholastic schools of Tibetan Buddhism[11] and the more yogic schools of Tibetan Buddhism and their respective approaches to liberation. In a similar way, we may apply this framework to our experiential realization of views in a moral phenomenological approach to environmental ethics.

The views that are conducive to a moral phenomenological approach to environmental ethics all require some degree of study to understand intellectually. Whether we are after an experiential realization of the ultimate ecological view of emptiness or an experiential understanding of a provisional view such as cause and effect, the suffering of nonhuman beings, the reality of climate change, deep and shallow ecology, or new materialism, these ideas can be complicated and must be studied and tested to be fully comprehended. This is where reflection comes in. Once we have encountered these views through listening, reading, watching, or what have you, they need to be intellectually tried, tested, played with, and challenged. As with any serious scientific or philosophical endeavor, one comes to a much greater degree of certainty about one's conclusions by considering opposing views and either refuting them or adapting one's own conclusion in light of them. This more comprehensive understanding of view is why debate is valorized in certain Tibetan Buddhist schools and why the teacher-student relationship is so important in others. It is not enough to simply read a book and then go off and meditate. One needs to make sure their view is correct by checking it against criticism, in debate, or by asking questions either to oneself or to one who understands the view in a more nuanced way. If this does not happen, then the ability for one to realize said view will be hampered. As Anne Klein states, "Direct [meditative] perception is hampered by a lack of ascertainment—of noticing what appears to it—and thought, despite being obstructed with respect to a clear and vivid appearance of impermanent things, is the instrument whereby one can cultivate ascertainment of what appears unnoticed to direct perception."[12] Regardless of which view we intend to mobilize toward a moral phenomenological approach to environmental ethics, they absolutely must be reflected upon such that our intellectual comprehension of the view is vast, deep, and nuanced.

Having come to this nuanced intellectual understanding of the view, one then meditates on the view to have a direct meditative experience of it. After having cultivated calm abiding, one directs their concentrated mind to the view in question to cultivate it, (perceptually) familiarize oneself with it, and bring it into one's experience of the world. This process amounts to the particular kind of understanding that we spelled out in chapter 5. Dreyfus notes how there is a gradient of acumen that increases when one moves from listening to contemplating to meditating and writes how this last acumen is one that "can lead to a more direct insight into the nature of persons and other phenomena, which gradually frees an individual from the bondage of negative emotions."[13] Thus, in a Buddhist soteriological sense, Dreyfus is implying that the acumen arising from listening and thinking does not actually address negative emotion or negative behavior. It is only through the meditative understanding of the view that one can overcome greed, hatred, and delusion and reorient ethically. Moreover, he writes that the meditative process "culminates in the full internalization of the content of the tradition."[14]

We might understand meditation in a similar way in ecological settings. Does their direct meditative realization address the root afflictions of greed, hatred, and delusion? Perhaps not. But they certainly address the errant views about and dispositions toward the more-than-human world that contribute to its degradation. Fully internalizing the view that nonhuman beings suffer from ecological collapse or the deep ecological view of the intrinsic value of nonhuman phenomena would allow us to reorient our conative mode such that our actions would naturally contribute to the flourishing of the more-than-human world (or at least would reduce our harm thereupon). Through *vipaśyanā*, we can bring these ecological views into our default perceptual mode through direct meditative experience and turn these intellectual understandings into embodied, nonconceptual, perceptual, and experiential understandings. In doing so, we radically shift our affect and our motivation such that our everyday experience produces a spontaneous concern for the more-than-human world, and we enact a moral phenomenological approach to environmental ethics. *This* is the contemplative approach to environmental ethics.

## Other Methods for Experiencing View

Given the ecological context of the current discussion, it is worth considering if there are other methods for experiencing the view outside of purely meditative contexts. The actual direct, perceptual experience of the view is more important than the method used to occasion that experience since it is the experience itself that reorients the individual's default perceptual mode. In Tibetan Buddhist soteriological contexts, meditation is the primary way of occasioning this experience due to both meditation's cultural availability and its effectiveness in engaging with very subtle concepts such as non-self, impermanence, and emptiness. If, however, we are engaging with more tangible and broad views such as cause and effect or the suffering of nonhuman beings, then perhaps there are other methods for directly experiencing these views outside of meditative contexts.

We have seen the nonmeditative occasioning of profound realization of views like these in Tibetan vegetarian contexts. Both Shabkar and Jigmé Lingpa came to an experiential realization of their complicity in the suffering of nonhuman animals not through meditation but through seeing animals awaiting slaughter. Similarly, His Holiness the seventeenth Karmapa came to this realization through watching a documentary on the abuse of nonhuman animals. It is clear then that there can be purely perceptual encounters with some of these views that can shock one into reorienting their perceptual experience in the same way that a meditative experience can. With the case of the suffering of nonhuman animals, there is a plethora of material online and many opportunities in our day-to-day lives to come face to face with the suffering of nonhuman animals. However, I would argue that one still has to be *primed* to respond in a certain way in these perceptual encounters. If one holds the ridiculous Cartesian view that nonhuman animals are automatons void of feeling and simply operating on instinct, then seeing nonhuman animals suffer would not have the same effect as it did on these figures. Shabkar, Jigmé Lingpa, and His Holiness the seventeenth Karmapa were all situated in a tradition where all sentient beings are seen as having been our mothers in a past life. Thus, as a consequence of this conceptual priming (or prior intellectual understanding of this particular view), they had a profound phenomenological shift upon seeing the suffering of nonhuman animals that reshaped their relationship with the more-than-human world.

This "conversion" experience wherein an individual has a profound shift in their view and subsequent action in the more-than-human world is a common theme in radical ecological writing. For example, Sarah Pike writes about the conversion of individuals to radical ecological activism in her book *For the Wild*, stating: "Conversion tends to take place on an internal and personal level. . . . In the context of conversion to activism, I explore the ways in which the love, wonder, rage, and grief that motivate radical activists develop through powerful, embodied relationships with nonhuman beings. Conversion to activism can happen in a matter of moments, during what some activists describe as a tipping point, or it can be a longer, more subtle internal process of shifting one's worldview."[15] Elsewhere, Pike calls this conversion an "internal revolution"[16] and says that, depending on the individual, it can occur through their "awe when they first encounter redwoods or anger when they first see a wilderness devastated by mining or logging."[17] Furthermore, like we find in the above accounts of seeing nonhuman animals in a new light, many of these eco-activists were primed to experience the more-than-human world through earlier encounters with nonhuman beings in their childhood and early adolescence.[18] Pike writes, "Because the boundaries between child self and nonhuman other were porous, loss of the other or its degradation were even more disturbing. Activists' remembered childhood worlds of wonder held pain and suffering when beloved childhood places were lost to roads, new houses, and shopping malls."[19] Thus, it is through a lifetime of encounters with the more than human that these eco-activists finally come to a "tipping point" where their conditioning as children and teenagers becomes a fully embodied care for the nonhuman.

While she doesn't use the language of moral phenomenology, we can easily see the parallels between Pike's ethnographic descriptions of activists' conversion experiences and the kind of shift that occurs in a moral phenomenological approach to environmental ethics. What she is identifying in these activists is a profound shift in how they view the more-than-human world and their place within it, which can result from either a gradual process or a singular profound encounter. Ultimately, however, these activists come to *see* the more-than-human world in way that is imbued with a great deal of affect (love, wonder, rage, grief, and so forth) that consequently compels these individuals to act accordingly. Thus, while the actual practice of meditation is typically not involved in Pike's population of study,[20] the move from an intellectual view to an experiential understanding of the more-than-human world is certainly present and clearly compels individuals to act in response to this perceptual shift. Simply encountering a view like the suffering of nonhuman animals in our day-to-day life may thus provide the impetus for ethical change, even if it's undirected and perhaps inconsistent when compared to meditation.

In the broader literature on environmental philosophy, we can also find several distinct methods that scholars and activists propose for enacting a similar kind of phenomenological shift in service of a larger eco-political goal. In *Staying with the Trouble*, Donna Haraway builds on the work of Vinciane Despret to articulate a practice of "worlding" where one develops an ability to "think-with other beings, human or not."[21] For Despret and Haraway, thinking with the other is a practice wherein individuals attend "not to what critters are supposed to be able to do, by nature or education, but to what beings evoke from and with each other that was truly not there before, in nature or culture."[22] This kind of practice is necessarily experiential in that it does away with former narratives around nonhumans and their relations to us and instead focuses on what is immediately available to us perceptually, affectively, and so on during our encounters with the more than human world. From this kind of encounter, Haraway claims that "the domain of ways of being and knowing dilates, expands, adds both ontological and epistemological possibilities, proposes and enacts what was not there before."[23] Intrinsic to this practice is its ability to disrupt the kinds of thinking that initiated and maintain our current epoch of the "Anthropocene, Capitalocene, and Cthulucene"[24] in order to respond to its demands and act in ethically efficient ways.

A similar practice can be found in Jenny Odell's recent work *How to Do Nothing: Resisting the Attention Economy*, where she advocates for a renewed attention to our immediate surroundings as a way to move out of capitalist modes of productivity and consumption and into a more embodied, care-filled relationship with our immediate more-than-human community. She critiques this attention economy and simultaneously promotes the "promise of bioregional awareness" because she sees "capitalism, colonialist thinking, loneliness, and an abusive stance toward the environment all coproducing one another."[25] This bioregional awareness is cultivated through a number of practices, including "contemplative walking,"[26] "Deep Listening,"[27] developing a sensitivity to the sentient beings we are in relationship with,[28] and cultivating a sustained attention to the natural phenomena around us, such as creeks, rocks, ferns, and so forth.[29] All of these encompass what Odell calls "doing nothing," which she defends against nihilistic interpretations of renouncing all worldly affairs by defining this practice as "an active process of listening that seeks out the effects of racial, environmental, and economic injustice and brings about real change."[30] This "doing nothing" is a perceptual practice. It involves paying attention to our environment and its inhabitants in a specific, intentional way to cultivate a particular way of seeing and being in the world. Further, like in a moral phenomenology, this kind of seeing evokes an ethical (and political) response that involves caring for our immediate surroundings and the phenomena we encounter on a daily basis.

Finally, outside of the Buddhist tradition, there are of course other classical contemplative practices that can elicit nonconceptual realizations of particular views, and these could perhaps be turned to in lieu of meditation. These contemplative practices include postural forms of yoga,[31] prayer, tai chi, qigong, and so forth. They can work with concepts and create embodied or experiential understandings of a view in a way that could resemble meditative practice. The Dalai Lama is quite famous for saying that people should not (or do not have to) convert to Buddhism but should practice the religions they were raised in. This being the case, it is likely that the contemplative practices native to other religious traditions could be used in place of Buddhist meditation in the contemplative framework of *lta sgom spyod gsum* to effect similar ethical change and extend this environmental moral phenomenology to other contemplative contexts.

We might also include plant medicine and psychedelic experiences under this category of nonmeditative ways of coming to an experiential realization of a view. These medicines, which include ayahuasca, psilocybin, LSD, and so forth, have been used in both indigenous and clinical settings to enact precisely this kind of phenomenological transformation. In indigenous settings, plant medicines have been used to initiate adolescents into the worldview of their culture in an experiential way, and their use in ceremony often marked their inclusion into the adult life of their community.[32] In contemporary clinical settings, psychedelics such as psilocybin have begun to be used to treat addiction, anxiety, depression, and PTSD, all of which are conceptually or narratively mediated.[33] In this latter case, a therapist first works with the patient to establish an appropriate mental set for the subsequent psychedelic experience through conventional cognitive behavioral therapy protocols. In other words, the therapist establishes a *view* that sets the basis for the subsequent *experience* in the psychedelic state.[34] In a sense, all of these modalities are engaging in a kind of moral phenomenology and are (perhaps inadvertently) functioning as the "meditation" in the framework of view, meditation, action to bring views into the default perceptual mode of practitioners. This is most explicit in the last of these modalities, clinical psychedelic therapy, where view is actively worked with prior to the experience and actively worked with in the psychedelic state to bring a certain narrative or perspective into how one experiences, and therefore acts within, the world. In Dzongsar Khyentse Rinpoche's book *What Makes You Not a Buddhist*, he claims that "even substances like peyote and mescaline might give us a vague notion of the illusory aspect of reality . . . but a drug cannot provide total awakening."[35] We might therefore conclude that psychedelics could be useful means for experiencing provisional views, but that the ultimate view of emptiness may evade those undergoing the psychedelic experience. Regardless, it's entirely possible that these contemplative practices and technologies could be used in place of meditation in a moral phenomenological approach to environmental ethics.


## Defending Meditation

All of this is to say that there are ways of enacting a moral phenomenological approach to environmental ethics that perhaps do not require a formal, seated meditation practice. We can see the kinds of experiential transformations that are central to moral phenomenology occurring through seeing animals suffer, feeling awe or anger when encountering nature and its destruction, the practice of worlding and thinking with other beings, and "doing nothing." We can also see how other contemplative practices could occasion a nonconceptual understanding of a view and act as possible substitutes for a systematic *śamatha* and *vipaśyanā*. However, I nonetheless hold that all of these nonmeditative approaches to linking view and action and bringing a particular concept in one's perceptual fold are less efficient than meditation.

The major reason for this claim is consistency and directness. The systematic cultivation of *śamatha* and the use of this calm, concentrated mind to develop direct insight into concepts are proven methods for occasioning nonconceptual realizations of view. To be clear, it is entirely possible that a practice like Odell's "doing nothing" could reliably bring an individual to see their immediate environment in a specific way or that a nonconceptual realization of some view regarding the nonhuman other could be brought about by Haraway and Despret's worlding and thinking with. However, these kinds of practices do not have the same history as meditative practice, and we therefore cannot say for certain that they will reliably produce a nonconceptual realization of an environmental view in the same way that we *know* meditation can.

Furthermore, Odell, Haraway, and Despret's given practices seem more or less inextricable from a specific philosophical context, and these authors link these practices to specific sociopolitical outcomes. This is completely fine in terms of their philosophical merit and sociopolitical utility, but it does detract from their usefulness in a moral phenomenological approach to environmental ethics. We have identified multiple views that could be relevant to an environmental ethic, including the ultimate view of emptiness and several provisional views that could lead to good environmental outcomes if brought into a moral phenomenology. To the extent that an individual has not yet realized emptiness, the more provisional views they are able to bring into their default perceptual mode, the stronger their motivation will be for acting in a way that promotes the flourishing of all being in the more-than-human world. Thus, if the method for installing view into one's default perceptual mode is linked to a single specific view or political program, then this method is limited in its applicability and its overall effectiveness in a moral phenomenological approach to environmental ethics.

Finally, with respect to the more general modes of contemplative practice, I again claim that meditation is the most effective method for a moral phenomenological approach to environmental ethics due to not only its consistency but also its precision. *Vipaśyanā* works directly with concepts to bring an individual to a nonconceptual realization of a given view. Perhaps one could direct one's postural yoga or taichi practice to realizing a particular view, but these practices are neither designed nor used for working with concepts in the way that meditation is. Thus, while they *may* be able to stand in for meditation, their utility in a moral phenomenological framework is questionable. Similarly, if we are to consider the use of plant medicines and psychedelics for enacting an applied moral phenomenology, we arrive more fully at this issue of precision. In meditation practice, one can carefully and systematically place one's mind on a particular concept with sustained attention. The nature of *śamatha* and *vipaśyanā* is such that these concepts can be brought into one's experience slowly and precisely. Contrastingly, these kinds of substances that can surely occasion a nonconceptual realization of a particular view are difficult to control. Once under their influence, all kinds of sensory and conceptual experience can occur, and even if one is guided by someone through the experience, the ability to call up and remain focused on a given view to actually experience that view nonconceptually is a difficult endeavor. Ironically, the ability to do so might be developed through a meditation practice, and there are contemporary instances of practitioners blending these two traditions together.[36]

Nonetheless, due to meditation's historical efficacy and the precision with which it can experientially approach any view brought into *vipaśyanā* practice, I claim that it is the best way for one to bring an ecological view into their default perceptual mode to enact a moral phenomenological approach to environmental ethics. We have seen some other methods for installing an ecological view into one's default experience of the world, but these methods lack the efficacy of meditation. This is not to say that they are unimportant or that they do not have a role to play in a contemplative approach to environmental ethics; they certainly can and, in many instances, do play key roles in bringing people to ecological consciousness. However, I suggest that they are simply less efficient for occasioning a direct experience of ecological views when compared to formal seated meditation. In this ecological context, the role of meditation is the same as in a general Buddhist moral phenomenology. First, one develops the ability to concentrate with a calm mind in *śamatha* practice, and then one directs this calm, attentive mind to a given conceptual object to come to a meditative, nonconceptual understanding of the given view. From this experiential understanding, one can adopt this view into their default perceptual mode and conduct themselves in the world from its basis. Thus, while the views and perhaps actions may differ from a general Buddhist moral phenomenology, meditation functions identical to a Buddhist moral phenomenology in an environmental ethical context.

## Ecological Action

With ecological meditation parsed, we can turn to the final piece in this moral phenomenological approach to environmental ethics: action. To understand action in this environmental context, it may be useful to call back to how action was understood in a general Buddhist moral phenomenology. In our definition of moral phenomenology, action is considered a *result* of experience. It is the *end* of moral phenomenological practice and emerges from an individual's direct experience of the world. Moral phenomenological practice is directed at the experience of the individual rather than the action that may be considered a by-product of this shift, even if it is the reason for conducting the experiential transformation in the first place. Thus, action is said to stem naturally from one's experience of the view that was brought into one's default perceptual mode through meditation.

We saw this notion of action and its relationship to view and meditation being forwarded by a number of Tibetan thinkers. For example, Dudjom Rinpoche explains the third step of *lta sgom spyod gsum* as "to experience [the view] continuously through action,"[37] implying that one's day-to-day actions are themselves aspects of the view. Similarly, Wangchuk Dorje instructs one's actions to accord with one's view when he states that to "maintain that view during any of the four actions is the conduct."[38] Finally, Gampopa states that "to continually abide in that [experience of the view] is the action."[39] In each of these statements, we can see not only how *action* is intimately tied to *view* but also how action is framed as the continuous experience of *view*. Another way to put this, as Milarepa does, is that "action is the mindfulness of this view in daily activities, meaning that the yogi is able to remember his meditation experience even during all the vicissitudes of his [*sic*] daily experience."[40] Thus, once one has meditatively familiarized oneself with the view, one must bring that experience with them into their daily happenings. In doing so, one's actions become informed by that particular view, and in turn, one practices moral phenomenology. It is through this understanding that we can understand Jigten Sumgön when he writes, "By acting in that state itself, it is the action."[41]

Further, we saw how some of the aforementioned sources refer to action as a specific *mode* of acting. Not only must one maintain the experience of the view during daily life, but one must also act in a way that accords with said experience. For example, Erik Pema Kunsang writes that action is "the implementation of that insight during the activities of daily life,"[42] and Barawa states that "always acting in that way is the action."[43] In other words, once an individual has meditatively implemented a particular view as their *default perceptual mode*, their actions will emerge naturally from that view such that they will spontaneously respond to the situations presented to them from that phenomenological position. This naturalness was described by Phagmodrupa in metaphor when he writes, "Their action needs to arise by itself like an old ox drinking water."[44] Similarly, it is described by Thubten Jinpa as follows: "Once you have formed a good habit through internalization and integration, you can move to the third stage: action. The kind of action we are talking about would arise naturally out of transformed states of mind."[45] Thus, when one puts moral phenomenology into practice by establishing a particular view intellectually and subsequently meditating on that view to bring it into one's experience, one's actions will be informed by this experience such that one can spontaneously and ethically respond to events as they happen.

This understanding of action carries over to a moral phenomenological approach to environmental ethics. This approach does not prescribe specific actions to be taken to promote the flourishing of the more-than-human world but instead simply primes individuals to respond to that end in their daily lives. In other words, an individual who has come to an experiential realization of emptiness or one of the provisional ecological views will go about their daily life informed by this way of experiencing the world and will reflexively act in a way that is conducive to the well-being of nonhuman beings and the ecological systems that support them. Of course, what this will actually look like may vary from person to person and situation to situation. It may change individuals' consumption patterns such that they lessen their impact on the environment; it may compel individuals to tend to their relationships with human and nonhuman beings in their immediate environment and work on supporting these beings by cleaning the local land, air, and water systems; or it may encourage individuals to mobilize politically to enact institutional change in the public and private sectors.

## The Nonprescriptive Character of an Eco-Buddhist Moral Phenomenology

Action can therefore manifest from an ecological view in myriad ways, and I will not speculate on *all* of the resultant forms of action here. Not only would that be a somewhat useless enterprise given how the list of actions would certainly not be exhaustive, but it takes away from the very point of a moral phenomenological approach. The merit in a moral phenomenological approach to environmental ethics comes from its ability to navigate daily life ethically and with ease. There need not be a complex moral calculus, an adherence to a rigid set of rules, or the development of certain qualities over others. Instead, individuals can naturally go about their day acting in a way that accords with whatever ecological view they brought into their experience. Actually bringing one of these ecological views into one's experience can be a difficult process, but once they are established as a part of one's default perceptual mode, then ethical action becomes effortless. This approach creates both a consistency and a flexibility where ethical situations can be navigated in a way that naturally creates the conditions for the flourishing of the more-than-human world.

This idea of context-specific, spontaneous ethical action is not limited to the Buddhist tradition alone. In fact, Lori Gruen's notion of entangled empathy in the feminist ethic-of-care tradition is a useful way of thinking about what this kind of action would look like. She writes primarily in the field of animal ethics, but her conclusions could easily be adapted to a more universal kind of moral phenomenology that encompasses all phenomena in the more-than-human world. Gruen defines the ethical practice of entangled empathy as "a type of caring perception focused on attending to another's experience of wellbeing. An experiential process involving a blend of emotion and cognition in which we recognize we are in relationships with others and are called upon to be responsive and responsible in these relationships by attending to another's needs, interests, desires, vulnerabilities, hopes, and sensitivities."[46] In other words, entangled empathy entails the development of a keen attention to the beings we are in relationships with to act in a way that supports their flourishing according to their specific needs and the specifics of the context.

Where her theory diverges from a moral phenomenology is in the way it is cultivated. While a moral phenomenological approach to environmental (or animal) ethics would begin with a view, work with meditation to experientially acclimate to this view, and finally see the world and act in a way that reflects this experience, Gruen begins her process in the third of these pieces: perception and action. She writes, "Empathy is a particular type of attention, what I think of as a kind of moral perception. Moral perception is not the same as ordinary sense perception, in that the latter doesn't often require reflection and correction, whereas moral perception does. Both types of perception aren't just interior processes; often in order to perceive accurately, we need to reflect in light of information."[47] Thus, rather than cultivate an experience of a view in order to perceive and act in the world in a particular way, perception comes prior to view and informs view in a constantly evolving manner.[48] In this way, Gruen's entangled empathy comes closer to a virtue ethic than a moral phenomenology insofar as it places the locus of moral cultivation on a specific quality rather than a specific experience. Elsewhere, we find this interpretation substantiated when she writes, "We are entangled in complex relationships and rather than trying to accomplish the impossible by pretending we can disentangle, we would do better to think about how to be *more* perceptive and *more* responsive to the deeply entangled relationships we are in."[49] Entangled empathy is therefore a distinct enterprise to moral phenomenology in that it cultivates a specific capacity of an individual to perceive and respond in a certain way rather than cultivates an experience of the world from which ethical concern naturally emerges.

Despite this difference, the notion of enacting morality through perception and a keen attention to the needs of the human and nonhuman beings that we are in relationship with results in a similar ethical outcome to that of a moral phenomenology. It entails clearly seeing the situation presented to oneself, the beings involved, and acting in a way that benefits them all. Like moral phenomenology, Gruen's entangled empathy "involves a particular blend of affect and cognition"[50] out of which action emerges and involves "attending to another's needs, interests, desires, vulnerabilities, hopes, and sensitivities."[51] These latter characteristics are not intrinsic to moral phenomenology per se, but this kind of action that naturally attends to the needs of other beings is precisely the kind of action that would emerge from a moral phenomenological approach to environmental ethics. Whether one can bring a view of emptiness, the suffering of nonhuman animals, deep ecology, new materialism, or another ecological view into one's experience, the resultant kind of action would be one that naturally places the flourishing of the more-than-human world as the conative basis for action.

I might also argue that this moral phenomenological approach is the most effective approach to environmental ethics available. Gruen's impetus for her ethical theorization is one shared by this project: the inadequacy of historical normative ethical theories. She writes, "In the face of the bewildering practical complexities associated with solving the world's problems, ethical theory should both motivate us and point us in the direction of what to do. Unfortunately, it rarely does either."[52] It goes without saying that our world is increasingly complex and that the causes, conditions, and effects of the ongoing degradation of the more-than-human world are difficult to fully comprehend. While the science on anthropogenic climate change is settled beyond any kind of doubt, the actions available to us individuals for addressing this problem change as technology develops, economic systems adapt, and politics shift.

The kinds of prescriptions we find in environmentalist literature from forty years ago *may* still hold, but many of these rules for living in an environmentally conscious way might have changed dramatically since. Similarly, a consequentialist or virtue-ethical approach may poise us to respond to changing environmental, social, and political conditions in an ethical way, but the factors to consider in a moral calculus or the qualities necessary for navigating situations regarding the environment are also subject to change. However, in a moral phenomenological approach to environmental ethics, these views and their experiential recognition remain relevant among changing external conditions. Surely, new views might emerge through either scientific or philosophical investigation that may be useful in a moral phenomenological approach to environmental ethics. After all, deep ecology only emerged in the seventies, and new materialisms have only been around for two decades. Nonetheless, the views we have explored in the previous chapter give us a solid foundation for any environmental action moving forward because they occasion a conative mode rather than a set of principles. Further, the general framework of a moral phenomenological approach to environmental ethics will maintain relevance amidst socioeconomic, political, or environmental change because any new view can be inputted into its contemplative framework. In this way, an individual's action can adapt in a moral phenomenological approach to environmental ethics such that any situation, encounter, or being that one is presented with will be responded to with care and a concern for the flourishing of all sentient beings involved.

## The Temporal Problem in Ecological Contexts

Now, suppose someone is convinced to implement this kind of approach to environmental ethics and begins developing a *śamatha* practice. Or perhaps someone with an established meditation practice wishes to direct their practice toward environmental ends and begins meditating on interdependence, the suffering of nonhuman animals, or the idea that ecological phenomena have noninstrumental value. When these folks finally come to an experiential realization of their chosen ecological views, they will be able to act naturally in a way that benefits the more-than-human world, but what are they to do up until that point? How are they to act in the weeks, months, or even years of walking the path toward this full phenomenological transformation?

Unsurprisingly, this temporal problem that we saw in chapter 3's articulation of moral phenomenology persists in ecological contexts. In fact, some scholars in the field have already pointed out this issue in their work on related topics. For example, Timothy Morton writes, "'If only we could see things differently' can be translated quickly into 'I won't act unless suitably stimulated and soothed by a picture of reality built to my preexisting specifications.'"[53] My approach to environmental ethics is precisely *seeing* a different way, but we should of course not hesitate to act prior to fully realizing an ecological view. In fact, the idea of "not acting" is absurd. Whatever we do (or don't do) has impacts on the more-than-human world, and simply "not acting" is functionally impossible. Morton is likely referring more specifically to not acting to alleviate the causes and effects of the climate crisis, and here I share their concern. In this moral phenomenological picture, if one has not sufficiently adopted an ecological view to the extent that their actions naturally support the flourishing of all sentient beings, then what are they to do in the meantime?

The answer here is again a kind of tiered, provisional ethic. Until the point where one has fully enacted a moral phenomenological transformation, one must rely on a different ethical system to guide their actions and navigate questions of environmental ethics. If we are staying within the realm of Buddhist environmental ethics, then this might mean adopting a rule-based approach or a character-based approach to environmental ethics. With respect to the former, we have seen how Padmasiri De Silva has articulated a rule-based approach to Buddhist environmental ethics through putting Pali sources into conversation with the life-based ethics of Paul Taylor and the ecological ethics of J. Baird Callicott. With respect to the latter, we might turn to an approach to environmental ethics that draws on the characterization of Buddhism as promoting a kind of virtue ethic as found in the work of Damien Keown, Pragati Sahni, and Simon P. James. These scholars each see the development of compassion, humility, openness, and so forth as ways to mitigate one's own impact on the environment and develop habits that contribute to its well-being.

Like the three vows of Tibetan Buddhism,[54] we can read these Buddhist approaches to environmental ethics in a tiered way. I have argued that a moral phenomenological approach to environmental ethics is not only the most consistent approach to Buddhist ethics as a whole but also is the most flexible and stable approach to environmental ethics in general. It allows one to effortlessly respond to the moral situations one is confronted with daily in a consistently ethical way. If this has yet to be realized, then we might turn to a Buddhist virtue-ethical approach to environmental ethics. While it is more rigid in its development of qualities rather than experience, it nonetheless gives the practitioner a basis for skillfully responding to novel ethical situations they may find themselves in. Finally, if neither of those can be practiced, one can adopt a rule-based approach to environmental ethics that may not encourage a practitioner to contribute to the flourishing of the more-than-human world but will at the very least protect them from actively creating harm. Thus, until one fully comes to an experiential understanding of an ecological view in a Buddhist moral phenomenological approach to environmental ethics, one should develop ecological virtues and/or adopt a rule-based environmental ethic.

We might also consider other modes of ethics that could be appropriate to adopt prior to a full realization of an ecological moral phenomenology. One ethical theory that remains largely absent in the literature on Buddhist environmental ethics is consequentialism. Though Charles Goodman has argued for a consequentialist interpretation of Buddhist ethics, no scholar has yet to apply this interpretation to the more-than-human world. That said, there are of course philosophers outside of the Buddhist tradition who have mobilized consequentialist arguments to the ends of animal and environmental ethics. The most obvious example of this is the work of Peter Singer, who directs the utilitarianism of Jeremy Bentham to nonhuman animals in his foundational work *Animal Liberation*. In the context of environmental ethics, several scholars have also drawn from the utilitarian position to articulate a concern for the environment (though this is less common than other modes of environmental ethics).[55] We might also consider a rights-based approach to an ethic of the more-than-human world as a provisional ethic. Again, this approach is most clearly seen in the realm of animal ethics and the work of Tom Regan, who articulates a rights-based approach to animal ethics on the basis of them being a "subject-of-a-life." However, we can also see rights-based approaches emerging in environmental ethics alongside modern legal attributions of "personhood" to rivers such as the Ganges and Yamuna in India, mountains such as Mount Taranaki in New Zealand, or all of "Mother Nature" in Bolivia.[56]

Regardless, if we are operating in a broader moral phenomenological approach to environmental ethics and are not restricting ourselves to Buddhist sources, then many existent environmental ethics could be used provisionally. What is important is that we do in fact rely on another kind of environmental ethic on our way to moral phenomenology so that we do not fall into Morton's legitimate critique of inaction on the way to seeing things properly. But suppose we *do* engage in contemplative practice and realize an environmental moral phenomenology—what might our behavior and our relationships with the more-than-human world actually look like?

## Contemporary Examples of Ecological Action

My exploration of a contemplative Buddhist environmental ethic has largely remained in the realm of theory, but if we take a brief look at the ethnographic work done on Buddhist environmental ethics, we can clearly see this novel, experiential-based approach to environmental ethics in practice. Barbra Clayton takes up an empirical-ethics approach in her article "Buddha's Maritime Nature: A Case Study in Shambhala Buddhist Environmentalism," where, through interviews, document analysis, and participant-observation at Windhorse Farm in Nova Scotia, she arrives at several conclusions about the nature of lived Buddhist environmental ethics. Importantly, what Clayton finds is an approach to the environment that eludes classification as a rule-based or character-based ethic. Instead, it greatly resembles our environmental moral phenomenology and provides us with a glimpse of what this contemplative environmental ethic might look like in the specific context of a Tibetan Buddhist community in Atlantic Canada.

The locus of environmental practice at Windhorse Farm is its surrounding forest and its sustainable forestry initiative. Clayton writes that Jim Drescher (who owns the farm) first moved from a Leopoldian land ethic focused on resource management and "trying to make a living from the forest while still respecting and not harming the other beings that lived there" to what he calls an environmental ethic that seeks to rewild the forest to its precolonial state.[57] Eventually, however, these both gave way to what Drescher and Clayton term a "Nothing Missing" ethic. This term is based in the teachings of Drescher's Shambhala Tibetan Buddhist community and draws from both his understanding of *tathāgatagarbha*,[58] which they translate as "basic goodness," and his understanding of the ultimate view of Mahāmudrā, which holds that "the nature of mind and reality is primordially pure, innately clear, and luminous."[59] The "Nothing Missing" ethos is one that understands that *"fundamentally* there is no problem, either with the forest or those who work in it. It is an approach to living that is based on appreciating oneself and the world, and celebrating the innate purity of reality."[60]

Clayton rightly identifies how this approach flies in the face of mainstream environmental discourse, which often holds that the environment is a "victim of humanity's greed and folly, and must be saved by, ironically, us humans, or else we all face certain doom."[61] However, these two positions are reconciled by the Shambhala community through an appeal to ultimate and conventional truth. The above ultimate view is to be held at the same time as the conventional or relative view, where "there is tremendous suffering, and innumerable situations require amelioration."[62] By seeing the world through these lenses simultaneously, Drescher states that "you can engage the world with a wakefulness that allows you to see and help the beings right in front of you. You respond appropriately to problems and challenges, without fixating on absolute ends, such as saving the planet or curing poverty once and for all."[63] Clayton notes how this approach eschews the normative approaches to Buddhist environmentalism that involve appeals to *pratītyasamutpāda* exclusively or that call for the cultivation of specific ecological virtues. While she sees the Windhorse Farm ethic as involving aspects of each of these approaches, she concludes that "the Windhorse ethic defies the demands put forth in theoretical discussions of Buddhist ethics, and reminds us that doctrines like conditioned arising are always interpreted in particular contexts."[64] In this particular context, living in the light of "Nothing Missing" involves mindfulness, seeing *tathāgatagarbha* in oneself and the world, and the recognition of the nonduality of *saṃsāra* and *nirvāṇa*, which Clayton notes are "aspects of Buddhist values not normally emphasized in scholarly discussions of Buddhist environmentalism."[65]

This "Nothing-Missing" ethic gestures to an experience-based ethical approach to the environment and mirrors the language of moral phenomenology by grounding ethical action in an ontological position. Clayton briefly brings this idea up in her conclusion when she reflects on how the environmental ethics of Windhorse Farm relates to a keynote address given by Damien Keown at the conference "Contemporary Perspectives on Buddhist Ethics."[66] She writes,

> This case study would appear to confirm the importance of one of the factors he identifies [as to why there are no systematic ethics in Buddhism], namely the focus on metaphysics and gnosis in Indian traditions. Because truth

in this tradition is eternally wedded to value, once one achieves gnosis and knows reality as it is (*yathābhutā*), the assumption is that one will automatically be and do what is good. Such a perspective might then undermine the need for systematic reflection on ethics, since ethics would be embedded within ontology.[67]

What Clayton is asserting (by way of Keown) is essentially a moral phenomenological approach to ethics. It is precisely this kind of ontologically embedded ethic that moral phenomenology asserts. An experiential understanding of a particular ontological position will reorient an individual's default perceptual mode and hence align their conative and affective modes with that position. In doing so, they "will automatically be and do what is good" in Clayton's terms. I therefore claim that Windhorse Farm presents an excellent example of what a Buddhist moral phenomenology looks like when applied to the issue of the environment. By approaching the environment primarily through their contemplative understandings of buddhanature, Mahāmudrā, and the suffering of the more-than-human world, those working at Windhorse Farm are able to manage their forest without recourse to rules, virtues, or moral calculi and ethically engage with their environment in an appropriate, ethical, context-specific way.

I think Clayton's exploration of the Nova Scotian Buddhist context is perhaps the most compelling case study of eco-Buddhist practice that exemplifies the particularist, experience-based approach to environmental ethics that can emerge from a deep commitment to Tibetan Buddhist contemplative practice. However, it's not the only instance of perceptual experience informing ecological action. We can also see this kind of contemplative environmental ethic emerging in three world-renown figures in Buddhism and environmentalism: His Holiness the Dalai Lama, Gary Snyder, and Dr. Gail Bradbrook.

Arguably, the most vocal proponent of a Buddhist environmental ethic is His Holiness the Dalai Lama. When he is taking up residence in Dharmsala, his home in exile, the Dalai Lama's day is filled with Buddhist study and contemplation. According to his official website, he wakes at 3:00 a.m., meditates until 5:00 a.m., eats a small breakfast, and then meditates from 6:00 a.m. to 9:00

a.m. Then he studies Buddhist texts until lunch is served at 11:30 a.m.[68] Half of his waking day is thus dedicated to contemplative practice, which grounds his ethical outlook. Abraham Vélez de Cea has analyzed the Dalai Lama's ethical discourse across several of his published works and locates the sources of his ethical transformation in this very meditation. He writes,

> The Dalai Lama uses traditional Buddhist meditations to encourage ethical restraint and transform ordinary compassion into great compassion. Some meditations focus on the organic nature of reality and the interrelatedness of our interests. Others focus on the doctrine of rebirth and view all living beings as having been one's mother in the past. Still others reflect on the sameness of our nature in that we all have a common aspiration to be happy and to avoid suffering. This meditation called "equalizing oneself and others" is usually accompanied by another meditation where one imaginatively exchanges oneself for others in a variety of happy and unhappy situations. All these meditations are intended to transform narrow and exclusivist conceptions of self-identity and gradually develop a bond of empathy and eventually compassion with all sentient beings.[69]

Through this daily practice, His Holiness the Dalai Lama lays the contemplative foundation for his ethics and can respond to ecological situations appropriately as they arise in his daily life.

And his response to ethical issues regarding the environment has been significant. In 1989, His Holiness the Dalai Lama won the Nobel Peace Prize in recognition of his "peaceful solutions based upon tolerance and mutual respect in order to preserve the historical and cultural heritage of his people" in response to the Chinese occupation of Tibet.[70] During his acceptance speech, the Dalai Lama laid out one of the key points of his peace plan: turning Tibet into a "zone of *ahimsa*," including an important ecological provision: "The Tibetan plateau would be transformed into the world's largest natural park or biosphere. Strict laws would be enforced to protect wildlife and plant life; the exploitation of natural resources would be carefully regulated so as not to damage relevant ecosystems; and a policy of sustainable development would be adopted in populated areas."[71] Since this award, the Dalai Lama has ceaselessly advocated for environmental justice. He includes the environment as a central value in his Three Principal Commitments of his life,[72] has been lauded by world figures such as Barack Obama for his work on climate change,[73] and has promoted activists such as Greta Thunberg at his Mind and Life Institute.[74] Of course, this advocacy isn't simply a consequence of the Dalai Lama's Buddhist view of the world. Instead, it is the Dalai Lama's deep experiential understanding of interdependence, his commitment to the alleviation of all *duḥkha* from all sentient beings, *and* the novel recognition of the environment as a source of this *duḥkha* that has led the Dalai Lama to his forceful advocacy. The Dalai Lama has said as much in conversation with Franz Alt:

> When I came from Tibet to India in 1959, I had no idea of the problems with the environment. When I first heard, "You cannot drink this water," I was surprised that it was polluted. . . . I learned about pollution and gradually about ecology. I now feel a deep concern about the environment, as it has become a question of our survival. I learned about this through awareness—not through meditation, but through awareness with help from experts.[75]

The Dalai Lama thus rejects the notion that meditation alone brought him to this position. Instead, it is through his education on ecology and pollution that he came to an environmentalist position. I read the Dalai Lama's approach to the environment to be precisely the kind outlined by a moral phenomenology. His daily contemplative practice laid the foundation for a strong Buddhist moral phenomenological ethic characterized by a conative mode of compassion and *bodhicitta*, and when he became knowledgeable about climate change, he naturally gravitated to and advocated for environmental justice.

There are instances of this contemplative approach to environmental ethics in the American context as well. Take, for example, the work of the renowned Beat poet Gary Snyder. Snyder is an eclectic figure. In the words of the scholar Jason M. Wirth,

"Gary Snyder is one of our Elders: a Zen teacher and shaman poet with his ear to the ground of the West Coast of Turtle Island, including its indigenous stories, and who inspires as much by practicing another mode of dwelling on earth as he does by his powerful poetic-philosophical-scientific articulation of it."[76] Snyder has argued for and worked to implement an anarchistic[77] bioregional approach to politics inclusive of human and nonhuman beings alike.[78] For Snyder, bioregionalism occurs when "a people and a place become one"[79] and involves an engagement with one's community, inclusive of human and nonhuman beings, in "search for the sustainable sophisticated mix of economic practices that would enable people to live regionally and yet learn from and contribute to a planetary society."[80] His political vision is informed by his deep ecological view wherein we should "take ourselves as no more and no less than another being in the Big Watershed. We can accept each other all as barefoot equals sleeping on the same ground."[81] And importantly, Snyder attributes his deep ecological approach to life and his vision of what an ethical bioregional society looks like to his Zen contemplative practice. In an interview with Doug Flaherty, Snyder recounts his ecological satori experiences that shaped his worldview and his political action:

> I don't lay claim to any great enlightenment experiences or anything like that, but I have had a very moving, profound perception a few times that everything was alive (the basic perception of animism) and that on one level there is no hierarchy of qualities in life—that the life of a stone or a weed is as completely beautiful and authentic, wise and valuable as the life of, say, an Einstein. And that Einstein and the weed know this; hence the preciousness of mice and weeds.[82]

Thus, Snyder's contemplative practice culminated in a "profound perception" that deeply informed his ethical, philosophical, and political life henceforth. Snyder's Buddhist environmental action is therefore intimately informed by what he has called the "yogic implications" of mountains and rivers.[83]

Outside of Buddhist contexts, the most striking example of a contemplative experience leading to committed environmental action is in the life of Dr. Gail Bradbrook. Bradbrook is a molecular biologist who has had a sincere interest in the more-than-human world since she was a young teenager. Spurred by an interest in animal rights, she joined the UK's Green Party at age fourteen,[84] and she spent the large part of her life engaging in activist work against oil companies and the financier class.[85] But it wasn't until she went on a psychedelic retreat in Costa Rica that she became inspired to found Extinction Rebellion (XR), the largest climate action initiative in recent history.[86] At this psychedelic retreat, Bradbook partook of ayahuasca, iboga, and kambo and prayed to the universe to show her "codes for social change."[87] She called this retreat "utterly transformative,"[88] and when she met Roger Hallam, a PhD student studying civil disobedience at King's College London who would eventually become XR's cofounder, she found these codes for social change and was thoroughly primed to begin the movement. Thus, while particulars of her action were context specific and informed by her English political situation, we might say that Bradbrook's contemplative psychedelic transformation laid the moral phenomenological foundation for creating XR (which itself has a Buddhist wing, XR Buddhists). It was the contemplative engagement with the views she already had through her political and activist career that became thoroughly realized in her psychedelic retreat that ultimately created one of the largest civil disobedience campaigns against climate change that the anglophone world has seen.

## A Test Case: Contextual Moral Veganism

To further illustrate how this contemplative approach to the more-than-human world might function, we can turn from these specific examples to the specific issue of eating animals. In his article "Toward an Ecological Ethic of Care," Deane Curtin uses vegetarianism as a test case to demonstrate the nuances of a feminist care ethic in ecological contexts. When the article was published in 1991, veganism was even more of a minority position than it is now and was not in any conversations about addressing climate change or environmental degradation. Today, however, we find a vegan diet at the forefront of individual responses to climate change[89] and recognize animal agriculture as one of (if not *the*) leading causes of climate change and environmental destruction.[90] Dan Smyer Yü contends that "vegetarianism, as an action of spiritual environmentalism, remains a nonenvironmental topic of debate between Buddhists and scholars,"[91] but this is a problem, especially among Tibetan Buddhist diaspora and convert communities. Given what we know about the relationships among animal agriculture, climate change, and environmental collapse, vegetarianism *needs* to become an environmental topic of debate in Buddhist scholarship. Thus, just as Curtin used vegetarianism as a test case for discerning what a feminist care ethic might look like in practice, veganism presents itself as a prime test case for thinking through what a Buddhist moral phenomenological approach to the more-than-human world might look like in in today's ecological emergency.

An eco-Buddhist moral phenomenology might conceive of two options as it relates to the question of veganism: its full-fledged adoption or its regrettable rejection. The full-fledged adoption of veganism (or, rather, the complete abstention from animal-based foods and goods) would be the ideal for a practitioner who wants to mitigate *duḥkha*, recognizes the reality of *pratītyasamutpāda*, and has *bodhicitta* as their operating conative mode. The most obvious reason for this adoption would be to not actively contribute to the immense suffering of sentient beings involved in the animal agriculture industry. Eating meat, eggs, and dairy involves paying others to murder sentient beings on one's behalf and is therefore perpetuating systems that subject more and more sentient beings to greater and greater amounts of *duḥkha*. Moreover, the Tibetan tradition consistently recognizes all sentient beings as having been one's mother in a past life. In the *Laṅkāvatāra Sūtra*, the Buddha tells Mahāmati that "it is not easy to find someone who was not once your father, mother, brother, sister, son, daughter, kinsman, friend, or the like at some point during the long ages of saṃsāra" and that "they have now changed their form and become wild animals, domestic animals, and birds, whatever their karma dictates."[92] This line of reasoning is later echoed by many prominent Tibetan vegetarians in their admonitions to their students, including Shabkar Tsogdruk Rangdrol, Chatral Rinpoche, and the eighth Karmapa Mikyö Dorje who has a treatise on vegetarianism titled "A Letter on the Unsuitability of Eating the Meat of Our Old Mothers."[93] Ecofeminism and care ethics emphasize the relational nature of our ethical lives and recognize the roles of emotion and intimacy as driving factors in ethical decision making. In a similar way, we find the reflection on all beings having been our mothers in a past life using emotion, intimacy, and relationship to drive home the argument for not harming nonhuman animals. If one truly wants to repay the kindness of *all* their mothers (a common trope in Tibetan religious literature), then one must extend care to all sentient beings. Given how one simply cannot at once care for nonhuman animals and pay for others to have them killed, veganism becomes the ideal default position in a Buddhist approach to environmental ethics.

This line of reasoning for abstaining from animal-based foods has a serious precedent in Tibetan contexts. In the history of Tibetan vegetarianism, there was a contentious debate on whether the eater of meat takes on the same negative karma of the hunter or butcher, and the famous vegetarian yogi Shabkar is unequivocal in his answer. In his treatise titled *The Nectar of Immortality* he writes,

> Let us imagine that there is a homestead in the vicinity of a large monastery where the monks eat meat. The inhabitants of the homestead calculate that if they kill a sheep and sell its best meat in spring to the monastic community, they will make a profit on the sheep since they will keep its tripe and offal, head, legs, and hide for themselves. And the monks, knowing full well that the sheep has been slaughtered and its meat preserved, come and buy it. The following year, the family will kill more sheep and sell the meat. And if they make a good living out of it, when the next year arrives, there will be a hundred times more animals slaughtered, and the family will get rich. Thus by trying to enrich themselves through the killing of sheep, they become butchers. They will teach this trade to their children and their grandchildren and all those close to them. And even if they do not actively teach it to others, other people will see their wicked work. They in turn will become butchers doing acts of dreadful evil, and they will set in motion

> a great stream of negativity that will persist until the
> ending of samsara. Now all this has happened for one
> reason only: the monastic community and others eat
> meat. Who therefore behaves in a more consistently evil
> manner than they?[94]

Thus, Shabkar recognizes the market forces behind the killing of nonhuman animals and the consequences of consuming animal products in this interdependent system. But he also frames his argument in positive terms centered around *karuṇā* (care). He writes,

> The Buddha has defined as evil any action that directly or
> indirectly brings harm to beings. And since what he says
> is true, it is clear that the eating of meat most certainly
> involves more injury to beings than the consumption of
> any other food. . . . I believe therefore that if one wishes
> to commit oneself to an ongoing habit of goodness, there
> is nothing better than the resolve to abstain from meat.
> Those few monks who do actually have compassion [Skt.
> *karuṇā*] should keep this in their hearts![95]

Shabkar argues that if one has indeed developed *bodhicitta* and is operating with care as their central conative mode, then abstaining from meat is the natural outcome. Shabkar's ethical writings thus quite clearly demonstrate the positive consequences of Buddhist moral phenomenology in a more-than-human world.

Knowing what we do today about the dire ecological consequences of animal-based foods, we might extend our reasoning for such abstention to include the effect of animal agriculture on humans and the broader environment. Toxic pig farms are set up near working-class people of color,[96] who consequently face high incidence of respiratory disease,[97] and slaughterhouse workers suffer some of the highest rates of workplace injury (and death) and leave their jobs beset with life-long mental health issues such as perpetrator-induced stress disorder.[98] Further, beyond simply being the potential greatest source of industrial greenhouse-gas emissions,[99] animal agriculture uses the highest amount of land[100] and water[101] per calorie, stifling efforts to draw down carbon emissions through rewilding[102] and preserve fresh water in the face of worsening droughts.[103] For these reasons, a Buddhist moral phenomenological approach to environmental ethics would most certainly place veganism as an ideal regardless of whether the immediate focus of one's *bodhicitta* is on humans, nonhuman animals, the environment, or (most likely) an intersectional more-than-human world inclusive of all three. As Curtin writes, "The caring-for approach responds to particular contexts and histories. It recognizes that the reasons for moral vegetarianism may differ by locale, by gender, as well as by class."[104] So too might the reason for ethical veganism differ from Buddhist to Buddhist, but it would nonetheless remain the ideal approach to eating in this Buddhist contemplative environmental ethic.

Despite the obviousness of this ideal, neither veganism nor vegetarianism was a major historical practice in Tibetan Buddhism, where meat was a dietary staple on the Tibetan plateau. While exceptional figures such as Shabkar advocated for and embraced vegetarianism, Geoffrey Barstow has shown how Tibetan Buddhism mostly held an ambivalent position on killing and consuming animals. The ideal of compassion was indeed a strong force in the direction of vegetarianism, but the material realities of the Tibetan plateau and the social discourses on health and masculinity provided an often stronger counterforce in the direction of carnism. Even today, Smyer Yü notes that the vegetables now available on the Tibetan plateau as a result of Chinese modernizing efforts offer little protein, making the feasibility of a nutritionally complete plant-based diet difficult.[105] Thus, vegetarianism was regrettably rejected due to largely material considerations by most historical Buddhists in Tibet, and this accords with the contextualism of a care ethic. Curtin writes,

> As a "contextual moral vegetarian," I cannot refer to an absolute moral rule that prohibits meat eating under all circumstances. There may be some contexts in which another response is appropriate. Though I am committed to moral vegetarianism, I cannot say that I would never kill an animal for food. Would I not kill an animal to provide food for my son if he were starving? Would I not generally prefer the death of a bear to the death of a

> loved one? I am sure I would. The point of a contextualist
> ethic is that one need not treat all interests equally as if
> one had no relationship to any of the parties.[106]

In my estimation, this position would fairly map onto a Buddhist
moral phenomenological approach to the more-than-human world.
While abstention from animal products may be the ideal, there also
may be context-specific reasons for one's care for the more-than-
human world not resulting in a strictly vegan diet.

Today, many Tibetan Buddhists live outside the Tibetan plateau either in diaspora or convert communities. As such, some of
the material reasons (i.e., lack of vegetables) and medicinal reasons no longer hinder the adoption of vegetarian or vegan diets.
As a result, we now find major figures such as the Dalai Lama[107]
and the Karmapa[108] encouraging their followers to abstain from
animal products. However, there are other barriers that may prevent an individual from realizing the ideal of ethical veganism.
Food deserts are rampant across large areas of working-class (and
often racialized) communities in North America, subsistence animal farming continues to be a necessary practice in intentionally
underdeveloped locales around the globe, and hunting remains a
necessary practice in extreme geographies such as the Canadian
arctic, where soaring food prices contribute to some of the highest
levels of food insecurity in Canada. In these cases, the contextual
nature of a moral phenomenological ethic would highlight the *positionality* of the individual and their capacity to adopt something
akin to a vegan diet. The present Karmapa is a major advocate
for vegetarianism and highlighted the necessity of reducing meat
consumption in a public address of 2007 but also recognized the
difficulty for some to do so, stating, "Some people give up meat
altogether, but some people cannot. But at least, one should reduce
it."[109]

Positionality of this kind is something endemic to the Tibetan
Buddhist tradition, which includes a reflection on the unique
capacities of a "precious human life" at the beginning of most of
its practices. Humans are uniquely poised to alleviate the *duḥkha*
of oneself, other humans, and nonhuman animals, and, as I argue
elsewhere, reflecting on this unique capacity can compel altruistic
behavior.[110] Beyond this, the reflection on the preciousness of a

human life also involves a recognition of how certain humans are better poised to actualize Buddhist soteriological and ethical ends than others. In *Words of My Perfect Teacher*, Patrul Rinpoche lists the five advantages of a human life as being born a human, being born in a central place where you can encounter the teachings, being born with all one's faculties, having a livelihood that allows one to practice *dharma*, and having confidence that the *dharma* teachings work.[111] Applied to the question of veganism, we might reframe these as being born as a human who can thrive on plants, being born in a central place where you have access to plant foods, not having any medical conditions that prevent the adoption of a vegan diet (i.e., someone who is allergic to all soy, nuts, gluten, and stone fruit), having a livelihood where you have time and energy to cook your own meals or can afford vegan takeout, and having confidence that a vegan diet is indeed the most caring way to eat. Even if these adapted advantages are a bit of an interpretive stretch, the overarching principle of positionality still rings true. There are those who have a greater capacity to achieve the ideal of ethical veganism than others, and this means that the onus to adopt a vegan diet as a consequence of one's compassionate conative mode is contextual according to the capacities and advantages of a given person.

Interestingly, for those who could (or would) not adopt vegetarianism in Tibet, a range of practices were developed to mitigate negative consequences of eating animals. Barstow notes how some tantric practitioners claimed that eating a nonhuman animal creates a karmic link between the animal and the *dharma* such that "eating the meat of an animal . . . was actually a form of kindness, causing some temporary suffering but ultimately benefiting the animal."[112] Other adepts such as Jigmé Lingpa dismissed this line of argument, stating "It's great if someone has given rise to the power of concentration, so that he is not tainted by obscurations and is able to benefit beings through a connection with their meat and blood. But I do not have this confidence."[113] Some religious leaders also instructed practitioners to recite prayers and mantras so that, in the words of Karma Chakmé, "the animal will be liberated from the lower realms,"[114] though this too was critiqued as mere performance by figures such as Shabkar. Others, however, were more material in their efforts to mitigate the negative consequences of eating meat. Some such as Nyamé Sherab Gyeltsen wrote that meat is only permissible in medical contexts but not as a staple of one's diet,[115] while others such as Shardza Tashi Gyeltsen advocated for a kind of protofreeganism and argued that animals who have died of natural causes were permitted to be eaten, likening them to harvesting mountain herbs.[116] While animal liberationists may be left wanting by these half-measures, they nonetheless express a certain degree of care when it comes to the relationship between a Buddhist practitioner and eating animals. In situations where a vegan diet is unattainable, a compassion born of a Buddhist moral phenomenological ethic can still inform one's relationship to food in a context-specific way.

In terms of understanding what a Buddhist moral phenomenological approach to the environment might look like, these half measures might actually reveal more than the ethical vegan ideal. There is an obvious compassionate motivation behind these practices that demonstrate how a fully developed moral phenomenology might present itself in an imperfect world. None of us can lead perfectly ethical lives. To travel, we must pollute, to call our families we need a phone produced under horrid economic conditions, and the vast majority of the food we eat comes wrapped in plastic that will remain in our oceans indefinitely. While those of us in much of the developed world are thankfully able to eat a nutritionally complete plant-based diet with relative ease, we can still see the compassionate intent behind some of the above practices designed to mitigate *duḥkha* while nonetheless engaging in an ethically imperfect action. These kinds of half measures show a degree of striving toward an ideal of liberating all sentient beings from *duḥkha* that we can better approximate today, both by directly not supporting animal agriculture and by indirectly lessening our consumption and lobbying institutions to implement better policy and regulation. They show what action might look for those who have contemplatively realized a Buddhist moral phenomenological ethic in an ethically contentious context and make the nonprescriptive nature of moral phenomenological ethics quite clear in ecological contexts.

Thus, I argue that a fully realized Buddhist moral phenomenological approach to the more-than-human world would be contextually vegan but would recognize the positionality and material barriers to achieving this ideal for certain individuals. If one is operating with *bodhicitta* as one's primary conative mode and has contemplatively recognized the interdependent nature of *duḥkha*, then abstaining from animal products is the ideal way to care for humans, nonhuman animals, and the environment in one's daily consumption. However, a Buddhist moral phenomenology would also understand the contextual nature of consumption and would recognize how positionality affects one's ability to choose between consumption and abstention. By directing a moral phenomenological ethic toward the more-than-human world and meditatively realizing ecological views, we can establish the experiential basis for acting in a way that benefits humans, nonhuman animals, and our broader ecological communities. By carrying a direct experience of an ecological view with us in our daily lives, we can navigate ethical issues in our personal, community, and broader political lives and skillfully work toward the liberation of all sentient beings. And by thinking through the case of ethical veganism, we can see how a Buddhist moral phenomenological approach to environmental ethics care might manifest in the lives of Buddhist practitioners and begin to see some of the nuances of this contemplative approach to the more-than-human world.

# Conclusion

In recent years, a concern for the environment has thankfully once again become a priority for both practicing Buddhists and scholars of Buddhism. The Dalai Lama has published several books on climate change,[1] Western Buddhists are engaging in direct action against the oil industry as a part of the Extinction Rebellion movement,[2] and excellent scholars like Deane Curtin[3] and Katie Javanaud[4] have begun creatively reconsidering the Buddhist role in addressing our planetary crisis. Likewise, Buddhist scholar-practitioners outside of the Tibetan tradition have begun constructively mobilizing Buddhist practice toward addressing climate change, as in Bhikkhu Anālayo's recent books *Mindfully Facing Climate Change* and *Mindfulness between Early Buddhism and Climate Change.*[5] As the environmental crisis becomes ever more dire, and the deadly consequences of climate change have become a headline on the daily news, global traditions such as Buddhism will have to prioritize thinking through how their philosophies and contemplative practices can play a part in ameliorating our collective situation.

Over the previous chapters, I have attempted to help in this constructive ecological effort by offering a novel, contemplative approach to the more-than-human world. This work first concerned itself with outlining precisely why Buddhism might be concerned with the environment and established the ideological basis of eco-Buddhism. Then it defended a moral phenomenological interpretation of Buddhist ethics and developed this theory through the framework of *lta sgom spyod gsum.* It reviewed how scholars such as Jay Garfield have argued for a moral phenomenological interpretation that I then defended by turning to the resources in the Vajrayāna tradition of Tibet and by raising and responding to possible issues in a Buddhist moral phenomenology. It then argued that view, meditation, action should be used as the framework for implementing a moral phenomenological praxis. It surveyed the ways this framework has been employed in Tibetan contexts before applying this framework to moral phenomenology specifically. It nuanced this approach by asking what *view* really means in the context of *lta sgom spyod gsum* and analyzed Madhyamaka, Mahāmudrā, and Dzogchen answers to this inquiry. Finally, it looked at the role of meditation in this framework and investigated the role of direct meditative experience in bringing these conceptual views into one's default perceptual mode to inform one's everyday action.

It then put forth a moral phenomenological approach to environmental ethics by searching for an ecological view, analyzing how meditation would function in this more-than-human context, and considering what the resultant action would look like. It argued that emptiness is the ecological view par excellence but that, in lieu of fully realizing this complex view, individuals could also approach an ecological moral phenomenology through the reality of climate collapse, the suffering of nonhuman beings, deep ecology, and new materialism. It looked at how these views could be brought into one's experience through various contemplative methods but ultimately argued that meditation is the most effective means to do so because of its consistency and its precision in occasioning direct, nonconceptual experiences of view. Finally, it explored what action might look like in these ecological contexts by examining ethnographic work on lived eco-Buddhism in Canada, the lives of major Buddhist and environmentalist figures, and thinking through eating animals as a theoretical case study. In doing so, I hope to have demonstrated the unique nature of Buddhist ethical theory, shown how this ethical system can be applied to contemporary issues outside of the specifics of the Buddhist tradition, and how it can provide novel approaches to solving issues such as climate change and the degradation of the more-than-human world. I have tried to present the Tibetan Buddhist tradition as a useful interlocutor in contemporary discussions about our global future and a robust intellectual and practical tradition that can offer important interventions in the broader philosophical discourse concerning the environment and nonhuman animals.

Of course, while this book focuses on a *Buddhist* moral phenomenological approach to environmental ethics, it is very possible that a contemplative approach to ecology could be articulated and practiced outside of Buddhist contexts. The idea of a moral phenomenology emerges out of Buddhist literature, but it need not be framed in exclusively Buddhist terms (see Dreyfus and Dreyfus's ethical comportment). Likewise, as chapter 5 and 6 parsed, there are a variety of ecological views and contemplative modalities outside of the Buddhist tradition that could take the place of emptiness and formal meditation in the contemplative framework of view, meditation, action. All one would need to do to implement this ethic outside of a Buddhist context is intellectually explore a view like those found in new materialisms, environmental science, or non-Buddhist notions of interdependence, engage in a form of contemplative practice such as mindfulness meditation, psychedelics, or "doing nothing" with that view in mind until it becomes the way you naturally see the world and then go about your day-to-day life operating from that view. Thus, whether in a Buddhist or non-Buddhist context, I see this contemplative approach to ecology as having merit and utility, and I hope that it offers both those who subscribe to a Buddhist worldview and those who do not a way to develop ethically and ameliorate our environmental conditions.

## Limitations of an Ecological Moral Phenomenology

Prior to formally concluding this work, it is worth pointing out some of its potential limitations. As Johan Elverskog writes in his book *The Buddha's Footprint*, Buddhism was used to support extractive economies throughout Asia and the systematic oppression of the environment, nonhuman animals, and human "others." Elverskog looks at how Pali and Sanskrit texts affirmed the value of affluence, the manipulation of natural environments, and the use of exotic materials for religious purposes and how these influenced state, market, and religious actors to exploit the more-than-human world. He thus crafts an argument that eco-Buddhism is a thoroughly modern project with little precedent in Buddhist history and that any claims of some sort of ecological essence to Buddhism are unfounded. He writes, "I will not be arguing that Buddhism and environmental thought are antithetical or that Buddhism cannot be used to promote environmental action . . . [But] these are *contemporary* interpretations that reflect the successful influence of modern environmental discourses on Buddhism and not vice versa."[6] Thus, he aims to show clearly that "ecological awareness is not inherent in the Buddhist tradition itself."[7] Further, Elverskog contends that projecting contemporary ecological interpretations of Buddhism into the past creates two problems: "First, it obscures from our awareness the environmental consequences of Buddhist activities across Asia historically. Second, because ahistorical claims of eternal environmental awareness have been roundly disproven by twenty years of Buddhological scholarship, maintaining this eco-Buddhist fantasy diminishes the moral authority of contemporary Buddhist environmentalism."[8] Thus, Elverskog contends that the Buddhist tradition was historically *not* eco-friendly and that claims to the contrary diminish the potency of a contemporary Buddhist approach to environmentalism.

While I certainly do not make the claim that Buddhism is inherently eco-friendly, this book has nonetheless argued that Buddhism can be of great intellectual and practical benefit in our current time of environmental catastrophe. The first half of this work articulated an interpretation of Buddhist ethics as a moral phenomenology, while the second half applied this ethical framework to the contemporary issues facing the more-than-human world and sought to construct an environmental ethic from this moral phenomenological foundation. However, this second half largely stayed in the realm of contemporary issues and made no claims as to the historicity of this kind of approach to environmental ethics. The one area where this issue of projecting environmental values into the past is in my placement of emptiness as the *ultimate* ecological view. The view of emptiness was the pinnacle of the Tibetan Buddhist philosophical tradition throughout its history, so are we in turn to claim that those historical persons who realized emptiness developed an ecological awareness?

To this I answer yes and no, and a moral phenomenological approach to ethics offers a unique way to navigate this potential objection. Recall how moral phenomenology is not prescriptive but provides the necessary conative and affective modes for navigating ethical situations. Those who realized emptiness in the history of Buddhism *did* in fact cultivate the necessary experiential foundation for acting in a way to support the flourishing of the more-than-human world, but the issues they were presented with were vastly different than the ones we have today. In other words, there was no environmental crisis to navigate, and we therefore do not find environmentalism in the history of Tibetan Buddhism. Furthermore, the scientific understanding that we have today concerning the environment and how human action affects the water, air, and earth systems was not present in premodern Tibet. We now know how the deterioration of ecological systems negatively affects the welfare of the sentient beings therein, but this understanding is a patently modern understanding. We therefore do not find calls to preserve forests, clean rivers, and stop open burns (in fact, we find quite the opposite as Elverskog shows). However, we do certainly find instances of highly realized Buddhists such as Shabkar and Jigmé Lingpa directly helping, caring for, and teaching nonhuman animals. In other words, one may argue that their deep experiential recognition of emptiness indeed led them to develop an ethic of the more-than-human world but that this was expressed differently according to the specific situations they were presented with and the specific cultural and scientific understanding of the more-than-human world of their time.

Beyond this historical interpretive issue, there is also a major material issue: the difficulty in translating the kind of highly theoretical environmental ethic that I propose to actual material, political praxis. While ethics usually lend well to political prescriptions, moral phenomenology is more concerned with an individual's experience of the world than it is with any set of universally applicable principles. That said, an argument could be made that a specific kind of political organization would emerge from a community who comes to an experiential recognition of emptiness, and politics are certainly not foreign to some of the Buddhist philosophers I have relied upon in crafting my argument for moral phenomenology. For example, Nāgārjuna's *Ratnāvalī* is itself a letter written to an Indian king and was meant to guide this monarch to create a society based on Buddhist principles. One may claim that these prescriptions came from Nāgārjuna's profound realization of emptiness and his natural action that emerged therefrom.

To give a more recent example in modern political terms, His Holiness the Dalai Lama claimed that he is "half-Marxist, half-Buddhist"[9] in the 1990s and has since reiterated this claim in his more recent talks.[10] In other words, his political identification as a Marxist comes from his Buddhist practice and the experience he has cultivated therein. I sympathize with this Buddhist socialist position and, while I don't have space to fully explore this position here, am partial to the idea that the only political organization that makes sense from a Buddhist ethical position is (eco-)socialism. We might therefore speculate that if a society full of individuals with the same realization as the Dalai Lama wishes to organize politically, it would resemble some form of socialist organization. In this sense, I follow Graham Priest in suggesting that the philosophical principles of Buddhism lend to this political reading more so than any other.[11]

However, this is not the only possible political outcome of a moral phenomenological ethic. Like mindfulness can be used to create better snipers just as it can better doctors,[12] the experiential kind of ethic that moral phenomenology forwards and its corollary contemplative framework of view, meditation, action could just as easily lend itself to a utopian socialist state as to a hyper-capitalist fascistic one. The distinction between these outcomes would lie simply in the views that precede contemplation. Thus, the notion of translating a moral phenomenological ethic into the kind of political system that can truly deal with the scale of climate change is problematic. It is the ontological views within the Buddhist tradition that lead the Dalai Lama to his particular political prescription, not the experience of those views themselves. Thus, we cannot really talk about a political extension to moral phenomenology because such an extension emerges from the philosophical views that come *prior* to a moral phenomenological ethic. We can of course talk about how someone who contemplatively realizes the gravity of the ecological situation would engage with the political sphere through this lens, but we cannot talk about the precise political systems or policy prescriptions that might emerge from an environmental moral phenomenology.

In other words, as I argue in chapter 6, moral phenomenology is inherently nonprescriptive. It primes individuals to respond naturally and spontaneously to the situations they are presented with in accordance with whatever view they have brought into their default perceptual mode, but this response is ultimately determined by the view. Ethical outcomes rely on the specific views that are brought into one's experience. It is for this reason that it is difficult to transcribe a moral phenomenological approach to ethics into a political prescription. Politics cannot simply emerge from experience but need to be articulated through philosophical or conceptual means. Thus, while moral phenomenology may prime an individual to organize politically or act toward political ends, the specifics of this politics are not determinable through a moral phenomenological framework alone.

To me, this is the most obvious practical issue of a moral phenomenological approach to ethics both generally and in terms of the more-than-human world. Work needs to be done *prior* to implementing a moral phenomenology to ensure that the view to which we are acclimating produces our desired outcomes. There are certainly other limitations to a moral phenomenological ethic that I have addressed neither here nor in preceding chapters, and I hope scholars continue identifying and addressing these issues to develop both the theory and the praxis of moral phenomenology.

## Moral Phenomenological Futures

Addressing these kinds of gaps in moral phenomenological theory is one area for future scholarship, but there are certainly other avenues for exploring and developing moral phenomenology and a Buddhist approach to environmental ethics. This book showed what an applied moral phenomenology would look like in an ecological context, but applied moral phenomenology does not end with environmental ethics. Moving forward, I hope to see more research on the relevance of this approach to other ethical arenas as well. Applying moral phenomenology and its supporting framework of view, meditation, action to other issues has the potential to benefit other contemporary struggles for justice, peace, and so forth by giving their advocates and activists theoretical, practical, and contemplative supports for their work. Some of this work has begun, such as Jessica Locke's application of moral phenomenology to antiracist contexts.[13] To the extent that we consider moral phenomenology as a promising way to understand and implement Buddhist ethics, or even simply a useful way of thinking about our ethical lives, directing moral phenomenological theory and praxis to these other contemporary struggles can support the efforts of engaged Buddhists around the world and further develop the theoretical and experiential basis for their work.

Further, this work operated squarely within a Tibetan Buddhist framework, but moral phenomenology need not be relegated to the Buddhist tradition either. It used Tibetan Buddhist sources for constructing its approach to moral phenomenological praxis, but there is nothing inherently Buddhist about *lta sgom spyod gsum* or the theory behind moral phenomenology. For this reason, I also hope to see this theory engaged with other strands of Buddhism and with the Western philosophical tradition in both a critical and a constructive way. There are certainly aspects of this approach that could be critiqued in light of contemporary work on environmental ethics, but there are likewise many ways that engaging a moral phenomenological approach to environmental ethics (or other ethical areas) could generate novel lines of inquiry. This kind of cross-cultural philosophical work is something we desperately need since problems such as climate change, economic inequality, and systemic violence are global problems that transcend the thin borders of nation-states and their local intellectual traditions. This cosmopolitan philosophical approach[14] can work to create greater global cooperation for solving these universal problems. To this end, I hope this book can contribute in a small way to developing these kinds of discussions and working toward liberating all humans, nonhuman animals, and ecosystems from all suffering and oppression.

# Notes

## Introduction

1. David Suzuki, "David Suzuki: The Fundamental Failure of Environmentalism," *The Georgia Straight* (Vancouver, 1 May 2012).

2. Johan Rockstrom et al., "A Safe Operating Space for Humanity," *Nature* 461, no. 472–75 (2009).

3. Rockstrom et al., "A Safe Operating Space for Humanity."

4. Measured as atmospheric carbon-dioxide concentration and change in radiative forcing, extinction rate, and amount of N2 removed from the atmosphere for human use respectively.

5. Peter Singer, *Animal Liberation: A New Ethics for Our Treatment of Animals* (New York: Avon Book, 1975), xiv.

6. Timothy Morton, *Dark Ecology: For a Logic of Coexistence* (New York: Columbia University Press, 2016), 11.

7. Ted Toadvine, *Merleau-Ponty's Philosophy of Nature* (Evanston: Northwestern University Press, 2009), 10.

8. Tib. *mdo.* A note on translation: Sanskrit terms will be used throughout where there are insufficient anglophone equivalents. Tibetan equivalents will be given in the footnotes the first time each term appears. In certain cases, Wylie renderings of Tibetan terms will be used where there are no direct Sanskrit or English parallels.

9. For an example of this, see Lily de Silva, "Early Buddhist Attitudes toward Nature," in *Dharma Rain: Sources of Buddhist Environmentalism*, ed. Stephanite Kaza and Kenneth Kraft (Boston: Shambhala, 2000). Also see the many *sūtras* in the collection *Dharma Rain* that the editors included because they have "potential environmental significance" in Stephanie Kaza and Kenneth Kraft, "Part One: Teachings from Buddhist Traditions—Introduction," *Dharma Rain: Sources of Buddhist Environmentalism*, ed. Stephanie Kaza and Kenneth Kraft (Boston: Shambhala, 2000), 13.

10. Marti Kheel, "From Heroic to Holistic Ethics: The Ecofeminist Challenge," in *Ecofeminism: Women, Animals, Nature,* ed. Greta Gaard (Philadelphia: Temple University Press, 1993), 255.

11. Quoted in David E. Cooper and Simon P. James, *Buddhism, Virtue and Environment* (Aldershot: Ashgate, 2005), 32.

12. Donald S. Lopez Jr., "Developments in Buddhist Studies, 2015: A Report on the Symposium 'Buddhist Studies Today,' University of British Columbia, Vancouver, July 7–9, 2015," *Canadian Journal of Buddhist Studies* 11 (2016).

13. Quoted in Lopez Jr., "Developments in Buddhist Studies, 2015," 7.

14. José Ignacio Cabezon, "Buddhist Theology in the Academy," in *Buddhist Theology: Critical Reflections by Contemporary Buddhist Scholars,* ed. John Makransky and Roger Jackson (Richmond: Curzon, 2000): 34.

15. John Makransky, "The Emergence of Buddhist Critical-Constructive Reflection in the Academy as a Resource for Buddhist Communities and for the Contemporary World," *Journal of Global Buddhism* 9 (2008): 115.

16. Makransky, "The Emergence of Buddhist Critical-Constructive Reflection," 124.

17. Makransky, "The Emergence of Buddhist Critical-Constructive Reflection," 137.

18. See Daniel Capper, *Roaming Free like a Deer: Buddhism and the Natural World* (Cornell University Press, 2022); Johan Elverskog, *The Buddha's Footprint: An Environmental History of Asia* (Philadelphia: University of Pennsylvania Press); Ian Harris, "Buddhist Environmental Ethics and Detraditionalization: The Case of EcoBuddhism," *Religion* 15, no. 3 (1995); Ian Harris, "Buddhism and the Discourse of Environmental Concern: Some Methodological Problems Considered," in *Buddhism and Ecology: The Interconnection of Dharma and Deeds,* ed. Mary Evelyn Tucker and Duncan Ryūken Williams (Cambridge: Harvard University Press, 1997).

19. Tib. *'bri gung bka' brgyud.*

20. Jay L. Garfield, *Engaging Buddhism: Why It Matters to Philosophy* (Oxford: Oxford University Press, 2014), 320.

21. Tib. *zhi gnas.*

22. Tib. *pad+ma'i ngang tshul,* c. 740–95.

23. Tib. *sgom rim*

24. Tib. *lhag mthong.*

25. Tib. *thos bsam sgom gsum.*

# Chapter 1

1. Donald K. Swearer, "An Assessment of Buddhist Eco-Philosophy," *Harvard Theological Review* 99, no. 2 (2006).

2. Ian Harris, "How Environmentalist Is Buddhism?," *Religion* 21 (1991): 101–14.

3. Lambert Schmithausen, "The Early Buddhist Tradition and Ecological Ethics," *Journal of Buddhist Ethics* vol. 4 (1997): 1–74.

4. Capper, *Roaming Free like a Deer.*

5. Simon P. James, "Against Holism: Rethinking Buddhist Environmental Ethics," *Environmental Values* 16 (2007): 451.

6. John J. Holder, "A Suffering (but Not Irreparable) Nature: Environmental Ethics from the Perspective of Early Buddhism." *Contemporary Buddhism* 8, no. 2 (2007): 125.

7. Padmasiri De Silva, *Environmental Philosophy and Ethics in Buddhism* (Houndmills: Macmillan, 1998), 114.

8. De Silva, *Environmental Philosophy and Ethics in Buddhism*, 118.

9. De Silva, *Environmental Philosophy and Ethics in Buddhism*, 119.

10. De Silva, *Environmental Philosophy and Ethics in Buddhism*, 119.

11. De Silva, *Environmental Philosophy and Ethics in Buddhism*, 110.

12. Keown, "Buddhism and Ecology," 110.

13. Pragati Sahni, *Environmental Ethics in Buddhism: A Virtues Approach* (London: Routledge, 2008), 92.

14. Simon P. James, *Zen Buddhism and Environmental Ethics* (Burlington: Ashgate, 2004), 58.

15. Cooper and James, *Buddhism, Virtue and Environment*, 118.

16. This sentiment occurs repeatedly in the apologetic eco-Buddhist collection *Dharma Gaia: A Harvest of Essays on Buddhism and Ecology*, especially the works of Patricia Donegan, Joan Halifax, and Ken Jones. See *Dharma Gaia: A Harvest of Essays in Buddhism and Ecology*, ed. Alan Hunt Badiner (Berkeley: Parallax Press, 1990).

17. Schmithausen, "The Early Buddhist Tradition and Ecological Ethics," 46; emphasis in original.

18. It is clear Schmithausen still affirms this possibility nearly thirty years later given his enthusiastic endorsement of Bhikkhu Anālayo's recent book *Mindfully Facing Climate Change*, in which he writes: "Starting from the four noble truths as a scaffolding for his presentation and from mindfulness as a central Buddhist practice, he analyzes the present situation and points out how a Buddhist should react and contribute to prevent further deterioration. To an admirable degree, Bhikkhu Anālayo succeeds in suggesting creative answers while faithfully preserving the spirit and the thought of early Buddhism." See Bhikkhu Anālayo, *Mindfully Facing Climate Change* (Barre: Barre Centre for Buddhist Studies, 2019), 2.

19. Lambert Schmithausen, *Buddhism and Nature* (Tokyo: International Institute for Buddhist Studies, 1991), 53–54; emphasis in original.

20. Ian Harris, "Causation and Telos: The Problem of Buddhist Environmental Ethics," *Journal of Buddhist Ethics* 1 (1994): 46.

21. Harris, "Buddhist Environmental Ethics and Detraditionalization," 207.

22. Ian Harris, "A Vast Unsupervised Recycling Plant: Animals and the Buddhist Cosmos," in *A Communion of Subjects: Animals in Religion, Science, and Ethics*, ed. Paul Waldau and Kimberley Patton (New York: Columbia University Press, 2006), 213.

23. Harris, "A Vast Unsupervised Recycling Plant," 213.

24. Johan Elverskog, *The Buddha's Footprint: An Environmental History of Asia* (Philadelphia: University of Pennsylvania Press), 76.

25. Elverskog, *The Buddha's Footprint*, 85.

26. Elverskog, *The Buddha's Footprint*, 101.

27. Elverskog, *The Buddha's Footprint*, 103. That said, there is notable opposition to Elverskog's conclusions. Julia Shaw has written several pieces contesting the historical relationship between Buddhist monasticism and extractive economies on both theoretical and archaeological grounds. Regardless, Elverskog's work clearly does show how the eco-Buddhist thesis that Buddhism is an inherently green religion is deeply flawed. See Julia Shaw, "Religion, 'Nature' and Environmental Ethics in Ancient India: Archaeologies of Human: Non-Human Suffering and Well-Being in Early Buddhist and Hindu Contexts," *World Archaeology* 48, no. 4 (2016): 517–43; Julia Shaw, "Buddhism and the 'Natural' Environment," in *The Oxford Handbook of Buddhist Practice*, ed. Kevin Trainor and Paula Arai (Oxford: Oxford University Press, 2022).

28. Geoffrey Barstow, *Food of Sinful Demons: Meat, Vegetarianism, and the Limits of Buddhism in Tibet* (New York: Columbia University Press, 2018), 114–67.

29. Tib. *rten 'brel du 'byung ba*.

30. Each of these translations of *pratītyasamutpāda* has a distinct history and is commonly associated with different Buddhist traditions that emphasize different aspects of the term in their interpretations. In this chapter, I will use these translations interchangeably to refer to a Mahāyāna understanding of *pratītyasamutpāda* as the causal matrix in which all phenomena are embedded as a result of their lack of independent existence. More will be said about this below. For a sustained analysis of the evolving interpretations of *pratītyasamutpāda* and its use in contemporary Buddhist contexts, see David L. McMahan, "A Brief History of Interdependence," in *The Making of Buddhist Modernism* (Oxford: Oxford University Press, 2009).

31. The nature/culture divide is subject to major critique in the realm of environmental philosophy, which I will not address here. For the purposes of this chapter, the term *natural world* will denote the nonhuman

fauna, flora, and abiotic phenomena that have not been produced by human industry.

32. Harris, "Buddhism and the Discourse of Environmental Concern," 380–81.

33. Ian Harris, "Buddhism," in *Attitudes to Nature*, ed. Jean Holm and John Bowker (New York: Pinter, 1994), 15.

34. Harris, "Buddhism and the Discourse of Environmental Concern," 205.

35. Capper, *Roaming Free like a Deer*, 8.

36. Harris, "Buddhism," 15–16; emphasis in original.

37. Tib. *'khor ba*. The cycle of rebirth at the heart of the Buddhist soteriological problem.

38. Capper, *Roaming Free like a Deer*, 9.

39. Holmes Rolston III, *A New Environmental Ethics: The Next Millenium for Life on Earth* (New York: Routledge, 2012), 37–38.

40. Capper, *Roaming Free like a Deer*, 218–20.

41. Capper, *Roaming Free like a Deer*, 215.

42. Mark Sagoff, "Animal Liberation and Environmental Ethics: Bad Marriage, Quick Divorce," *Osgoode Hall Law Journal* 22 (1984), 304.

43. Rolston, *A New Environmental Ethics*, 67–68.

44. Capper, *Roaming Free like a Deer*, 217–18.

45. Arne Naess, *Ecology, Community, and Lifestyle: Outline of an Ecosophy*, trans. David Rothenberg (Cambridge: Cambridge University Press, 1989), 164–71.

46. Capper, *Roaming Free like a Deer*, 10; emphasis added.

47. Rolston, *A New Environmental Ethic*, 122.

48. Rolston, *A New Environmental Ethic*, 218.

49. However, this may be markedly less difficult in East Asian Buddhist contexts, which explicitly ascribe buddhanature (Skt. *tathāgatagarbha*) to plants, mountains, waters, and other traditionally nonsentient phenomena. See James, *Zen Buddhism and Environmental Ethics*, 64–69.

50. The extent to which sentience is distributed across biotic lifeforms is a matter of debate. In traditional cosmologies (which persistently inform Buddhist understandings of life today), there were six classes of sentient beings: gods, demigods, humans, animals, hungry ghosts, and hell beings. Only humans and animals would therefore be considered sentient in constructing a cosmopolitan environmental ethic. However, recent speculation on how scientific understanding of plant, bacteria, and AI cognition complicate these traditional understandings, and contemporary (and, to a lesser extent, historical) Tibetan teachers have begun ascribing sentience beyond the traditional six realms. See Colin H. Simonds, "Expanding

Sentience: Tibetan Buddhism and the Possibility of Plant, Bacteria, and AI Sentience," *Canadian Journal of Buddhist Studies* 18 (2023).

51. Capper, *Roaming Free like a Deer*, 217–18.

52. Clayton, *Moral Theory in Śāntideva's Śikṣāsamuccaya*, 112–18.

53. William Edelglass, "Buddhist Ethics and Western Moral Philosophy," in *A Companion to Buddhist Philosophy*, ed. Steven M. Emmanuel. Malden: Wiley-Blackwell, 2014.

54. Garfield, *Engaging Buddhism*, 278–79.

55. Garfield, *Engaging Buddhism*, 279. Emphasis in original.

56. I will do so specifically from an Indo-Tibetan Mahāyāna Buddhist philosophical perspective, but I expect scholars and philosophers of other Buddhist traditions to agree with some of the views presented here.

57. Tib. *bdag las ma yin gzhan las min / gnyis las ma yin gyu med min / dngos po gang dag gang na yang / skye ban am yang yod ma yin.* Sourced from Nāgārjuna, *The Root Stanzas of the Middle Way*, 111.

58. Tib. *rten cing 'brel bar 'bying ba gang / de ni stong pa nyid du bshad / de ni brten nas gdags pa ste / de nyid dbu ma'I lam yin no / gang phyir rten 'breng ma yin pa'i / chos 'ga' yod pa ma yin pa / de phyir strong pa ma yin pa'i / chos 'ga' yod pa ma yin no.* Sourced from Nāgārjuna, *The Root Stanzas of the Middle Way*, 159.

59. Anthony Weston, "Beyond Intrinsic Value: Pragmatism in Environmental Ethics," in *Environmental Pragmatism*, ed. Eric Katz and Andrew Light (London: Routledge, 1996), 308.

60. Weston, "Beyond Intrinsic Value," 311–12; emphasis in original.

61. This might be read as a kind of moral pragmatism or pluralism that ascribes relative value to all phenomena but nonetheless holds that "we possess different moral obligations derived from different principles for these distinct entities." As Edelglass has argued in his analysis of Śāntideva's *Bodhicaryāvatārā*, this approach to ethics is characteristic of Mahāyāna Buddhist moral thought. See William Edelglass, "Moral Pluralism, Skillful Means, and Environmental Ethics," *Environmental Philosophy* 3, no. 1 (2006): 10.

62. Aldo Leopold, *A Sand County Almanac with Essays on Conservation from Round River* (New York: Ballantine Books, 1970), 262.

63. Capper, *Roaming Free like a Deer*, 9.

64. Tsoknyi Rinpoche, "A New Meaning of Chu ("Beings") and No ("Environment") Has Emerged," in *A Buddhist Response to the Climate Emergency*, ed. John Stanley, David R. Loy, and Gyurme Dorje (Boston: Wisdom, 2009).

65. Which the *bodhisattva* vow itself admits in its common East Asian articulation codified by Zhiyi: "Sentient beings are innumerable, I vow to save them all. The afflictive emotions are inexhaustible, I vow

to overcome them. Dharma gates are limitless, I vow to master them all. The Buddha way is unsurpassable, I vow to accomplish it." See Robert F. Rhodes, "The Four Extensive Vows and Four Noble Truths in T'ien-t'ai Buddhism," *Annual Memoirs of the Otani University Shin Buddhist Comprehensive Research Institute* 2 (1987).

66. Tib. *byang chub sems dpa'*. An enlightened being who forestalls their own liberation to help others also achieve enlightenment.

67. This is at least the predominant interpretation in the work of the pioneering scholars of Buddhist ecology surveyed earlier in the paper. Contemporary figures in the Theravada tradition (being the modern-day representation of this Early Buddhist tradition) indeed have articulated quite nuanced responses to the climate crisis grounded in their readings of the Pali suttas. See Bhikkhu Anālayo, *Mindfully Facing Climate Change*.

68. Timothy Morton, *Hyperobjects: Philosophy and Ecology after the End of the World* (Minneapolis: University of Minnesota Press, 2013), 14.

69. Levi R. Bryant and Eileen A. Joy, "Preface: Object/Ecology," *O-Zone: A Journal of Object-Oriented Studies* 1 (2014); Drew M. Dalton, 2018, "Towards an Object-Oriented Ethics: Schopenhauer, Spinoza, and the Physics of Objective Evil," *Open Philosophy* 1 (2018).

70. John Clark, "On Being None with Nature: Nagarjuna and the Ecology of Emptiness," *Capitalism Nature Socialism* 19, no. 4 (2008): 12.

71. Tib. *sgam po pa bsod nams rin chen*, b.1079–d.1153.

72. Tib. *dam chos yid bzhin nor bur in po che'i rgyan*.

73. Gampopa, *The Jewel Ornament of Liberation: The Wish-Fulfilling Gem of the Noble Teachings*, trans. Khenpo Konchog Gyaltsen Rinpoche, ed. Ani K. Trinlay Chodron (Boulder: Snow Lion, 1998), 126–30.

74. Tib. *'dul ba*. The rules of monastic discipline.

75. Charles S. Prebish, *Buddhist Monastic Discipline: The Sanskrit Prātimokṣa Sūtras of the Mahāsāṃghikas and Mūlasarvāstivādins* (University Park: Pennsylvania State University Press, 1975), 76–77, 88–89.

76. The local deities and water serpents considered to be sentient beings living in the landscape in the Tibetan cosmological imagination.

77. Emily Woodhouse, Martin A. Mills, Philip J. K. McGowan, and E. K. Milner-Gulland, "Religious Relationships with the Environment in a Tibetan Rural Community: Interactions and Contrasts with Popular Notions of Indigenous Environmentalism," *Human Ecology* 43 (2015).

78. *The Life of Shabkar: The Autobiography of a Tibetan*, 139.

79. Rachel H. Pang, "Taking Animals Seriously: Shabkar's Narrative Argument for Vegetarianism and the Ethical Treatment of Animals," *Journal of Buddhist Ethics* 29 (2022).

80. Capper, *Roaming Free like a Deer*, 180.

81. Capper, *Roaming Free like a Deer*, 180.

82. Capper, *Roaming Free like a Deer*, 180.

83. J. Baird Callicott, "Animal Liberation: A Triangular Affair," *Environmental Ethics* 2, no. 4 (1980): 336–37.

84. Callicott, "Animal Liberation," 337.

85. Callicott, "Animal Liberation," 337.

86. Sagoff, "Animal Liberation and Environmental Ethics," 304.

87. Mary Anne Warren, "The Rights of the Nonhuman World," *Environmental Philosophy*, ed. Robert Elliot and Arran Gare (New York: University of Queensland Press, 1983), 110.

88. Warren, "The Rights of the Nonhuman World," 110.

89. Warren, "That Rights of the Nonhuman World," 129–30.

90. Warren, "The Rights of the Nonhuman World," 131.

91. J. Baird Callicott, "Animal Liberation and Environmental Ethics: Back Together Again," *Between the Species* 4, no. 3 (1988): 163.

92. Callicott, "Animal Liberation and Environmental Ethics," 164.

93. Callicott, "Animal Liberation and Environmental Ethics," 166.

94. Callicott, "Animal Liberation and Environmental Ethics," 166.

95. Dale Jamieson, "Animal Liberation Is an Environmental Ethic," *Environmental Values* 7, no. 1 (1998).

96. Jamieson, "Animal Liberation Is an Environmental Ethic," 46.

97. Jamieson, "Animal Liberation Is an Environmental Ethic," 47.

98. Jamieson, "Animal Liberation Is an Environmental Ethic," 49.

99. Jamieson, "Animal Liberation Is an Environmental Ethic," 47.

100. Jamieson, "Animal Liberation Is an Environmental Ethic," 47.

101. Jamieson, "Animal Liberation Is an Environmental Ethic," 51.

102. Tib. *'khor ba*.

103. Capper, *Roaming Free like a Deer*, 217–18.

104. Harvey, *An Introduction to Buddhist*, 51.

105. Clayton, "Buddha's Maritime Nature: A Case Study in Shambhala Buddhist Environmentalism."

106. Edelglass, "Moral Pluralism, Skillful Means, and Environmental Ethics."

107. Kheel, "From Heroic to Holistic Ethics," 255.

108. Jamieson, "Animal Liberation Is an Environmental Ethic," 47.


# Chapter 2

1. Tib. *mya ngan las 'das pa*.

2. Damien Keown, *The Nature of Buddhist Ethics* (New York: Palgrave Macmillan, 1992), 230–31.

3. Tib. *zhi ba lha*, c. 685–763.

4. Tib. *thogs med*, fl. fourth century C.E.

5. Peter Harvey, *An Introduction to Buddhist Ethics: Foundations, Values and Issues* (Cambridge: Cambridge University Press, 2000), 51.

6. Barbra Clayton, *Moral Theory in Śāntideva's Śikṣāsamuccaya: Cultivating the Fruits of Virtue* (New York: Routledge, 2006), 112.

7. Clayton, *Moral Theory in Śāntideva's Śikṣāsamuccaya*, 113.

8. Clayton, *Moral Theory in Śāntideva's Śikṣāsamuccaya*, 118.

9. Tib. *byang chub sems dpa'i spyod pa la 'jug pa*.

10. Jay L. Garfield, "What Is It Like to Be a Bodhisattva? Moral Phenomenology in Śāntideva's *Bodhicaryāvatāra*," *Journal of the International Association of Buddhist Studies* 33, no. 1–2 (2010): 334.

11. Garfield, *Engaging Buddhism*, 278–79.

12. Garfield, *Engaging Buddhism*, 279.

13. Garfield, *Engaging Buddhism*, 279.

14. Skt. *caturapramana*. Tib. *tshad med bzhi*.

15. While the following discussion will primarily take part in the Tibetan Buddhist tradition, the *brahmavihārās* are an active part of Tibetan Buddhism as well as Theravada Buddhism. The *brahmavihārās* are not found in the Theravada tradition alone (in the *Dīgha Nikāya* and the *Visuddhimagga*) but are also present in Mahāyāna and Vajrayāna traditions in texts such as the *Lotus Sūtra* and *Mahāparinirvāṇa Sūtra* and Bön texts such as the *mdzod phug* (*A Cavern of Treasures*). Thus, Garfield's words on them are relevant to the broader discussion of moral phenomenology in Tibetan Buddhism.

16. Tib. *snying rje*. Typically translated as "compassion," though Garfield prefers "caregiving" or "caring for" due to the former's lack of engagement. Compassion is a feeling, while caregiving is both a feeling *and* an action. Though I agree that the active component of compassion should be stressed, I will be using the more common "compassion" to translate *karuṇa* to be consistent with the majority of Buddhist scholars who translate it as such.

17. Garfield, *Engaging Buddhism*, 289.

18. Garfield, *Engaging Buddhism*, 289.

19. Tib. *sdug bsngal*. *Duḥkha* is often translated as "suffering" but also refers to "dissatisfaction" or "unease." These terms will be used interchangeably in this book.

20. Pali. Skt. *maitrī*. Tib. *byams pa*. Eng. Lovingkindness.

21. Garfield, *Engaging Buddhism*, 289–90.

22. Garfield, *Engaging Buddhism*, 290.

23. Garfield, *Engaging Buddhism*, 290.

24. Tib. *btang snyoms*.

25. Garfield, *Engaging Buddhism*, 290.

26. Garfield, *Engaging Buddhism*, 291.

27. Garfield, *Engaging Buddhism*, 294.

28. Garfield, *Engaging Buddhism*, 296.

29. Garfield, *Engaging Buddhism*, 296–97.

30. Garfield, *Engaging Buddhism*, 296.

31. Tib. *bya bral sangs rgyas rdo rje*. A wandering yogi (Tib. *'khyams pa*) and Dzogchen master of the Longchen Nyinthig (Tib. *klong chen snying thig*) lineage. 1913–2015.

32. Tib. *gnad gzhan pha byang chub smon 'jug sems / 'di theg chen rtsa ba yin pa'i phyir*. Sourced from: *sangs rgyas rdo rje*, "zhal gdams snying gi thig le," *sngags mang zhib 'jug* (3), ed. hum chen he ru ka, nyi zla he ru kah, and ye shes sgrol ma (Zi Ling: mtsho ngong zhing chen nang bstan rig gnas zhib 'jug lte gnas, 2002), 114–15.

33. Each of which he dedicates a chapter to exploring in his book *The Concept of Bodhicitta in Śāntideva's Bodhicaryāvatarā*. See Francis Brassard, *The Concept of Bodhicitta in Śāntideva's Bodhicaryāvatarā* (Albany: State University of New York Press, 200).

34. Brassard, *The Concept of Bodhicitta*, 150.

35. Tib. *khu nu bla ma bstan 'dzin rgyal mtshan*. A Nyingma and Kagyu yogi who notably taught the *Bodhicaryāvatarā* to His Holiness the Dalai Lama. 1895–1977.

36. Tib. *sems can re re'i skyon kun sel / re re'ng yon tan mtha' klas pa / skyed 'dod byang chub sems mchog ste / rmad byung las kyang 'di rmad byung*. Sourced from bstan 'dzin rgyal mtshan, *byang chub sems kyi stod pa rin chen sgron ma* (Dharamsala: dga' ldan pho brang, 2018), 7. For an alternate translation, see Khunu Rinpoche, *Vast as the Heavens, Deep as the Sea*, trans. Gareth Sparham (Somerville: Wisdom, 1999), 31.

37. Tib. *smon pa sems bskyed* and *'jug pa sems bskyed*. Śāntideva makes this distinction in his *Bodhicaryāvatarā* (1.15), which states, "In brief, one should know that *bodhicitta* has two aspects: the mind which aspires to enlightenment and the very application of enlightenment." Tib. *byang chub sems de mdor 'bsdus na / rnam pa gnyis su shes bya ste / byang chub smon pa'i sems dang ni / byang chub 'jug pa nyid yin no*. Sourced from *Bodhicaryāvatarā of Śāntideva*, ed. Vidhushekhara Bhattacharta. (Calcutta: Asiatic Society, 1960), 6.

38. Dilgo Khyentse Rinpoche, *The Heart Treasure of the Enlightened Ones*, trans. Padmakara Translation Group (Boston: Shambhala, 1992), 2.

39. Tib. *sbyin pa tshul khrims bzod pa brtson 'grus bsam tan te / thabs spyod pa'i phyogs kyi pha rol tu phyin pa lnga / shes rab ye shes kyi tsogs te drug yin*. Sourced from *rdza dpal sprul 'jigs med chos kyi dbang po, kun bzang bla ma'i zhal lung* (Lha sa: ser gtsug nang bstan dpe rnying 'tshol bsdu

phyogs sgrig khang, 2016), 309. For an alternate translation, see Patrul Rinpoche, *Words of My Perfect Teacher*, trans. Padmakara Translation Group (New Haven: Yale University Press, 2011), 234.

40. Dilgo Khyentse Rinpoche, *Heart Treasure of the Enlightened Ones*, 4.

41. Garfield, "What Is It Like to Be a Bodhisattva?," 334–35.

42. Garfield, "What Is It Like to Be a Bodhisattva?," 334–35.

43. Garfield, "What Is It Like to Be a Bodhisattva?," 347.

44. Garfield, "What Is It Like to Be a Bodhisattva?," 347–48.

45. Tib. *ma rig pa*.

46. Tib. *phung po*. This is the fundamental claim of *anātman* or *bdag med*: We feel like we have a Self, but when we analyze the aggregates (*skandhas*) which make up the Self, no Self can be found. The *skandhas* are form, feeling, perception, mental activity, and consciousness. Our sense of self only emerges when all of these are together, but when we analyze each individually, we are unable to locate where the Self is and, hence, our sense of self dissipates.

47. Daniel Timothy Aitken, "Experience and Morality: Buddhist Ethics as Moral Phenomenology," PhD dissertation (University of Tasmania, 2016), 113.

48. Aitken, "Experience and Morality," 117.

49. Tib. *kun 'gro lnga*.

50. Tib. *tshor ba*. I follow Aitken's translation of the terms here, but this is also commonly translated as "sensation."

51. Tib. *'du shes*. Also commonly translated as "perception."

52. Tib. *sems pa*.

53. Tib. *reg pa*.

54. Tib. *yid la byed pa*.

55. Aitken, "Experience and Morality," 119–20.

56. Aitken, "Experience and Morality," 157.

57. Garfield, "What Is It Like to Be a Bodhisattva?," 334–35.

58. Garfield, "What Is It Like to Be a Bodhisattva?," 341–42.

59. Garfield, "What Is It Like to Be a Bodhisattva?," 341–42.

60. Tib. *phags pa lha*.

61. Tib. *rnal 'byor spyod pa bzhi brgya pa*.

62. Aitken, "Experience and Morality," 159.

63. Aitken, "Experience and Morality," 166.

64. *The Foundation for Yoga Practitioners: The Buddhist Yogācārabhūmi Treatise and Its Adaptation in India, East Asia, and Tibet, Volume 1.*, ed. Ulrich Timme Kragh, Harvard Oriental Series 75 (Cambridge: Department of South Asian Studies, Harvard University, 2013), 144.

65. Aitken, "Experience and Morality," 177.

66. Aitken, "Experience and Morality," 160.

67. Tib. *lus la lus dbang ji bzhin du / gti mug kun la gnas gyur te / de phyir nyon mongs thams cad kyang / gti mug bcom pas bcom par 'gyur / / rten cing 'brel par 'byung ba ni / mthong na gti mug 'byung mi 'gyur / de phyir 'bad pas kun gyis 'dir / gtam de kho na bsnyad par bya.* Sourced from Aitken "Experience and Morality," 177.

68. Aitken, "Experience and Morality," 180.

69. Aitken, "Experience and Morality," 179.

70. Tib. *rdo rje theg pa.*

71. Tib. *sa ma ya.*

72. Tib. *dbang.*

73. Tib. *yi dam.*

74. Such as the unique Kālacakra vows, which have their own series of downfalls that constitute breaches in the Kālacakra pledge. Tsongkhapa goes over these in his *Fruit Clusters of Siddhis,* but we will instead focus on the more universal downfalls that are shared among the other Highest Yoga Tantra systems. There were also disputes between scholars as to the nature and scope of these vows, such as Vibhūticandra's rebuttal to Dragpa Gyaltsen's *Explanation of the Three Codes* (Tib. *rtsa ba'i ltung ba bcu bzhi pa'i 'grel pa,* on which Sakya Pandita based his important *Explanation of the Three Codes*) titled *Light Garland of the Three Codes.* For more about this particular dispute, see Cyrus Stearns, "The Life and Tibetan Legacy of the Indian Mahāpaṇḍita Vibhūticandra," *Journal for the International Association of Buddhist Studies* 19, no. 1 (1996): 127–68.

75. Tsongkhapa traces this division between "root downfalls" and "gross downfalls" back to the text *Vajrāvalī of Maṇḍala Rituals.* See Tsongkhapa, *Tantric Ethics: An Explanation of the Precepts for Buddhist Vajrayana Practice,* trans. Gareth Sparham (Boston: Wisdom, 2005), 87.

76. This is a difficult point and is formulated differently in different texts—I follow the *Ornament of the Vajra Essence Tantra's* exposition, which phrases this point as "False imagination about what is inexorably empty." As quoted in Tsongkhapa, *Tantric Ethics,* 113.

77. Phrased in my own words for clarity. Sourced from rta byangs "rdo rje theg pa rtsa ba'i ltung ba bsdus pa," in *bstan 'gyur dpe sdur ma* vol. 27 (Pe cin: krung go'i bod rig pa'i dpe skrun khang, 1994–2008). For an alternate translation, see Aśvaghoṣa, *Summary of the Root Downfalls of the Vajra Vehicles,* trans. Adam Pearcey (Lotsawa House, 2018).

78. Tib. *bde bar gshegs pa.* An epithet of the Buddha meaning one who has "gone to bliss."

79. Tib. *dbu ma rtsa ba shes rab.*

80. Tib. *klu sgrub.*

81. Tib. *rten cing 'brel bar 'byung ba gang / de ni stong pa nyid du bshad / de ni brten nas gdags pa ste / de nyid dbu ma'i lam yin no // gang phyir rten 'byung ma tin pa'i / chos 'gal yod pa ma yin pa / de phyir stong pa ma yin pa'i / chos 'ga' yod pa ma yin no.* Sourced from Nāgārjuna, *The Root Stanzas of the Middle Way: The Mūlamadhyamakakārikā*, trans. Padmakara Translation Group (Boulder: Shambhala, 2016), 159.

82. Tib. *'di kun ngo bos stong ba dang / 'di las 'di 'bras 'byung ba yi / nges pa gnyis po phan tshun du / gegs med par ni grogs byed pa.* Excerpted from tsong kha pa blo bzang grags pa, "rten 'grel stod pa," in *dge lugs pa'i chos spyod phyogs bsgrigs* (Zi Ling: Mtsho sngong mi rigs dpe skrun khang, 1995), 263. For an alternate translation, see Lobsang Gyatso and Graham Woodhouse, *Tsongkhapa's Praise for Dependent Relativity* (Boston: Wisdom, 2011), 4.

83. Robert Thurman, *The Jewel Tree of Tibet: The Enlightenment Engine of Tibetan Buddhism* (New York: Free Press, 2006), 111.

84. Thurman, *The Jewel Tree of Tibet*, 111.

85. Tib. *rin chen phreng ba.*

86. For the phrase in context, see Jeffrey Hopkins, *Nāgārjuna's Precious Garland: Buddhist Advice for Living and Liberation* (Boulder: Snow Lion, 2007), 218. The full Tibetan verse is as follows: *kha cig la ni gnyis mi bten / zab mo khu 'khrig can 'jigs pa / stong nyid snying rje'i snying po can / byang chub bsgrub pa kha cig la'o.*

87. Hopkins, *Nāgārjuna's Precious Garland*, 147. Bhikshu Steve Carlier's translation is "its essence is emptiness and compassion." In either case, the way Thurman and I translate the phrase in isolation differs from how Hopkins and Chodron translate the phrase in context. While I read Hopkins and Carlier's translations as appropriate in the context of the verse, I nonetheless stand by the utility of the phrase in isolation and its applicability to this discussion. See Khensur Jampa Tegchok, *Practical Ethics and Profound Emptiness: A Commentary on Nāgārjuna's Precious Garland*, trans. Bhiksu Steve Carlier, ed. Bhiksuni Thubten Chodron (Somerville: Wisdom, 2017), 323.

88. Tib. *so so'i bslab par bya ba dang / sems bskyed pa yi gnad rnams dang / stong nyid snying rje'i snying po dang / rim pa gnyis kyi gsang tshig dang.* Sourced from Sakya Pandita Kunga Gyaltsen, *A Clear Differentiation of the Three Codes: Essential Distinctions among the Individual Liberation, Great Vehicle, and Tantric Systems*, trans. Jared Douglas Rhoton, ed. Victoria R. M. Scott (Albany: State University of New York Press, 2002), 278.

89. Sakya Pandita, *A Clear Differentiation of the Three Codes*, 40.

90. Tib. *mda' bsnun.*

91. Tib. *lta sgom spyod pa 'bras bu'i do ha'i glu.*

92. Tib. *zung 'jug phyag rgya blo 'das chen po ni | bde gsal mi rtog nam mkha lta bu ste | khyab cig rgya chen sying rje chen po'i ngor*. Sourced from: sa ra ha, "lta sgom spyod pa 'bras bu'i do ha'i glu," in *sa ra ha pa'i rdo rje'i gsung rnams phyogs bsgrigs, sde tshan ra* (Kathmandu: Thrangu tashi choling, 2011), 425.

93. Later in this verse, Saraha alludes to how the view of Mahāmudrā goes beyond even the claims of Madhyamikas in his statement: "While clear, the fundamental state is free from all extreme and middling designations." "Extreme designations" refer to those of eternalists and nihilists, which Madhyamikas refute while "middling" (*dbu*) refers to the views of those Madhyamikas themselves. Thus, Saraha asserts that his view of Mahāmudrā goes beyond even that of the Prasangika-Madhyamaka, which is lauded as the highest philosophical position in Tibetan doxography. Tib. *gsal yang tha snyad mtha' dbus kun dang bral*. Sourced from sa ra ha, "lta sgom spyod pa 'bras bu'I do ha'i glu," 425.

94. Tib. *sems kyi ngo bo*.

95. Pure awareness.

96. Tib. *sems kyi ngo bo zhes bya ba ni | rig pa 'dus ma byas pa'I rang ngo rjen par bla ma'I byin rlabs zhugs shing man ngag gis ngo 'phrad pa la bya ba yin | de'i ngo bo ci lta bu zhe na | ng obo stong pa dmigs su med pa | rang bzhin gsal ba lhun gyis grub pa | thugs rje kun khyab 'gags pa med pa | sku gsum dbyer med kyi rig pa yin te*. Sourced from mi pham rgya mtsho, "sems kyi ngo bo," in *gsung 'bum mi pham rgya mtsho* (Khreng tu'u: Gangs can rig gzhung dpe rnying myur skyobs lhan tshogs, 2007), 369. For an alternate translation, see Mipham Rinpoche, *The Essence of Mind*, trans. Adam Pearcey (Lotsawa House, 2016).

97. Joanna Macy, "The Ecological Self: Postmodern Ground for Right Action," in *Worldview, Religion, and the Environment: A Global Anthology*, ed. Richard C. Foltz (Belmont: Wadsworth/Thomson Learning, 2003), 445.

98. Tib. *thogs med*.

99. Tib. *byams pa*.

100. *A Feast of the Nectar of the Supreme Vehicle: An Explanation of the Ornament of the Mahāyāna Sūtras — Maitreya's Mahāyānasūtrālamkāra with a Commentary by Jamgön Mipham*, trans. Padmakara Translation Group (Boulder: Shambhala, 2018), 14.

101. Tib. *de phyir ji srid ngar 'dzin pa | sel ba'i chos 'di ma shes pa | de srid sbyin dang tshul khrims dang | bzod pa'i chos la gus par mdzod*. Sourced from Hopkins *Nāgārjuna's Precious Garland*, 183. For an alternate translation, see Hopkins *Nāgārjuna's Precious Garland*, 112.

102. Tib. *sdom gsum*.

103. Tib. *so thar gyi sdom pa*.

104. Tib. *byan chub sems dpa'i sdom pa*. A typical formulation of these vows is: Sentient beings are innumerable, I vow to save them. The afflictive emotions are inexhaustible, I vow to extinguish them. The *dharma* is immeasurable, I vow to master it. Buddhahood is incomparable, I vow to attain it.

105. Tib. *gsang sngags kyi sdom pa*.

106. Tib. *de ltar rig byas gzhan don la / rtak tu brtson par gnas par bya / thugs rje mnga' ba ring gzigs pas / bkag pa rnams kyang de la gnang*. Sourced from: *Bodhicaryāvatarā of Śāntideva*, 73.

107. Geoffrey Barstow addresses this in the context of vegetarianism in monastic settings and quotes Tūlku Urgyen, saying, "The reason I didn't take ordination at that time or any time after was simply that I didn't trust that I could keep the vows. Not only did Samten Gyatso never touch women, he never even touched meat or liquor. Uncle Sangngak was not different. If you take monk's vows, you should keep them pure, like my uncles or like Karmé Khenpo. I have great respect for anyone who does so, but not for the half-hearted renunciate so common nowadays. Maybe it was my lack of pure perception, but I didn't see that many pure monks even then." See Barstow, *Food of Sinful Demons*, 65. For its original context, see Tulku Urgyen Rinpoche, *Blazing Splendor: The Memoirs of Tulku Urgyen Rinpoche*, trans. Erik Pema Kunsang (Boudhanath: Rangjung Yeshe, 2015), 198.

108. Tib. *'brug pa kun legs*.

109. Terry Horgan and Mark Timmons, "Moral Phenomenology and Moral Theory," *Philosophical Issues* 15 (2005): 72.

110. Kriegel, "Moral Phenomenology," 1.

111. Horgan and Timmons, "Moral Phenomenology and Moral Theory," 62–63.

112. Horgan and Timmons, "Moral Phenomenology and Moral Theory," 240–44.

113. Gilligan theorized her care ethic in response to the modes of androcentric ethical theories that tend to dominate ethical discussion. Specifically, Kohlberg's chauvinistic development scale, which categorized women as less morally developed than men, was heavily criticized by individuals such as Gilligan, who argued that the way in which he conducted his research was fraught with error. Kohlberg uses the moral dilemma of whether a man should steal from the pharmacy a drug that he cannot afford to save his dying wife and, according to Dreyfus and Dreyfus, concludes that men "tended to answer that Heinz should steal the drug because the right to life Is more basic than the right to private property. Women, however, seemed unable to deal with the dilemma in a

mature, logical way." However, Gilligan contests this narrative and suggests that the women in Kohlberg's study show a greater understanding of the nuance of the situation and writes, "Seeing in the dilemma not a math problem with humans but a narrative of relationships that extends over time, Amy envisions the wife's continuing need for her husband and the husband's continuing concern for his wife and seeks to respond to the druggist's need in a way that would sustain rather than sever connection." See Hubert L. Dreyfus and Stuart E. Dreyfus, "What Is Morality? A Phenomenological Account of the Development of Ethical Expertise," in *Universalism vs. Communitarianism: Contemporary Debates in Ethics*, ed. David Rasmussen (Cambridge: MIT Press, 1990), 251; Carol Gilligan, *In a Different Voice: Psychological Theory and Women's Development* (Cambridge: Harvard University Press, 2003), 28.

114. Dreyfus and Dreyfus, "What Is Morality?," 254.

115. Elsewhere, I have explored some of the parallels between the Buddhist moral phenomenological tradition and the care-ethics tradition pioneered by Gilligan in ecological contexts and have argued that when Buddhist moral phenomenology is applied to ecological situations, it presents as an ecological ethic of care. See Colin H. Simonds, "Toward a Buddhist Ecological Ethic of Care," *Religions* 14 (2023).

116. Dreyfus and Dreyfus, "What Is Morality?," 256.

# Chapter 3

1. As in Yeshe Tsogyal's hagiography of Padmasambhava, which states, "As the road to freedom, practice the view, meditation, and [action]." See Yeshe Tsogyal, *The Lotus-Born: The Life Story of Padmasambhava*, trans. Erik Pema Kunsang, ed. Marcia Binder Schmidt (Boston: Shambhala, 1999), 186.

2. As in Saraha's *Spontaneous Song of View, Meditation, Action, and Fruition*, which states, "In brief, by acting in whatever way benefits the practice of view, meditation, and action, one acts according to the natural state." Tib. *mdor na lta sgom spyod pa nyams len la / ji ltar phan pa'i spyod pas rnal byor spyod*. Sourced from sa ra ha, "lta sgom spyod pa 'bras bu'i do ha'i glu," 13.

3. As in Rangjung Dorje's *Prayer of Mahāmudrā*, which states, "To cut through misconceptions of the ground is to have confidence in the view. To maintain that view without distraction is the crucial point of meditation. To train in all objects of meditation is the supreme form of action. May I possess the confidence of view, meditation, and action." Tib. *gzhi la sgro 'dogs chod pa lta ba'i gdengs / de la ma yengs skyong ba sgom*

*pa'i gnad / sgom don kun la rtsal sbyong spyod pa'i mchog / lta sgom spyod pa'i gdeng dang ldan par shog.* Sourced from rang byung rdo rje, *nges don phyag rgya chen po'i smon lam dang sa bcad zur bkol blo gsar 'jug bde* (rdo rje gdan: bka' brgyud sang+g+ha smon lam chen mo, 2004), 4.

4. As in Jigmé Lingpa's "Prayer of the Ground, Path, and Fruition," which states: "Since it is primordially pure, even the word *view* does not exist. Through the awareness of one's true nature, it emerges from the sheath of causal meditation. Since it is without grasping at concepts, it is free from the fetters of [restrained] action. This is the spontaneously entered nature, the state of naked simplicity. May there be no wrong directions on the way to this crucial point of the path!" Tib. *ye nas dag pas lta ba'i ming yang med / rang ngo rig pas sgom rgyu'i shubs nas 'don / gza' gtad med pas spyod pa'i sgrog dang dral / rang bzhin lhums zhugs spros bral rjen pa'i ngang / lam gyi gnad la gol phyogs med par shog.* Sourced from 'jigs med gling pa, "klong chen snying gi thig le las gzhi lam 'bras bu'i smon lam," in *gsang chen snga 'gyur ba'i bka' gter zhal 'don phyogs bsgrigs* (zi ling: mtsho sngon zhing chen mtsho lho dge 'os slob grwa'i khang, 1998), 433.

5. As in Dudjom Rinpoche's *Light of Primordial Wisdom*, which organizes its text around the framework, stating: "1) Deciding through the view; 2) Adopting it as one's experience through meditation; 3) To experience continuously through action, and; 4) Bringing the fruition to realization." Tib. *lta bas thag bcod pa / sgom pas nyams su blang ba / spyod pas rgyun skyong ba / 'bras bu mngon du byed pa'o.* Sourced from bdud 'joms rin po che, "bdud 'dul dbang drug rdo rje gro lod kyi rdzogs rim ka dag gi khrid yig ye shes snang ba," in *bdud 'joms 'jigs bral ye shes rdo rje'i gsung 'bum dam chos rin chen nor bu'i bung mdzod,* vol. 15 (kalimpong: dupjung lama, 1979–1975), 427.

6. As in Padmasambhava's *A Garland of Views*, which uses the framework as an organizational tool, such as when he states, "Regarding the view of those who engage in the *bodhisattva* vehicle, all phenomena which are either totally disturbed or completely refined, are without inherent existence on the ultimate level, and on the conventional level, are merely illusions with distinct, individual characteristics. As a result of their [meditative] training in the ten perfections, practitioners gradually progress along the ten grounds, and in the end seek to accomplish the unsurpassed enlightenment." Tib. *byang chub sems dpa'i theg pa la zhugs pa rnams kyi lta ba ni / kun nas nyon mongs pa dang rnams par byang ba'i chos thams cad don dam par ni rang bzhin med pa yin la / kun rdzob du ni sgyu ma stam du so so'i mthan nyid ma 'dres par yod de / pha rol tu phyin pa bcu spyad pa'i 'bras bus a bcu rim gyis bgrod pa'i mthar bl ana med pa'i byang chub tu 'grub par 'dod pa yin no.* Sourced from pad+ma 'byung gnas, *man ngag lta ba'I phreng ba* (Bylakuppe: Ngagyu nyingma Institute, 2001), 5–6.

7. Tib. *sa ra ha*, fl. eighth century C.E.

8. Tib. *mdor na lta sgom spyod pa nyams len la / ji ltar phan pa'i spyod pas rnal byor spyod.* Sourced from sa ra ha, "lta sgom spyod pa 'bras bu'i do ha'i glu," 13.

9. Tib. *nor brang o rgyan gyis bsgrigs*, b. 1933.

10. Tib. *chos rnam kun btus.*

11. Tib. 1. *nang pa'i chos lugs kyi lta ba gtso bor bshad pa'i mdo sde'i sde snod / 2. ting nge 'dzin sgom tshul gtso bor bshad pa'i mngon pa'i sde snod / 3. kun spyod gtso bor bshad pa'i 'dul ba'i sde snod bcos gzhung gsum la sde snod gsum zer.* Sourced from: nor brang o rgyan gyis bsgrigs, chos rnam kun btus, vol. 1 (pe cin: krung go'i bod rig pa dpe skrun khang, 2008), 265.

12. Tib. *mi la ras pa*, c. 1040–1123.

13. *The Hundred Thousand Songs of Milarepa, Volume 1,* trans. Garma C. C. Chang (Boulder: Shambhala, 1977), 72.

14. Yeshe Tsogyal, *The Lotus-Born*, 286; Chökyi Nyima Rinpoche, *The Union of Mahamudra and Dzogchen,* trans. Erik Pema Kunsang, ed. Marcia B. Schmidt (Kathmandu: Rangjung Yeshe, 1989), 239.

15. Tib. *zhe sar gzigs pa dang / rtogs bya'i lta ba.* Sourced from Gegen Dorje Tharchin, *[Tibetan-Tibetan Dictionary] vol. 2* (Kalimpong: Tibet Mirror, 1950–1976), 1007.

16. Erik Pema Kunsang, Ives Waldo, Jim Valby, Gyurme Dorje, Thomas Doctor, and Matthieu Ricard, "lta ba," *Rangjung Yeshe Wiki Dharma Dictionary* (Tsadra Foundation, 2021).

17. Tib. *sems rtse gcig tu gnas pa . . . thugs sgom zer ba sogs la'ngo.* Sourced from Gegin Dorje Tharchin, *[Tibetan-Tibetan Dictionary] vol. 1*, 568.

18. Hopkins, *Jeffrey Hopkins' Tibetan-Sanskrit-English Dictionary*, 317.

19. Erik Pema Kunsang, Ives Waldo, Jim Valby, Gyurme Dorje, Thomas Doctor, and Matthieu Ricard, "sgom pa," *Rangjung Yeshe Wiki Dharma Dictionary* (Tsadra Foundation, 2021).

20. Jim Valby's dictionary is a desktop application, but his entries can also be found on the Tibetan and Himalayan Library translation tool. The above connotations can be seen under "JV" when one searches for *sgom pa.* See: "THL Tibetan to English Translation Tool."

21. Tib. *lta spyod ya bral te / spyod pa rtsing ba / spyod pa zhib pa / spyod pa rgya chen po / spyod pa mi gsal ba sogs.* Sourced from Gegin Dorje Tharchin, *[Tibetan-Tibetan Dictionary] vol. 1*, 656.

22. For a survey of some of these descriptive uses, see Colin H. Simonds, "*Lta sgom spyod gsum:* A Tibetan Approach to Moral Phenomenological Praxis," *Journal of Buddhist Ethics* 30 (2023): 105–10.

23. Tib. *dbang phyug rdo rje*, c. 1556–1603.

24. Tib. *phyag chen ma rig mun sel.*

25. Tib. *bya bas gzung 'dzin kun dang bral zhing yang dag pa'i gnas lugs la blta b ani lta ba | de don yengs med du bsgom pa ni sgom pa | bya byed thams cad dang bral zhing | spyod pa bzhi gang rung skyong ba spyod pa dang | mar 'khor bar lhung dogs dang yar sangs rgyas thob 'dod sogs re dogs | bsgom bya sgom byed thams cad bral b ani 'bras bu ste | lta sgom spyod 'bras kyi don yang | de zhin du shes par byas la brtson pa bskyed cing.* Sourced from kar ma pa dbang phyug rdo rje, "phyag-chen ma-rig mun-sel," *Study Buddhism by Berzin Archives* (Berzin Archives, 2021). For an alternate translation, see Wang-ch'ug Dor-je, *The Mahāmudrā: Eliminating the Darkness of Ignorance* (Dharamsala: Library of Tibetan Works and Archives, 1978), 150.

26. Tib. *rang byung rdo rje,* c. 1284–1339.

27. Tib. *gzhi la sgro 'dogs chod pa lta ba'i gdengs | de la ma yengs skyong ba sgom pa'i gnad | sgom don kun la rtsal sbyong spyod pa'i mchog | lta sgom spyod pa'i gdeng dang ldan par shog.* Sourced from rang byung rdo rje, *nges don phyag rgya chen po'i smon lam dang,* 4.

28. Tib. *bdud 'joms 'jigs bral ye shes rdo rje,* c. 1904–1987.

29. In general, tantric practice in Vajrayāna Buddhism consists of two parts: the generation stage (Tib. *bskyed rim*) and the completion stage (Tib. *rdzogs rim*). In the generation stage, one visualizes a particular meditative deity (Tib. *yi dam*) either in front of, on top of, or as oneself. In the completion stage, one collapses this visualization and rests in a nonclinging meditative equipoise, the description of which changes from practice to practice but can be said to be akin to the view of Dzogchen or Mahamudra. For example, this particular text defines the view of the natural state as: "The ultimate Dorje Drolo which is empty clarity, is not to be looked for anywhere but here, this naked, self-arisen awareness. In the great lord which is the whole of *saṃsāra* and *nirvāṇa,* this great primordial nature, be resolved." Tib. *stong gsal don gyi gr obo lod | gzhan nas mi 'tshol rang byung gi | rig pa rjen pa 'di ka ste | 'khor 'das yongs kyi khyab bdag che | ye babs chen por la bzla'o.* Sourced from bdud 'joms rin po che, "bdud 'dul dbang drug rdo rje gro lod kyi rdzogs rim ka dag gi khrid yig ye shes snang ba," 427.

30. Tib. *gnyis pa dngos gzhi lhag mthong gi ye shes bskyed pa la bzhi | lta bas thag gcod pa | sgom pas nyams sub lang ba | spyod pas rgyun skyong ba | bras bu mngon du byed pa'o.* Sourced from bdud 'joms rin po che, "bdud 'dul dbang drug rdo rje gro lod kyi rdzogs rim ka dag gi khrid yig ye shes snang ba," 427.

31. Tib. *dpal sprul rin po che,* c. 1808–1887.

32. Tib. *thog mtha' bar gsum du dge ba'i gtam lta sgom spyod gsum nyams len dam pa'i snying nor zhes bya ba.*

33. Tib. *dil mgo mkhyen brtse rin po che,* c. 1910–1991.

34. Dilgo Khyentse Rinpoche, *The Heart Treasure of the Enlightened Ones*, 9.

35. Dilgo Khyentse Rinpoche, *The Heart Treasure of the Enlightened Ones*, 167.

36. Elsewhere in the text, Dilgo Khyentse Rinpoche states: "To establish the view means to acquire complete certainty about the absolute truth, which is that the phenomenal world, though obviously appearing and functioning, is utterly devoid of any ultimate reality. This view of all phenomena as appearing yet void is the seed from which the perfect fruit of enlightenment will grow." See Dilgo Khyentse Rinpoche, *The Heart Treasure of the Enlightened Ones*, 9.

37. Sonam Thakchoe, *The Two Truths Debate: Tsongkhapa and Gorampa on the Middle Way* (Somerville: Wisdom, 2007), 79.

38. Tib. *yang thang rin po che*, c. 1930–2016.

39. Tib. *lta sgom spyod gsum nang nas lta ba gtso / 'khul med lta bar togs pa shin tu gal / lta ba ma rtogs sgom gzhi gang yang med / 'khrul med lta ba dngos sur togs pa'i rjes / de nas bsgom pas nyams su len pa'i skabs / rang ngo 'phrod pa'i lta ba'I ngang de la / bzhugs yun bsting nas 'bad pas bsgom pa yin / de bas sgom rgyu gzhan zhig logs na med.* Sourced from yang thang rin po che, "lta sgom spyod gsum mdor bsdus," *Lotsawa House* (Lotsawa House, 2021).

40. Tib. *rim gul sprul sku rin po che*, b. 1952.

41. Ringu Tulku Rinpoche, "The Bodhisattva Path at a Time of Crisis" in *A Buddhist Response to the Climate Emergency*, ed. John Stanley, David R. Loy, and Gyurme Dorje (Boston: Wisdom, 2009), 130.

42. Tib. *klu sgrub*, fl. second–third centuries, CE.

43. Khensur Jampa Tegchok, *Practical Ethics and Profound Emptiness*, 47.

44. Tib. *de ltar bdag med kyi lta ba rnam par dag pa la / spyod pa rnam par dag pa dgos / dper na bya gshog pa gnyis 'dzom gyi nam kha' la 'phur nus / gshog pa ya gcig bzang kyang gar yang mi phyin ba ltar / lta spyod zung du 'brel ba'i nyams len la bsten nas / rnam pa thams cad mkhyen ba'i go 'phang thob nas / lta spyod dang rung gcig bzang kyang sa lam gar yang phyin mi nus / o na lta spyod zung du 'brel ba'i nyams len ji ltar bya snyam na / mdor hril gyis dril bas lag len la sngon gyis bka' gdams pa'i skyes chen dam pa rnams kyis 'khor ba'i sdug bsngal thams cad bskyed pa'i rtsab bdag med la bdag tu 'dzin pa'i ma rig pa 'di yin par ma khyen nas / gcig dang du bral gyis rig pas gang zag dang chos kyi bdag med gtan la phab nas / mnyam bzhag nam kha' lta bu'i stong nyid dang / rjes thob sgyu ma lta bu'i stong pa nyid la bslab pas lta spyod zung 'brel gyis lam rnam par dag.* Sourced from zhabs dkar tshogs drug rang grol, *'jam dbyangs sprul pa'i glegs bam*, 395–96. For an alternate translation, see Shabkar Tsogdruk Rangdrol, *The Emanated Scripture of Manjushri: Shabkar's*

*Essential Meditation Instructions from Lam-Rim to Mahāmudrā and Dzogchen,* trans. Sean Price (Boulder: Snow Lion, 2020), 98–99.

45. Tib. *chos ldan rin po che,* c. 1930–2015.

46. Chöden Rinpoche, *Mastering Meditation: Instructions on Calm Abiding and Mahāmudrā,* trans. Tenzin Gache (Somerville: Wisdom, 2020), 98.

47. Chöden Rinpoche, *Mastering Meditation,* 98.

48. Chöden Rinpoche, *Mastering Meditation,* 186.

49. Chöden Rinpoche, *Mastering Meditation,* 13.

50. Garfield, *Engaging Buddhism,* 296–97.

51. Garfield, *Engaging Buddhism,* 296–97.

52. Tib. *lta bas thag bcod pa.* Sourced from bdud 'joms rin po che, "bdud 'dul dbang drug rdo rje gro lod kyi rdzogs rim ka dag gi khrid yig ye shes snang ba," 427.

53. Tib. *gzhi la sgro 'dogs chod pa lta ba'i gdengs.* Sourced from rang byung rdo rje, *nges, don phyag rgya chen po'i smon lam dang,* 4.

54. Dilgo Khyentse Rinpoche, *The Heart Treasure of the Enlightened Ones,* 9.

55. Tib. *de don yengs med du bsgom pa ni sgom pa.* Sourced from kar ma pa dbang phyug rdo rje, "phyag-chen ma-rig mun-sel."

56. Tib. *sgom pas nyams sub lang ba.* Sourced from bdud 'joms rin po che, "bdud 'dul dbang drug rdo rje gro lod kyi rdzogs rim ka dag gi khrid yig ye shes snang ba," 427.

57. Tib. *sgom pa la brten nyams myong skye.* Sourced from dbang phyug rdo rje, "lhan cig skyes sbyor gyi zab khrid nges don rgya mtsho'i snying po 'phrin las 'od 'phro," in *karma pa sku phreng rim byon gyi gsung 'bum phyogs bsgrigs, vol.* 85 (Lha sa: dpal brtsegs bod yig dpe rnying zhib 'jug khang, 2013), 434.

58. Tib. *de la ma yengs skyong ba sgom pa'i gnad.* Sourced from rang byung rdo rje, *nges don phyag rgya chen po'i smon lam dang,* 4.

59. Dilgo Khyentse Rinpoche, *The Heart Treasure of the Enlightened Ones,* 9.

60. Tib. *spyod pas rgyun skyong.* Sourced from bdud 'joms rin po che, "bdud 'dul dbang drug rdo rje gro lod kyi rdzogs rim ka dag gi khrid yig ye shes snang ba," 427.

61. Tib. *spyod pa bzhi gang rung skyong ba spyod pa dang.* Sourced from kar ma pa dbang phyug rdo rje, "phyag-chen ma-rig mun-sel."

62. Tib. *dwags po rin po che,* also known as *sgam po pa bsod nams rin chen,* c. 1079–1159.

63. Tib. *de la rgyun du gnas pa spyod pa yin.* Sourced from dbang phyug rdo rje, "lhan cig skyes sbyor gyi zab khrid nges don rgya mtsho'i snying po 'phrin las 'od 'phro," 434.

64. *The Hundred Thousand Songs of Milarepa, Volume 1*, 72.

65. Yeshe Tsogyal, *The Lotus Born*, 286; Chökyi Nyima Rinpoche, *The Union of Mahamudra and Dzogchen*, 239.

66. Tib. *'ba' r aba*, c. 1310–1391.

67. Tib. *rgyun du spyod pas spyod pa yin*. Sourced from dbang phyug rdo rje, "lhan cig skyes sbyor gyi zab khrid nges don rgya mtsho'i snying po 'phrin las 'od 'phro," 436.

68. Tib. *de nyid la spyod pas spyod pa*. Sourced from dbang phyug rdo rje, "lhan cig skyes sbyor gyi zab khrid nges don rgya mtsho'i snying po 'phrin las 'od 'phro," 436.

69. Thubten Jinpa, "From Value to Action: A Buddhist Perspective," in *Ecology, Ethics, and Interdependence: The Dalai Lama in Conversation with Leading Thinkers on Climate Change*, ed. John Dunne and Daniel Goleman (Somerville: Wisdom, 2018), 202–4.

70. Tib. *phag mo gru pa*, c. 1110–1170.

71. Tib. *spyod pa shugs las byung bag lang rgan chu btung ba lta bu zhig dgos*. Sourced from dbang phyug rdo rje, "lhan cig skyes sbyor gyi zab khrid nges don rgya mtsho'i snying po 'phrin las 'od 'phro," 436.

72. Tib. *bya rtsol med na spyod pa'i rgyal po yin*. Sourced from dbang phyug rdo rje, "lhan cig skyes sbyor gyi zab khrid nges don rgya mtsho'i snying po 'phrin las 'od 'phro," 436.

73. For a comparison of Buddhist moral phenomenology and the ethic-of-care tradition, see Simonds, "Toward a Buddhist Ecological Ethic of Care."

74. Tib. *dbu rdzogs phyag gsum bsdams pa rnams ston pas | drin can bla ma nying dbus su bzhugs shig*. Sourced from zhabs dkar tshogs drug rang grol, *'jam dbyangs sprul pa'i glegs bam*, 432–33. For an alternate translation, see Rangdrol, *The Emanated Scripture of Manjushri*, 132.

75. Shabkar Tsogdrug Rangdrol, "The View, Meditation, and Action of Mahamudra," in *Perfect Clarity: A Tibetan Buddhist Anthology of Mahamudra and Dzogchen*, trans. Erik Pema Kunsang (Kathmandu: Rangjung Yeshe, 2012), 43.

76. Tib. *nges don gyi lta sgom nyams su lent shul ji lta bar ston pa rdo rje'i mdo 'dzin*.

77. Tib. *bden gnyis zung 'jug mtha' bral dbu ma dang | gnas lugs ma bcos ye shes phyag rgya che | gdod ma'i kun bzang ka dag rdzogs chen rnams | ma lus dgongs pa gcig tu mthun pa'i don*. Sourced from rtse le sna tshogs rang grol, "nges don gyi lta sgom nyams su lent shul ji lta bar ston pa rdo rje'i mdo 'dzin," *rtse le sna tshogs rang grol gyi gsung gdams zab phyogs bsgrigs*, vol. 1 (Kathmandu: Khenpo shedup tenzin and lama thinley Namgyal, 2007), 13. For an alternate translation, see Tsele Natsok Rangdrol, *Heart Lamp: Lamp of Mahamudra & The Heart of the Matter*, trans. Erik Pema Kunsang (Kathmandu: Rangjung Yeshe, 2009), 107.

78. Tib. *'ga' zhig gis ni shin tu khyad yod par / gsung ba'ng yod la 'gag don snying po ni / lta ba'i rang bzhin nyid ni mthun na yang / blo yis bcos dang ma bcos khyad par ram / zhe 'dod der 'dzin yod med khyad par ni.* Sourced from rtse le sna tshogs rang grol, "nges don gyi lta sgom nyams su lent shul ji lta bar ston pa rdo rje'i mdo 'dzin," 8–9. For an alternate translation, see Tsele Natsok Rangdrol, *Heart Lamp*, 101–2.

79. Chökyi Nyima Rinpoche, *The Union of Mahamudra and Dzogchen*, 40.

80. Ogyen Trinley Dorje, *Interconnected: Embracing Life in Our Global Society* (Somerville: Wisdom, 2018), 138–39.

# Chapter 4

1. Tib. *sgom rim.*

2. Tib. *pad+ma'i ngang tshul*, c. 740–95.

3. Tib. *bsam yas*

4. Van Shaik uses *Zen* out of convenience for an English audience who is likely more familiar with the term than *Chan*, which was the Chinese school represented in Lhasa at the time. Japanese Zen developed out of Chinese Chan and hence shares many of the same assumptions, approaches, and practices.

5. Sam Van Shaik, *Tibet: A History* (New Haven: Yale University Press), 37.

6. Van Shaik, *Tibet*, 37.

7. Tib. *zhi bu 'tsho*, c. 725–88.

8. Tib. *hwa shang.*

9. Van Shaik, *Tibet*, 38.

10. R. A. Stein, *Tibetan Civilization* (Stanford: Stanford University Press, 1972), 66–67.

11. Van Shaik, *Tibet*, 39.

12. Tib. *klong chen pa*, 1308–63

13. Sam Van Shaik, "The Great Perfection and the Chinese Monk: rNying-ma-pa Defences of Hwa-Shang Mahāyāna in the Eighteenth Century," in *Buddhist Studies Review* 20, no. 2 (2003).

14. Tib. *gnubs chen sangs rgyas ye shes*, fl. ninth century CE.

15. Yaroslav Komarovski, *Tibetan Buddhism and Mystical Experience* (Oxford: Oxford University Press, 2015), 135.

16. Tib. *sems rtse gcig tu gnas pa . . . thugs sgom zer ba sogs la'ngo.* Sourced from Tharchin, [*Tibetan–Tibetan Dictionary*], vol. 1, 568.

17. Tib. *zhi gnas de ni rnyed pa la sogs pa la 'dod pa la mi lta zhing tshul khrims la legs par gnas la sdug bsngal la sogs pa dang du len pa'i dang tshul can du gyur la brtson 'grus brtsams na shin tu myur du 'grub bo / de bas na*

*'phags pa dgongs pa nges par 'grel ba la sogs pa las kyang sbyin pa la sogs pa gong ma'i yang gong ma'i rgyu nyid yin par bstan to.* Sourced from pad+ma'i ngang tshul, "sgom rim dang po," in *sgom rim thog mtha' bar gsum dang rim gyis 'jug pa'i bsgom don sogs* (Gangtok: gonpo tseten, 1977), 52–53.

18. Tib. *ting 'dzin tshogs.* Samādhi is the Sanskrit for concentration, deep contemplation, or meditative stabilization.

19. Tsong–kha–pa, *Calming the Mind and Discerning the Real: Buddhist Meditation and the Middle View from the Lam Rim Chen Mo,* trans. Alex Wayman (New York: Columbia University Press, 1978), 98.

20. Tsong–kha–pa, *Calming the Mind and Discerning the Real,* 98–99.

21. Tib. *de la thog mar re zhig mdor bsdu na rnam pa ji snyed kyis rnam par dpyad pa dbya ba dngos po mtha' dag 'du bar 'gyur ba'i dngos po gang yin pa de la sems gzhag par bya'o / dngos po 'dus pa ni gzugs can dang / gzugs can ma yin pa'i bye brag gis rnam pa gnyis te.* Sourced from: pad+ma'i ngang tshul, "sgom rim dang po," 54.

22. Tib. *de la thog mar re zhig zhi gnas bsgrub par bya ste / phyi rol gyi yul la rnam par gyeng ba zhi gnas nang du dmigs pa la rgyun du rang gi ngang gis 'jug la dga' ba dang shin tu sbyangs pa dang ldan pa'i sems nyid la gnas pa ni zhi gnas zhes bya'o.* Sourced from pad+ma'i ngang tshul, "sgom rim bar ba," in *sgom rim thog mtha' bar gsum dang rim gyis 'jug pa'i bsgom don sogs* (gangtok: gonpo tseten, 1977), 147–48.

23. Tsong–kha–pa, *Calming the Mind and Discerning the Real,* 141–42.

24. Tib. *sems gnas thabs dgu'i sgo nas zhi gnas sgrub tshul la dang po 'jog pa ni / phyi rol la g.yeng ba'i sems bsdus te dmigs rten gyis steng du sems 'jog / gnyis pa rgyun du 'jog pa ni / bzhag pa'i dmigs rten de nyid las gzhan du mi yengs par dmigs pa de la rgyun du 'jog / gsum pa slan te 'jog pa ni / brjed ngas kyi dbang gis phyi rol du g.yeng na de shes par byas nas slar dmigs rten de nyid la slan te 'jog / bzhi pa nye bar 'jog pa ni / sems rang bzhin gyis rgya che ba'i yang nas yang du nang du bsdus te phra bar byas nye bar 'jog / lnga pa dul bar byed pa ni / ting 'dzin gyis yon tan bsam nas ting 'dzin la dga' bas sems dul bar byed / drug pa zhi par byed pa ni / rnam g.yengs la skyon du bltas nas ting 'dzin la mi dga' ba zhi bar byed / bdun pa rnam par zhi bar byed pa ni / chags sems dang yid mi bde byid rmugs sogs las byung pa rnam par zhi bar byed / brgyud pa rtse gcig tu 'jog pa ni / rab tu 'bad nas bying rgod kyi bar chad pa med pa byas rgyun chag su ting nge 'dzin la rtse gcig tu 'jog par byed / dgu pa mnyam par 'jog pa ni / bying rgod kyi rnam par g.yen ba thams cad dang bral nas / 'bad med lhun grub tu ting nge 'dzin la ngam ngam shugs kyi 'jug pa'i tshe rtsol ba'i 'du shes med par btang snyom su glod nas mnyam par 'jog pa'o.* Sourced from: zhabs dkar tshogs drug rang drol, *'jam dbyans sprul pa'i glegs bam,* 367–68. For an alternate translation, see Shabkar Tsogdruk Rangdrol, *The Emanated Scripture of Manjushri,* 89–90.

25. Tib. *las dang po pa'i rnam par g.yeng ba'i nyes pa bsal ba'i phyir re zhig 'dus pa de la ni dmigs pa'i rigs so / gang gi tshe yid la byed pa khugs par gyur pa de'i tshe phung po dang khams la sogs pa'i bye brag gis rgyas par yang dmigs par byed pa kho na ste.* Sourced from pad+ma'i ngang tshul, "sgom rim dang po," 54.

26. Tsong–kha–pa, *Calming the Mind and Discerning the Real,* 109.

27. Tsong–kha–pa, *Calming the Mind and Discerning the Real,* 109.

28. Tsong–kha–pa, *Calming the Mind and Discerning the Real,* 111.

29. Tsong–kha–pa, *Calming the Mind and Discerning the Real,* 106.

30. Tsong–kha–pa, *Calming the Mind and Discerning the Real,* 112.

31. Tib. *sngon 'gro.*

32. Daniel Aitken and Jetsunma Tenzin Palmo, "Jetsunma Tenzin Palmo: Emptiness, Dzogchen, and Women in Buddhism," *Wisdom Podcast* (Somerville: Wisdom, 2021).

33. Daniel Aitken and Jetsunma Tenzin Palmo, "Jetsunma Tenzin Palmo."

34. Tsong–kha–pa, *Calming the Mind and Discerning the Real,* 112.

35. Chöden Rinpoche, *Mastering Meditation,* 104.

36. Tib. *byang chub lam gyi sgron ma.*

37. Tib. *zhi gnas grub pa ma yin pas / mngon shes 'byung bar mi 'gyur bas / de phyir zhi gnas bsgrub pa'I phyir / yang dang yang du 'bad par bya / zhi gnas yan lag rnam nyams pas / rab tu 'bad de bsgom byas kyang / lo na stong phrag dag gis kyang / ting 'dzin 'grub par mi 'gyur ro.* Sourced from Richard Sherburne, *The Complete Works of Atīśa Śrī Dīpaṁkara Jñāna, Jo–Bo–rJe: The Lamp for the Path and Commentary, Together with the Newly Translated Twenty–Five Key Texts* (New Delhi: Adiya Prakashan, 2000), 12. For an alternate translation, see Sherburne, *The Complete Works of Atīśa Śrī Dīpaṁkara Jñāna,* 13.

38. Even if Choden Rinpoche is correct when he notes, "Given the apparent centrality of the dhyanas and formless absorptions in Buddhist practice in general and Mahāyāna practice in particular, many readers may be surprised to see hardly any mention of them in Tibetan practice texts." While the particulars of the meditative states of absorption are not at the fore of Tibetan practice texts, instructions for actualizing *samatha* are still a present and important part of its meditative system. See Chöden Rinpoche, *Mastering Meditation,* 14.

39. Tib. *'di ltar shes pa'i snang ba byung bas kun tu rmongs pa'i sa bon shin tu spong bar 'gyur ro / de lta ma yin na mu ste gas can rnams kyi bzhin du ting nge 'dzin tsam gyis nyon mongs pa spong bar mi 'gyur ro.* Sourced from pad+ma'i ngang tshul, "sgom rim dang po," 54.

40. Tsong–kha–pa, *Calming the Mind and Discerning the Real,* 174.

41. Tsong–kha–pa, *Calming the Mind and Discerning the Real*, 176.

42. Tib. *shing rta chen po.*

43. Longchen Rabjam, *The Practice of Dzogchen: Longchen Rabjam's Writings on the Great Perfection*, trans. Tulku Thondup, ed. Harold Talbott (Boston: Snow Lion, 2014), 278.

44. Longchen Rabjam, *The Practice of Dzogchen*, 277.

45. Longchen Rabjam, *The Practice of Dzogchen*, 279.

46. Longchen Rabjam, *The Practice of Dzogchen*, 279.

47. Longchen Rabjam, *The Practice of Dzogchen*, 281.

48. Longchen Rabjam, *The Practice of Dzogchen*, 282.

49. Longchen Rabjam, *The Practice of Dzogchen*, 282–83.

50. Longchen Rabjam, *The Practice of Dzogchen*, 287.

51. Longchen Rabjam, *The Practice of Dzogchen*, 287.

52. Tib. *sgyu ma'i dpe brgyud.*

53. Tib. *sgyu ma ngal gso.*

54. Tib. *dri za.*

55. For an exposition of these eight examples in English, see Longchenpa, *Finding Rest in Illusion: The Trilogy of Rest, Volume 3*, trans. Padmakara Translation Group (Boulder: Shambhala, 2019).

56. Longchen Rabjam, *The Practice of Dzogchen*, 288.

57. Tib. *dbyig gnyen*, c. 316–96.

58. Tib. *chos mngon pa'i mdzod.*

59. Vasubandhu, *Abhidharmakośabhasyam of Vasubandhu*, ed. P. Pradhan (Patna: Jayaswal Institute, 1975), 341–42.

60. Khensur Jampa Tegchok, *Practical Ethics, Profound Emptiness*, 45.

61. Tib. *dang por rgya cher thos pa mang du btsal / bar du gzhung lugs thams cad gdams par shar / tha mar nyin mtshan kun tu nyams su blangs / kun kyang bstan pa rgyas pa'i ched du bsngos.* Sourced from Georges B. J. Dreyfus, *The Sound of Two Hands Clapping: The Education of a Tibetan Buddhist Monk* (Berkeley: University of California Press, 2003), 371.

62. *The Life of Shabkar: The Autobiography of a Tibetan Yogi*, trans. Matthieu Ricard (Ithaca: Snow Lion, 2003), 128.

63. Tib. *thos pa las byung ba'i shes rab, bsam byung las byung ba'i shes rab, sgom byung gi shes rab.* Dreyfus, *The Sound of Two Hands Clapping*, 165–66.

64. "Acumen" here is Dreyfus's translation of the word *shes rab*, which is typically parsed as "wisdom." It can also be translated as "knowledge, insight, discrimination, intelligence, and understanding." He is using "wisdom" because of the mystical connotations of the term, which detract from the intellectual nature of *shes rab*.

65. Dreyfus, *The Sound of Two Hands Clapping*, 165.

66. Dreyfus, *The Sound of Two Hands Clapping*, 165.

67. Dreyfus, *The Sound of Two Hands Clapping*, 166.

68. Dreyfus, *The Sound of Two Hands Clapping*, 166.

69. Dreyfus, *The Sound of Two Hands Clapping*, 166.

70. Dreyfus, *The Sound of Two Hands Clapping*, 166.

71. Dreyfus, *The Sound of Two Hands Clapping*, 166.

72. Tib. *chos kyi grags pa,* fl. seventh century C.E.

73. John Dunne, "Realizing the Unreal: Dharmakīrti's Theory of Yogic Perception," in *Journal of Indian Philosophy* 34, no. 6 (2006), 514.

74. Anne C. Klein, *Knowledge and Liberation: Tibetan Buddhist Epistemology in Support of Transformative Religious Experience* (Ithaca: Snow Lion, 1986), 28.

75. Klein, *Knowledge and Liberation*, 120.

76. Klein, *Knowledge and Liberation*, 120.

77. Klein, *Knowledge and Liberation*, 120.

78. Klein, *Knowledge and Liberation*, 120.

79. Klein, *Knowledge and Liberation*, 215.

80. Klein, *Knowledge and Liberation*, 121.

81. Klein, *Knowledge and Liberation*, 32.

82. Klein, *Knowledge and Liberation*, 121.

83. Klein, *Knowledge and Liberation*, 182.

84. Klein, *Knowledge and Liberation*, 206.

85. Sourced from gser mdog pan chen shakya mchog lden, "shing rta chen po'i srol gnyis kyi rnam par dbye ba bshad nas nges don gcig tu bsgrub pa'I bstan bcos kyi rgyas 'grel," in *Two Controversial Mādhyamika Treatises*, ed. Trayang Samten and Jamyang Samten (New Delhi: n.p. 1974), 390.

86. Klein, *Knowledge and Liberation*, 15.

87. William James, *The Varieties of Religious Experience*, ed. Matthew Bradley (Oxford: Oxford University Press, 2012), 290–91.

88. James, The *Varieties of Religious Experience*, 291.

89. Tib. *'khrul med lta ba dngos sur togs pa'i rjes / de nas bsgom pus nyams su len pa'i skabs / rang ngo 'phrod pa'i lta ba'i ngang de la / bzhugs yun bsring nas 'bad pas bsgom pa yin.* Sourced from: yang thang rin po che, "lta sgom spyod gsum mdor bsdus."

90. James, *The Varieties of Religious Experience*, 291.

91. Klein, *Knowledge and Liberation*, 13.

92. Komarovski, *Tibetan Buddhism and Mystical Experience*, 4.

93. Much has been written about Zen and mystical experience and a general pan–Buddhist approach to mysticism but little about Tibetan Buddhism specifically.

94. Klein, *Knowledge and Liberation*, 14.

95. There are of course more divisions in the study of mysticism, including dualistic and monistic experience, apophatic and kataphatic

experience, theurgic and nontheurgic experience, and so forth. However, for our purposes, these two are the most relevant, so the discussion will be limited to them.

96. See Aldous Huxley, *The Perennial Philosophy* (New York: Harper & Brothers Publishers, 1945).

97. W. T. Stace, *Mysticism and Philosophy* (London: Macmillan, 1961), 79.

98. Stace, *Mysticism and Philosophy*, 79.

99. Stace, *Mysticism and Philosophy*, 86.

100. Stace, *Mysticism and Philosophy*, 86.

101. See *The Problem of Pure Consciousness*, ed. Robert K. C. Forman (Oxford: Oxford University Press, 1990).

102. Steven T. Katz, "Language, Epistemology, and Mysticism," in *Mysticism and Philosophical Analysis*, ed. Steven T. Katz (Oxford: Oxford University Press, 1978), 26.

103. Katz, "Language, Epistemology, and Mysticism," 27; emphasis added.

104. Roland Fischer, "A Cartography of the Ecstatic and Meditative States," in *Science* 174, no. 4012 (1971): 2.

105. Fischer, "A Cartography of the Ecstatic and Meditative States," 2.

106. Indeed, Forman makes use of this spectrum in his advocacy for pure consciousness events. See: Robert K. C. Forman, "Introduction: Mysticism, Constructivism, and Forgetting" in *The Problem of Pure Consciousness*, ed. Robert K. C. Forman (Oxford: Oxford University Press, 1990), 5–9.

107. Forman, "Introduction," 28; emphasis in original.

108. Robert K. C. Forman, *Mysticism, Mind, Consciousness* (Albany: State University of New York Press, 1999), 151.

109. Forman, *Mysticism, Mind, Consciousness*, 170.

110. Forman, *Mysticism, Mind, Consciousness*, 167.

111. For example, the article "Mystical Experience among Tibetan Buddhists: The Common Core Thesis Revisited" surveys 240 Tibetan Buddhists and seeks to find statistically significant evidence for the validation of the perennialist thesis. However, in doing so, the Chen, Hood, Yang, and Watson make strange claims about Tibetan Buddhism that bring its relevance into question such as when they relate Tibetan Buddhism to Chinese Pure Land Buddhism and write: "This characteristic [of invoking Amitābha] obviously distinguishes it from Tibetan Buddhism, which encourages meditative practice rather than knowledge acquisition and upholds no one God as more authoritative than others." Both calling Amitābha a God (with a capital G) and ascribing any sort of authority to a "God' demonstrates a fundamental misunderstanding of the tradition, and claiming that Tibetan Buddhism is uninterested in knowledge acquisition is a farcical

representation of a tradition with such a rich scholastic tradition. See Zhuo Chen, Ralph W. Hood Jr., Lijun Yang, P. J. Watson, "Mystical Experience among Tibetan Buddhists: The Common Core Thesis Revisited," *Journal for the Scientific Study of Religion* 50, no. 2 (2011): 337

112. Komarovski, *Tibetan Buddhism and Mystical Experience*, 5.

113. Komarovski, *Tibetan Buddhism and Mystical Experience*, 95–96.

114. Komarovski, *Tibetan Buddhism and Mystical Experience*, 102.

115. Komarovski, *Tibetan Buddhism and Mystical Experience*, 96.

116. Komarovski, *Tibetan Buddhism and Mystical Experience*, 96.

117. Forman, *Mysticism, Mind, Consciousness*, 22.

118. Komarovski, *Tibetan Buddhism and Mystical Experience*, 96.

119. Komarovski, *Tibetan Buddhism and Mystical Experience*, 76.

120. Tib. *lam.*

121. A common list of these factors numbers thirty seven and includes the four foundations of mindfulness, the four right efforts, the four bases of power, the five faculties, the five strengths, the seven factors of enlightenment, and the eightfold path. These thirty-seven factors can be found in more scholastic texts such as Gampopa's *Jewel Ornament of Liberation* and yogic texts such as Jigten Sumgön's *Single Intent*, which states, "The thirty-seven factors of enlightenment are present in the core of a Sugata." See Jigten Sumgon, *Gongchig: The Single Intent, the Sacred Dharma, with Commentary Entitled "The Lamp Dispelling the Darkness" by Rigdzin Chökyi Drakpa* (Munich: Otter Verlag, 2009), 14.

122. Komarovski, *Tibetan Buddhism and Mystical Experience*, 13.

123. Komarovski, *Tibetan Buddhism and Mystical Experience*, 241.

124. Komarovski, *Tibetan Buddhism and Mystical Experience*, 241.

# Chapter 5

1. Woodhouse et al., "Religious Relationships with the Environment in a Tibetan Rural Community."

2. See Elverskog, *The Buddha's Footprint*, 85.

3. Charles S. Brown and Ted Toadvine, "Eco-Phenomnology: An Introduction," *Eco-Phenomenology: Back to the Earth Itself*, ed. Charles S. Brown and Ted Toadvine (Albany: State University of New York Press, 2003), xii–xiii.

4. Quoted in Brown and Toadvine, "Eco-Phenomenology," 11.

5. Neil Evernden, *The Natural Alien* (Toronto: University of Toronto Press, 1993), 34.

6. David Wood, "What Is Ecophenomenology?," *Research in Phenomenology* 31 (2002).

7. Macy, "The Ecological Self: Postmodern Ground for Right Action," 445.

8. David Abram, *The Spell of the Sensuous: Perception and Language in a More-Than-Human World* (New York: Vintage Books, 1997), x.

9. Charles S. Brown, "The Real and the Good: Phenomenology and the Possibility of an Axiological Rationality," in *Eco-Phenomenology: Back to the Earth Itself*, ed. Charles S. Brown and Ted Toadvine (Albany: State University of New York Press, 2003), 10.

10. Brown, "The Real and the Good," 11.

11. Brown, "The Real and the Good," 12.

12. Brown, "The Real and the Good," 14.

13. Brown, "The Real and the Good," 15.

14. Brown, "The Real and the Good," 15.

15. Brown, "The Real and the Good," 16.

16. Don E. Marietta Jr., "Back to Earth with Reflection and Ecology," in *Eco-Phenomenology: Back to the Earth Itself*, ed. Charles S. Brown and Ted Toadvine (Albany: State University of New York Press, 2003), 121.

17. Marietta Jr., "Back to Earth with Reflection and Ecology," 128–29.

18. Marietta Jr., "Back to Earth with Reflection and Ecology," 124.

19. Arne Naess, "The World of Concrete Contents," *Inquiry* 28 (1985): 424.

20. Rockstrom et al., "A Safe Operating Space for Humanity."

21. Martina Igini, "'Impossible Not to Feel Hopeless'—Guardian Survey of IPCC Scientists Reveals 1.5C Goal out of Reach," *Earth.org* (Hong Kong, May 9, 2024).

22. Humans are, of course, also animals, and many of those working on animal philosophy and animal rights like to use the terms *human animal* and *nonhuman animal* to make this mere difference of degree explicit. While I appreciate the performative aspect of this distinction, I will simply use *human* and *animal* in my work for the sake of clarity, though I do acknowledge that the difference in these categories is quite tenuous.

23. Jim Mason, *An Unnatural Order: Uncovering the Roots of Our Domination of Nature and Each Other* (New York: Simon & Schuster, 1993), 163.

24. Singer, *Animal Liberation*, 7.

25. Mason, *An Unnatural Order*, 188–89.

26. Karen J. Warren, "The Power and the Promise of Ecofeminism, Revisited," in *Environmental Philosophy: From Animal Rights to Radical Ecology*, ed. Michael Zimmerman, J. Baird Callicott, Karen J. Warren, Irene Klaver, and John Clark (Upper Saddle River: Pearson Prentice Hall, 2005), 252.

27. David Naguib Pellow, *Total Liberation: The Power and Promise of Animal Rights and the Radical Earth Movement* (Minneapolis: University of Minnesota Press, 2014), 20.

28. Morton, *Dark Ecology*, 11.

29. Morton, *Hyperobjects*, 48.

30. Morton, *Hyperobjects*, 27.

31. Klein, *Knowledge and Liberation*, 15.

32. Kari Marie Norgaard, *Living in Denial: Climate Change, Emotions, and Everyday Life* (Cambridge: MIT Press, 2011), 64–65.

33. Paul Kellstedt, Sammy Zahran, and Arnold Vedlitz, "Personal Efficacy, the Information Environment, and Attitudes toward Global Warming and Climate Change in the United States," *Risk Analysis* 28, no. 1 (2008): 120.

34. Norgaard, *Living in Denial*, 68.

35. Norgaard, *Living in Denial*, 68.

36. Norgaard, *Living in Denial*, 89.

37. Norgaard, *Living in Denial*, 91.

38. As seen in the work of Geoffrey Barstow, who traces this move toward vegetarianism in Tibetan contexts that remain predominantly *non-vegetarian* today. Even in Buddhist settings such as China, which expressly mandate vegetarianism for monastics, these mandates were relatively late developments in the history of Buddhist thought. See Barstow, *Food of Sinful Demons*; Eric M. Greene, "A Reassessment of the Early History of Chinese Buddhist Vegetarianism," *Asia Major* 29, no. 1 (2016).

39. For a robust account of this early Buddhist understanding of animals, see Reiko Ohnuma, *Unfortunate Destiny: Animals in the Indian Buddhist Imagination* (Oxford: Oxford University Press, 2017.

40. Tib. *sangs rgyas rnams kyis chos bstan pa / bden pa gnyis la yang dag brten / 'jig rten kun rdzob bden pa dang / dam pa'i don gyi bden pa'o.* Sourced from Nāgārjuna, *The Root Stanzas of the Middle Way*, 158.

41. Tib. *'di kun ngo bos stong ba dang / 'di las 'di 'bras 'byung ba yi / nges pa gnyis po phan tshun du / gegs med par ni grogs byed pa.* Excerpted from tsong kha pa blo bzang grags pa, "rten 'grel stod pa," 263. For an alternate translation, see Lobsang Gyatso and Woodhouse, *Tsongkhapa's Praise for Dependent Relativity*, 4.

42. For example, in song 11 of his work *Flight of the Garuda*, Shabkar sings, "From the natural expression of this luminous and empty mind, an unlimited variety of appearances arise. Though these arise, like reflections in a mirror, there is no duality, since they are one in the state of being empty. This is how appearances are empty." See Shabkar, *The Flight of the Garuda*, trans. Erik Pema Kunsang (Kathmandu: Rangjung Yeshe, 1988), 45.

43. Tib. *bla ma chos kyi rgyal mtshan.*

44. This particular piece titled "The Rediscovery of Turtle Island" was originally a talk given to the University of California Humanities Research Institute in 1992, though he updated and revised his talk for publication.

45. Gary Snyder, *A Place in Space: Ethics, Aesthetics, and Watersheds* (Washington: Counterpoint, 1995), 246.

46. Martine Batchelor, "Even the Stones Smile: Selections from the Scriptures," in *Buddhism and Ecology*, ed. Martine Batchelor and Kerry Brown (London: Cassell, 1992).

47. Cooper and James, *Buddhism, Virtue and Environment*, 97.

48. Cooper and James, *Buddhism, Virtue and Environment*, 131.

49. Cooper and James, *Buddhism, Virtue and Environment*, 146–47.

50. Schmithausen, *Buddhism and Nature*, 32.

51. Clark, "On Being None with Nature," 12.

52. Ogyen Trinley Dorje, H.H. 17th Gyalwang Karmapa, "Walking the Path of Environmental Buddhism through Compassion and Emptiness," *Conservation Biology* 25, no. 6 (2011): 1094.

53. Ogyen Trinley Dorje, "Walking the Path of Environmental Buddhism through Compassion and Emptiness," 1095.

54. Ogyen Trinley Dorje, "Walking the Path of Environmental Buddhism through Compassion and Emptiness," 1095.

55. Ogyen Trinley Dorje, "Walking the Path of Environmental Buddhism through Compassion and Emptiness," 1095.

56. Thich Nhat Hanh, *The Heart of the Buddha's Teaching* (New York: Broadway Books, 1999), 226.

57. Thich Nhat Hanh, *The Heart of the Buddha's Teaching*, 225–26.

58. Thich Nhat Hanh, *The Heart of the Buddha's Teaching*, 90.

59. Thich Nhat Hanh, "The Five Mindfulness Trainings," *Plum Village* (Plum Village, 2025).

60. Christopher Ives, "Resources for a Buddhist Environmental Ethic," *Journal of Buddhist Ethics* 20 (2013), 552.

61. The ultimate validity of cause and effect is well challenged in Nāgārjuna's *Mūlamadhyamakakārikā*, though the Madhyamaka school nonetheless holds it to be conventionally true.

62. Tib. *yid ches pa'I dad pa ni / yul las dang 'bras bu dang sdug bsngal gyi bden pa dang kun 'byung gi bden pa la brten nas skye ba yin te / de yang dge ba'i las byi 'bras bus 'dod khams kyi bde ba 'byung bar yid ches / mi dge ba'i las kyi 'bras bus 'dod khams kyi sdug bsngal 'byung bar yid ches.* Sourced from: sgam po pa bsod nams rin chen, *dwags po thar rgyan* (Lha sa: ser gtsug nang bstan dpe rnying 'tshol bsdu phyogs sgrig khang), 25. For an alternate translation, see sGam.po.pa, *The Jewel Ornament of Liberation*, trans. Herbert V. Guenther (Boston: Shambhala, 1986), 20.

63. Norgaard, *Living in Denial*, 68.

64. Tib. *sems can ni / 'gro ba / skye 'gro / sems ldan / skye ldan / skye bo / sems pa can / srog chags / shes ldan / lus ldan / skye bu ste ming gi rnam grangs.* Sourced from Gegen Dorje Tharchin, [Tibetan-Tibetan Dictionary], vol. 5, 924.

65. Tib. *bla ma chos kyi rgyal bsthan*, Mark Webber.

66. Lama Mark Webber, *Union of Loving-kindness and Emptiness* (n.p., 2011), 54–56.

67. Webber, *Union of Loving-Kindness and Emptiness*, 56–57.

68. Lambert Schmithausen, *The Problem of the Sentience of Plants in Earliest Buddhism* (Tokyo: International Institute for Buddhist Studies, 1991).

69. Peter Wohlleben, *The Hidden Life of Trees: What They Feel, How They Communicate*, trans. Jane Billinghurst (Vancouver: Greystone Books, 2016).

70. Monica Gagliano, Mavra Grimonprez, Martial Depczynski, and Michael Renton, "Tuned In: Plant Roots Use Sound to Locate Water," *Oecologia* 184, no. 1 (2017).

71. Simonds, "Expanding Sentience."

72. *The Life of Shabkar*, 18.

73. Quoted in Shabkar, *Food of Bodhisattvas: Buddhist Teachings on Abstaining from Meat*, trans. Padmakara Translation Group (Boston: Shambhala, 2004), 12.

74. Quoted in Barstow, *Food of Sinful Demons*, 82.

75. Barstow, *Food of Sinful Demons*, 82.

76. *A Feast of the Nectar of the Supreme Vehicle*, 14.

77. Barbara McDonald, "'Once You Know Something, You Can't Not Know It': An Empirical Look at Becoming Vegan," *Society & Animals* 8, no. 1 (2000): 6.

78. Ogyen Trinley Dorje, "Walking the Path of Environmental Buddhism through Compassion and Emptiness," 1096.

79. See James Powell, "Scientists Reach 100% Consensus on Anthropogenic Global Warming," *Bulletin of Science, Technology & Society* 37, no. 4 (2017); Mark Lynas, Benjamin Z. Houlton, and Simon Perry, "Greater than 99% Consensus on Human Caused Climate Change in the Peer-Reviewed Scientific Literature," *Environmental Research Letters* 16, no. 11 (2021).

80. For example, the lifestylism-versus-revolution debate in anarchist theory which extends to green and vegan anarchisms. See Brian A. Dominick, *Animal Liberation and Social Revolution* (n.p., 1997), 16–17; Brian A. Dominick, "Anarcho-Veganism Revisited," in *Anarchism and Animal Liberation: Essays on Complementary Elements of Total Liberation*, ed. Anthony J. Nocella II, Richard J. White, and Erika Cudworth (Jefferson: McFarland, 2015).

81. Katharine Hayhoe and Tia Nelson, "Climate Change: The Case for Hope and Healing with Katharine Hayhoe and Tia Nelson," *New York Public Library*. New York: New York Public Library, September 29, 2021.

82. Rhianna Schmunk, "595 People Were Killed by Heat in B.C. This Summer, New Figures from Coroner Show," *CBC News*. CBC News, November 1, 2021; Sandy Erni et al., "Exposure of the Canadian Wildland-Human Interface and Population to Wildland Fire, under Current and Future Climate Conditions," *Canadian Journal of Forest Research* 51, no. 9 (2021).

83. Arne Naess, "The Deep Ecological Movement: Some Philosophical Aspects," in *Deep Ecology for the 21st Century: Readings on the Philosophy and Practice of New Environmentalism*, ed. George Sessions (Boston: Shambhala, 1995), 68.

84. This position of deep ecology as ontology is defended in Warwick Fox, *Approaching Deep Ecology: A Response to Richard Sylban's Critique of Deep Ecology* (Hobart: University of Tasmania Environmental Studies Occasional Paper 20, 1986).

85. Naess, *Ecology, Community and Lifestyle*, 166.

86. Naess, *Ecology, Community and Lifestyle*, 165.

87. Naess, *Ecology, Community and Lifestyle*, 163.

88. Slavoj Žižek, *Heaven in Disorder* (New York: OR Books, 2021), 69.

89. Another term to denote this tendency is *radical ecology*, which philosophers such as Carolyn Merchant and Frederic L. Bender use in place of *nonanthropocentric* or *deep ecology*. See Carolyn Merchant, *Radical Ecology: The Search for a Livable World* (New York: Routledge, 1992); Frederic L. Bender, *The Culture of Extinction: Toward a Philosophy of Deep Ecology* (Amherst: Humanity Books, 2003), 339–80.

90. Vandana Shiva and Maria Miles, *Ecofeminism* (Halifax: Fernwood, 1993).

91. Ariel Salleh, *Ecofeminism as Politics: Nature, Marx and the Postmodern* (New York: St. Martins, 1997).

92. Leopold, *A Sand County Almanac*.

93. J. Baird Callicott, *In Defense of the Land Ethic: Essays in Environmental Philosophy* (Albany: State University of New York Press, 1989).

94. Pellow, *Total Liberation*.

95. Christopher N. Gamble, Joshua S. Hanan, and Thomas Nail, "What Is New Materialism?," *Angelaki* 24, no. 6 (2019): 111.

96. Gottfried Wilhelm Leibniz, "Specimen Dynamicum," in *Philosophical Papers and Letters, Volume 2*, trans. Leroy E. Loemker (London: Kluwer Academic, 1989), 445.

97. Jane Bennett, *Vibrant Matter: A Political Ecology of Things* (Durham: Duke University Press, 2010), vii.

98. Bennett, *Vibrant Matter*, vii.

99. Gamble, Hanan, and Nail, "What Is New Materialism?," 120.

100. Graham Harman, *Prince of Networks: Bruno Latour and Metaphysics* (Melbourne: re.press, 2009), 25.

101. Quoted in Gamble, Hanan, and Nail, "What Is New Materialism?," 121.

102. Steven Shaviro, *The Universe of Things: On Speculative Realism* (Minneapolis: University of Minnesota Press, 2014), 66–67.

103. Graham Harman, *Tool-Being: Heidegger and the Metaphysics of Objects* (New York: Open Court, 2011), 293.

104. Gamble, Hanan, and Nail, "What Is New Materialism?," 121.

105. Timothy Morton, "Here Comes Everything: The Promise of Object-Oriented Ontology," *Qui Parle: Critical Humanities and Social Studies* 19, no. 2 (2011): 177.

106. Morton, "Here Comes Everything," 165.

107. Gamble, Hanan, and Nail, "What Is New Materialism?," 122.

108. Gamble, Hanan, and Nail, "What Is New Materialism?," 122.

109. Gamble, Hanan, and Nail, "What Is New Materialism?," 122.

110. Gamble, Hanan, and Nail, "What Is New Materialism?," 123.

111. Karen Barad, *Meeting the Universe Halfway: Quantum Physics and the Entanglement of Matter and Meaning* (Durham: Duke University Press, 2007), 149.

112. Gamble, Hanan, and Nail, "What Is New Materialism?," 123.

113. Vicky Kirby, *Telling Flesh: The Substance of the Corporeal* (New York: Routledge, 1997), 127.

114. Vicky Kirby, *Quantum Anthropologies: Life at Large* (Durham: Duke University Press, 2011), x.

115. Bennett, *Vibrant Matter*, xi; emphasis in original.

116. Bennett, *Vibrant Matter*, 13.

117. Bennett, *Vibrant Matter*, 14.

118. Levi Bryant, Nick Srnicek, and Graham Harman, "Toward a Speculative Philosophy," *The Speculative Turn: Continental Realism and Materialism*, ed. Levi Bryant, Nick Srnicek, and Graham Harman (Melbourne: re.press, 2011), 3.

119. Morton, "Here Comes Everything," 163.

120. Morton, *Hyperobjects*, 183.

121. Morton, *Dark Ecology*, 159.

122. Timothy Morton, *Humankind: Solidarity with Nonhuman People* (New York: Verso, 2019), 139–40.

123. Barad, *Meeting the Universe Halfway*, 33.

124. Kirby, *Quantum Anthropologies*, 136.

125. Barad, *Meeting the Universe Halfway*, 392.

126. Barad, *Meeting the Universe Halfway*, 393.

127. Barad, *Meeting the Universe Halfway*, 394.

# Chapter 6

1. Aitken and Jetsunma Tenzin Palmo, "Jetsunma Tenzin Palmo: Emptiness, Dzogchen, and Women in Buddhism."

2. See Jenny Odell, *How to Do Nothing: Resisting the Attention Economy* (Brooklyn: Melville House, 2019).

3. Tsong-kha-pa, *Calming the Mind and Discerning the Real*, 98.

4. Tsong-kha-pa, *Calming the Mind and Discerning the Real*, 98–99.

5. Tsong-kha-pa, *Calming the Mind and Discerning the Real*, 109.

6. Aitken and Jetsunma Tenzin Palmo, "Jetsunma Tenzin Palmo: Emptiness, Dzogchen, and Women in Buddhism."

7. Tsong-kha-pa, *Calming the Mind, Discerning the Real*, 112.

8. These are the three main sources of the contemporary mindfulness movement. See Wilson, *Mindful America*, 13–42.

9. As taught in recent introduction classes for the general public by Khenpo Gyaltsen at Rangjung Yeshe Institute.

10. Khensur Jampa Tegchok, *Practical Ethics, Profound Emptiness*, 45.

11. Such as the Sakyapa and Tsongkhapa's Gelug school.

12. Klein, *Knowledge and Liberation*, 211.

13. Dreyfus, *The Sound of Two Hands Clapping*, 166.

14. Dreyfus, *The Sound of Two Hands Clapping*, 166.

15. Sarah M. Pike, *For the Wild: Ritual and Commitment in Radical Eco-Activism* (Oakland: University of California Press, 2017), 16.

16. Pike, *For the Wild*, 20.

17. Pike, *For the Wild*, 101.

18. Pike devotes an entire chapter to the role of early encounters with the more-than-human world as formative experiences in eco-activists in *For the Wild*. See Pike, "Childhood Landscapes of Wonder and Awe," *For the Wild*, 71–103.

19. Pike, *For the Wild*, 73.

20. There is, however, a great overlap between Indian spiritual practice and eco-activism by way of the Hare Krishnas and their presence in the hardcore punk movement. See Pike, " 'Liberation's Crusade Has Begun': Hare Krishna Hardcore Youth and Animal Rights Activism," in *For the Wild*, 137–61.

21. Donna J. Haraway, *Staying with the Trouble: Making Kin in the Cthulucene* (Durham: Duke University Press, 2016), 7.

22. Haraway, *Staying with the Trouble*, 7.

23. Haraway, *Staying with the Trouble*, 126–27.

24. Haraway, *Staying with the Trouble*, 7.

25. Odell, *How to Do Nothing*, xviii.

26. Odell, *How to Do Nothing*, 7.

27. Odell, *How to Do Nothing*, 7.

28. Odell, *How to Do Nothing*, 24.

29. Odell, *How to Do Nothing*, 125–26.

30. Odell, *How to Do Nothing*, 22.

31. I say *postural* to make a distinction between the meditative yogas we find in the Tibetan tradition, the *Upaniṣads*, and Patanjali's *Yoga Sūtra* and the more body-oriented practices that we can find in Tibetan traditions

of *rtsa rlung 'khrul 'khor*, the yoga of the *Haṭhayogapradīpikā*, and the modern postural yoga tradition emerging from the figure of Krishnamacarya in 1930s Mysore. See Mark Singleton, *Yoga Body: The Origins of Modern Posture Practice* (Oxford: Oxford University Press, 2010).

32. Such as the use of iboga in Gabon, datura in the Chumash, and Pituri in Australian indigenous cultures. See James W. Fernandez, *Bwiti: An Ethnography of the Religious Imagination in Africa* (Princeton: Princeton University Press, 2019); Richard B. Applegate, "The Datura Cult amongst the Chumash," *Journal of California Anthropology* 2, no. 1 (1975); Marlene Dobkin de Rios and Ronni Stachalek, "The *Duboisia* Genus, Australian Aborigines and Suggestibility," *Journal of Psychoactive Drugs* 31, no. 2 (1999).

33. Kenneth W. Tupper, Evan Wood, Richard Yensen, and Matthew W. Johnson, "Psychedelic Medicine: A Re-Emerging Therapeutic Paradigm," *Canadian Medical Association Journal* 187, no. 14 (2015).

34. Elsewhere, I've argued that the Tibetan framework of view, meditation, action should be used to inform clinical approaches to psychedelic therapy. See: Colin H. Simonds, *"View, Meditation, Action*: A Tibetan Framework to Inform Psychedelic-Assisted Therapy," *Journal of Psychedelic Studies* 7 (2023): 58–68.

35. Dzongsar Jamyang Khyentse, *What Makes You Not a Buddhist* (Boston: Shambhala Publications, 2007), 67.

36. Such as Spring Washam's "Lotus Vine Journeys" which merges the meditative tradition of the Insight Meditation Society and ayahuasca ceremony in Costa Rica.

37. Tib. *spyod pas rgyun skyong.* Sourced from: bdud 'joms rin po che, "bdud 'dul dbang drug rdo rje gro lod kyi rdzogs rim ka dag gi khrid yig ye shes snang ba," 427.

38. Tib. *spyod pa bzhi gang rung skyong ba spyod pa dang.* Sourced from kar ma pa dbang phyug rdo rje, "Phyag-chen ma-rig mun-sel."

39. Tib. *de la rgyun du gnas pa spyod pa yin.* Sourced from dbang phyug rdo rje, "lhan cig skyes sbyor gyi zab khrid nges don rgya mtsho'i snying po 'phrin las 'od 'phro," 434.

40. *The Hundred Thousand Songs of Milarepa, Volume 1,* 72.

41. Tib. *de nyid la spyod pas spyod pa.* Sourced from dbang phyug rdo rje, "lhan cig skyes sbyor gyi zab khrid nges don rgya mtsho'i snying po 'phrin las 'od 'phro," 436.

42. Yeshe Tsogyal, *The Lotus Born,* 286; Chökyi Nyima Rinpoche, *The Union of Mahamudra and Dzogchen,* 239.

43. Tib. *rgyun du spyod pas spyod pa yin.* Sourced from dbang phyug rdo rje, "lhan cig skyes sbyor gyi zab khrid nges don rgya mtsho'i snying po 'phrin las 'od 'phro," 436.

44. Tib. *spyod pa shugs las byung bag lang rgan chu btung ba lta bu zhig dgos.* Sourced from dbang phyug rdo rje, "lhan cig skyes sbyor gyi zab khrid nges don rgya mtsho'i snying po 'phrin las 'od 'phro," 436.

45. Thubten Jinpa, "From Value to Action: A Buddhist Perspective," 202–4.

46. Gruen, *Entangled Empathy*, 3.

47. Gruen, *Entangled Empathy*, 39.

48. That said, elsewhere in the text Gruen does somewhat explore an ontological basis for her ethic. Interestingly, to do this, she turns to Karen Barad and her performative new materialism that we briefly looked at in the previous chapter. Gruen writes,

> [Karen Barad's] Intra-actions are what makes those separate things possible in the first place. So the idea of "intra-action queers the familiar sense of causality (where one or more causal agents precede and produce an effect) and more generally unsettles the metaphysics of individualism (the belief that there are individually constituted agents or entities, as well as times and place)." There can be no individuals that exist prior to and separate from the entangled intra-actions that constitute them. But, importantly, the individual that emerges from her entanglements is distinctly constituted by particular intra-actions. understanding and reflection on our entanglements are part of what it takes to constitute our selves because there is no self or other prior to our intra-actions.

While Gruen simply uses this ontology as a foundation for her ethical argument, one might also see how an ethic like the one Gruen proposes could emerge from an experiential recognition of Barad's view in a moral phenomenological sense. See Gruen, *Entangled Empathy*, 65.

49. Gruen, *Entangled Empathy*, 63–64; emphasis added.

50. Gruen, *Entangled Empathy*, 66.

51. Gruen, *Entangled Empathy*, 3.

52. Gruen, *Entangled Empathy*, 7–8.

53. Timothy Morton, *The Ecological Thought* (Cambridge: Harvard University Press, 2010), 124.

54. The *prātimokṣa* vows, the *bodhisattva* vows, and the *samaya* vows.

55. See Daniel Holbrook, "Utilitarianism on Environmental Issues Reexamined," *International Journal of Applied Philosophy* 7, no.1 (1992); Mfonobong Udoudom, "The Value of Nature: Utilitarian Perspective," *Gnosi: An Interdisciplinary Journal of Human Theory and Praxis* 4, no. 1 (2021).

56. See Avi Brisman, "Environmental and Human Rights," *Encyclopedia of Criminology and Criminal Justice*, ed. Gerben Bruinsma and David Weisburd (New York: Springer, 2014); Yesudas Choondassery, "Rights-based Approach: The Hub of Sustainable Development," *Discourse and Communication for Sustainable Education* 8, no. 2 (2017).

57. Cooper and James, *Buddhism, Virtue and Environment*, 577.

58. Tib. *de gshegs snying po*.

59. Barbra Clayton, "Buddha's Maritime Nature: A Case Study in Shambhala Buddhist Environmentalism," *Journal of Buddhist Ethics* 20 (2013): 578.

60. Clayton, "Buddha's Maritime Nature," 579.

61. Clayton, "Buddha's Maritime Nature," 580.

62. Clayton, "Buddha's Maritime Nature," 581.

63. Clayton, "Buddha's Maritime Nature," 581.

64. Clayton, "Buddha's Maritime Nature," 586.

65. Clayton, "Buddha's Maritime Nature," 587.

66. Damien Keown, "Keynote One: Damien Keown," *Contemporary Perspective on Buddhist Ethics* (New York: Center for Buddhist Studies, 2007).

67. Clayton, "Buddha's Maritime Nature," 587.

68. Dalai Lama, "Routine Day," *His Holiness the 14th Dalai Lama of Tibet* (Office of His Holiness the Dalai Lama, n.d).

69. Abraham Vélez de Cea, "The Dalai Lama and the Nature of Buddhist Ethics," *Journal of Buddhist Ethics* 20 (2013): 532.

70. "The Nobel Peace Prize 1989," *The Nobel Prize* (Nobel Prize Outreach AB, 2024).

71. The 14th Dalai Lama, "Nobel Lecture," *The Nobel Prize* (Nobel Prize Outreach AB, 2024).

72. Dalai Lama, "Principal Commitments," *His Holiness the 14th Dalai Lama of Tibet* (Office of His Holiness the Dalai Lama, n.d.).

73. "Readout of the President's Meeting with His Holiness the XIV Dalai Lama," *The White House* (White House Office of the Press Secretary, 15 June 2016).

74. "The Dalai Lama with Greta Thunberg and Leading Scientists: A Conversation on the Crisis of Climate Feedback Loops," *Mind & Life Institute* (Mind & Life Institute, 2020). See also Susan Bauer-Wu, *A Future We Can Love: How We Can Reverse the Climate Crisis with the Power of Our Hearts and Minds* (Boulder: Shambhala, 2023).

75. His Holiness the Dalai Lama and Franz Alt, *Our Only Home: A Climate Appeal to the World* (London: Bloomsbury, 2020), 56.

76. Jason M. Wirth, *Mountains, Rivers, and the Great Earth: Reading Gary Snyder and Dōgen in an Age of Ecological Crisis* (Albany: State University of New York Press, 2017), xvii.

77. See: Gary Snyder, "Buddhist Anarchism," *Journal for the Protection of All Beings #1* (City Lights, 1961).

78. For an excellent, comprehensive look at Snyder's Buddhist-inspired eco-political vision, see David Landis Barnhill, "Great Earth Saṅgha: Gary Snyder's View of Nature as Community," in *Buddhism and Ecology: The Interconnection of Dharma and Deeds*, ed. Mary Evelyn Tucker and Duncan Ryūken Williams (Cambridge: Harvard University Press, 1997).

79. Gary Snyder, *A Place in Space: Ethics, Aesthetics, and Watersheds* (Washington DC: Counterpoint, 1995), 95.

80. Snyder, *A Place in Space*, 247.

81. Gary Snyder, *The Practice of the Wild* (San Francisco: North Point, 1990), 24.

82. Gary Snyder, *The Real Work: Interviews & Talks 1964–1979*, ed. Wm. Scott McLean (Toronto: George J. McLeod, 1980), 17.

83. Quoted in Robert Kern, "Mountains and Rivers are Us: Gary Snyder and the Nature of the Nature of Nature," *College Literature* 27, no. 1 (2000): 121. Original quote from Gary Snyder, *Mountains and Rivers without End* (Washington DC: Counterpoint, 1996), 155.

84. Susannah Butter, "Extinction Rebellion's Co-Founder on Bringing London to a Standstill," *The Standard* (23 July 2019).

85. Sam Knight, "Does Extinction Rebellion Have the Solution to the Climate Crisis?" *The New Yorker* (21 July 2019).

86. Nin Kirkham and Chris Letheby, "Psychedelics and Environmental Virtues," *Philosophical Psychology* 37, no. 2 (2022).

87. Eliza Mackintosh, "A Psychedelic Journey, a Radical Strategy and Perfect Timing: How The World's Fastest-Growing Climate Movement Was Made," *CNN World* (25 Dec. 2019).

88. Mackintosh, "A Psychedelic Journey, a Radical Strategy and Perfect Timing."

89. Joseph Poore and Thomas Nemecek, "Reducing Food's Environmental Impacts Through Producers and Consumers," *Science* 360, no. 6392 (2018).

90. Veerasamy Seijan, Iqbal Hyder, T. Ezeji, J. Lakritz, Raghavendra Bhatta, J. P. Ravindra, Cadaba S. Prasad, and Rattan Lal, "Global Warming: Role of Livestock," in *Climate Change Impact on Livestock: Adaptation and Mitigation*, ed. Veerasamy Sejian, John Gaughan, Lance Baumgard, and Cadaba Prasad (New Delhi: Springer, 2015); Michael B. Eisen and Patrick O. Brown, "Rapid Global Phaseout of Animal Agriculture Has the Potential to Stabilize Greenhouse Gas Levels for 30 Years and Offset 68 Percent of $CO_2$ Emissions This Century," *PLOS Climate* (2022).

91. Dan Smyer Yü, "Freeing Animals: Sino-Tibetan Buddhist Environmentalism and Ecological Challenges," *Religions* 14, no. 110 (2023): 11.

92. Geoffrey Barstow, "Canonical Precedents: The *Laṅkāvatāra* and *Mahāparinirvāṇa Sūtras*," in *The Faults of Meat: Tibetan Buddhist Writings on Vegetarianism*, ed. Geoffrey Barstow (Somerville: Wisdom, 2019), 39.

93. Barstow, *Food of Sinful Demons*, 263.

94. Shabkar, *Food of Bodhisattvas*, 100–1.

95. Shabkar, *Food of Bodhisattvas*, 101–2.

96. Steve Wing, Dana Cole, and Gary Grant,"Environmental Injustice in North Carolina's Hog Industry," *Environmental Health Perspectives* 108, no. 3 (2000).

97. Floor Borlée, C. Joris Yzermans, Bernadette Aalders, Jos Rooijackers, Esmeralda Krop, Catharina B. M. Maassen, François Schellevis, Bert Brunekreef, Dick Heederik, and Lidwien A. M. Smit, "Air Pollution from Livestock Farms is Associated with Airway Obstruction in Neighboring Residents," *American Journal of Respiratory and Critical Care Medicine* 196, no. 9 (2017).

98. Andrew Wasley, and Alexandra Heal, "Revealed: Shocking Safety Records of UK Meat Plants," *The Bureau of Investigative Journalism* (2018); Karen Victor, and Antoni Barnard, "Slaughtering for a Living: A Hermeneutical Phenomenological Perspective on the Well-Being of Slaughterhouse Employees," *International Journal of Qualitative Studies in Health and Well-Being* 11 (2016).

99. Seijan et al., "Global Warming: Role of Livestock"; Sailesh Rao, "Animal Agriculture Is the Leading Cause of Climate Change—A Position Paper," *Journal of Ecological Society* 33 (2021).

100. Poore and Nemecek, "Reducing Food's Environmental Impacts."

101. Mesfin M. Mekonnen and Arjen Y. Hoekstra, "A Global Assessment of the Water Footprint of Farm Animal Products," *Ecosystems* 15 (2012).

102. Joris P. G. M. Cromsigt, Mariska te Beest, Graham I. H. Kerley, Marietjie Landman, Elizabeth le Roux, and Felisa A. Smith, "Trophic Rewilding as a Climate Change Mitigation Strategy?," *Philosophical Transactions of the Royal Society B: Biological Sciences* 373, no. 1761 (2018); Troy Vettese and Drew Pendergrass, *Half-Earth Socialism: A Plan to Save the Future from Exctinction, Climate Change, and Pandemics* (London: Verso Books, 2022).

103. Brent F. Kim, Raychel E. Santo, Allysan P. Scatterday, Jillian P. Fry, Colleen M. Synk, Shannon R. Cebron, Mesfin M. Mekonnen, Arjen Y. Hoekstra, Saskia de Pee, Martin W. Bloem, Roni A. Neff, and Keeve E. Nachman, "Country-Specific Dietary Shifts to Mitigate Climate and Water Crises," *Global Environmental Change* 62 (2020).

104. Deane Curtin, "Toward an Ecological Care Ethic," *Hypatia* 6, no. 1 (1999): 96.

105. Smyer Yü, "Freeing Animals," 11.

106. Curtin, "Toward and Ecological Care Ethic," 98.

107. "His Holiness the Dalai Lama Urges Promotion of Vegetarianism, Says the World Can't Do without Animals," *Central Tibetan Administration* (2020).

108. Karmapa Orgyen Trinley Dorje, "Talk on Vegetarianism." Paper presented at the Twenty-Fourth Annual Great Kagyu Monlam, Bodhgaya, India, January 3, 2007.

109. Karmapa Orgyen Trinley Dorje, "Talk on Vegetarianism," 5.

110. Colin H. Simonds, "This Precious Human Life: Human Exceptionalism and Altruism in Tibetan Buddhism," *Worldviews* 25 (2021).

111. Patrul Rinpoche, *Words of My Perfect Rinpoche*, 22.

112. Barstow, *Food of Sinful Demons*, 105.

113. Barstow, *Food of Sinful Demons*, 107.

114. Barstow, *Food of Sinful Demons*, 178.

115. Barstow, *Food of Sinful Demons*, 176.

116. Barstow, *Food of Sinful Demons*, 174.

# Conclusion

1. His Holiness the Dalai Lama and Franz Alt, *Our Only Home*; His Holiness the Dalai Lama, *This Fragile Planet: His Holiness the Dalai Lama on Environment*, ed. Michael Buckley. Manotick: Sumeru, 2021); Susan Bauer-Wu, *A Future We Can Love*.

2. Zoe Zielke, "Contesting Religious Boundaries with Care: Engaged Buddhism and Eco-Activism in the UK," *Religions* 14, no. 8 (2023).

3. Deane Curtin, "To Live as a Lotus among the Flames: Buddhist Awakening in the Middle of the Climate Crisis," *Worldviews: Global Religions, Culture, and Ecology* 21, no. 1 (2017).

4. Katie Javanaud, "The World on Fire: A Buddhist Response to the Environmental Crisis," *Religions* 11, no. 381 (2020).

5. Anālayo, *Mindfully Facing Climate Change*; Bhikkhu Anālayo, *Mindfulness between Early Buddhism and Climate Change* (Barre: Barre Center for Buddhist Studies, 2024).

6. Elverskog, *The Buddha's Footprint*, xiii.

7. Elverskog, *The Buddha's Footprint*, xiii.

8. Elverskog, *The Buddha's Footprint*, xiii.

9. His Holiness the Dalai Lama, *Beyond Dogma: The Challenge of the Modern World*, trans. Alison Anderson, ed. Marianne Dresser (New Delhi: Rupa, 1999), 110.

10. Ed Halliwell, "Of Course the Dalai Lama's a Marxist," *The Guardian* (Guardian News & Media Limited, 20 June 2011).

11. See Graham Priest, *Capitalism — Its Nature and Its Replacement: Buddhist and Marxist Insights* (New York: Routledge, 2021).

12. Ronald Purser, *McMindfulness: How Mindfulness Became the New Capitalist Spirituality* (London: Repeater Books, 2019).

13. Jessica Locke, "Making Consciousness an Ethical Project: Moral Phenomenology in Buddhist Ethics and White Anti-Racism," in *Buddhism and Whiteness: Critical Reflection*, ed. George Yancy and Emily McCrae (New York: Lexington Books, 2019).

14. Specifically of the kind employed by the late, great Michael Jamal Brooks in Michael Brooks, *Against the Web: A Cosmopolitan Answer to the New Right* (Washington: Zero Books, 2020).

# Bibliography

## Works in Tibetan


bdud 'joms rin po che. "bdud 'dul dbang drug rdo rje gro lod kyi rdzogs rim ka dag gi khrid yig ye shes snang ba." In *bdud 'joms 'jigs bral ye shes rdo rje'i gsung 'bum dam chos rin chen nor bu'i bang mdzod*, 423–434. Kalimpong: dupjung lama, 1979–1975. W20869.

*Bodhicaryāvatarā of Śāntideva*. Edited by Vidhushekhara Bhattacharta. Calcutta: Asiatic Society, 1960.

bstan 'dzin rgyal mtshan. *byang chub sems kyi stod pa rin chen sgron ma*. Dharamsala: dga' ldan pho brang, 2018. BDRC: W8LS66303.

dbang phyug rdo rje. "lhan cig skyes sbyor gyi zab khrid nges don rgya mtsho'i snying po 'phrin las 'od 'phro." In *karma pa sku phreng rim byon gyi gsung 'bum phyogs bsgrigs, vol. 85*, 175–458. Lha sa: dpal brtsegs bod yig dpe rnying zhib 'jug khang, 2013. BDRC: W3PD1288.

Gegen Dorje Tharchin. *[Tibetan-Tibetan Dictionary] vols. 1–5*. Kalimpong: Tibet Mirror, 1950–1976.

gser mdog pan chen shakya mchog lden. "shing rta chen po'i srol gnyis kyi rnam par dbye ba bshad nas nges don gcig tu sgrub pa'i bstan bcos kyi rgyas 'grel." In *Two Controversial Mādhyamika Treatises*. Edited by Trayang Samten and Jamyang Samten. New Delhi: n.p., 1974.

'jigs med gling pa. "klong chen snying gi thig le las gzhi lam 'bras bu'i smon lam." In *gsang chen snga 'gyur ba'i bka' gter zhal 'don phyogs bsgrigs*, 432–434. Zi ling: mtsho sngon zhing chen mtsho lho dge 'os slob grwa'i khang, 1998. BDRC: W25186.

kar ma pa dbang phyug rdo rje. "phyag-chen ma-rig mun-sel." *Study Buddhism by Berzin Archives*. Berzin Archives, 2021. https://studybuddhism.com/bo/bod-kyi-nang-chos/ma-dpe-khag/sngags-kyi-dpe-cha/phyag-rgya-chen-po-ma-rig-mun-sel/phyag-chen-gyi-sgom-gong-du-spel-ba.

mi pham rgya mtsho. "sems kyi ngo bo." In *gsung 'bum mi pham rgya mtsho*. Khreng tu'u: gangs can rig gzhung dpe rnying myur skyobs lhan tshogs, 2007. BDRC: W2DB16631.

nor brang o rgyan gyis bsgrigs. *chos rnam kun btus, vol. 1*. Pe cin: krung go'i bod rig pa dpe skrun khang, 2008. BDRC: W1KG2733.

pad+ma 'byung gnas. *man ngag lta ba'I phreng ba*. Bylakuppe: ngagyu nyingma institute: 2001. BDRC: W24519.

pad+ma'i ngang tshul. "sgom rim bar ba." *sgom rim thog mtha' bar gsum dang rim gyis 'jug pa'i bsgom don sogs*. Gangtok: gonpo tseten, 1977. BDRC: W23190.

pad+ma'i ngang tshul. "sgom rim dang po." *sgom rim thog mtha' bar gsum dang rim gyis 'jug pa'i bsgom don sogs*. Gangtok: gonpo tseten, 1977. BDRC: W23190.

rang byung rdo rje. *nges don phyag rgya chen po'i smon lam dang*. Rdo rje gdan: bka' brgyud sang+g+ha smon lam chen mo, 2004. BDRC: W1KG3409.

rdza dpal sprul 'jigs med chos kyi dbang po. *kun bzang bla ma'i zhal lung*. Lha sa: ser gtsug nang bstan dpe rnying 'tshol bsdu phyogs sgrig khang, 2016. BDRC: W1KG25095.

rta byangs. "rdo rje theg pa rtsa ba'i ltung ba bsdus pa." In *bstan 'gyur dpe sdur ma vol. 27*. Pe cin: krung go'i bod rig pa'i dpe skrun khang, 1994–2008. BDRC: W1PD95844.

rtse le sna tshogs rang grol. "nges don gyi lta sgom nyams su lent shul ji lta bar ston pa rdo rje'i mdo 'dzin." *rtse le sna tshogs rang grol gyi gsung gdams zab phyogs bsgrigs, vol. 1*, 1–48. Kathmandu: Khenpo Shedup Tenzin and Lama Thinley Namgyal, 2007. BDRC: W1KG4338.

sangs rgyas rdo rdje, "zhal gdams snying gi thig le." In *sngags mang zhib 'jug (3)*, edited by hum chen he ru ka, nyi zla he ru kah, and ye shes sgrol ma, 114–115. Zi Ling: mtsho ngong zhing chen nang bstan rig gnas zhib 'jug lte gnas, 2002. BDRC: W2DB4605.

sa ra ha. "lta sgom spyod pa 'bras bu'i do ha'i glu." In *sa ra ha pa'i rdo rje'i gsung rnams phyogs bsgrigs, sde tshan ra*, 445–448. Kathmandu: thrangu tashi choling, 2011. BDRC: W1KG10746.

sgam po pa bsod nams rin chen. *dwags po thar rgyan*. Lha sa: ser gtsug nang bstan dpe rnying 'tshol bsdu phyogs sgrig khang, n.d. BDRC: MW1AC220.

tsong kha pa blo bzang grags pa "rten 'grel stod pa." In *dge lugs pa'i chos spyod phyogs bsgrigs*. Zi Ling: mtsho sngong mi rigs dpe skrun khang, 1995. BDRC: W19999.

yang thang rin po che. "lta sgom spyod gsum mdor bsdus." *Lotsawa House*. Lotsawa House, 2021. https://www.lotsawahouse.org/bo/tibetan-masters/yangthang-rinpoche/view-meditation-action.

zhabs dkar tshogs drug rang drol. *'jam dbyans sprul pa'i glegs bam*. N.p., n.d. BDRC: W6468.

## Works in English

Abram, David. *The Spell of the Sensuous: Perception and Language in a More-Than-Human World*. New York: Vintage Books, 1997.

Aitken, Daniel Timothy. "Experience and Morality: Buddhist Ethics as Moral Phenomenology." PhD dissertation. University of Tasmania, 2016.

Aitken, Daniel, and Jetsunma Tenzin Palmo. "Jetsunma Tenzin Palmo: Emptiness, Dzogchen, and Women in Buddhism." *Wisdom Podcast*. Somerville: Wisdom, 2021. https://wisdomexperience.org/wisdom-podcast/126-jetsunma-tenzin-palmo.

Anālayo, Bhikkhu. *Mindfulness between Early Buddhism and Climate Change*. Barre: Barre Center for Buddhist Studies, 2024.

Anālayo, Bhikkhu. *Mindfully Facing Climate Change*. Barre: Barre Center for Buddhist Studies, 2019.

Applegate, Richard B. "The Datura Cult amongst the Chumash." *Journal of California Anthropology* 2, no. 1 (1975): 7–17.

Aśvaghoṣa. *Summary of the Root Downfalls of the Vajra Vehicle*. Translated by Adam Pearcey. Lotsawa House, 2018. Accessed 6 June 2021. https://www.lotsawahouse.org/indian-masters/ashvaghosha/root-downfalls.

Barad, Karen. *Meeting the Universe Halfway: Quantum Physics and the Entanglement of Matter and Meaning*. Durham: Duke University Press, 2007.

Barnhill, David Landis. "Great Earth Saṅgha: Gary Snyder's View of Nature as Community." In *Buddhism and Ecology: The Interconnection of Dharma and Deeds*, edited by Mary Evelyn Tucker and Duncan Ryūken Williams, 187–218. Cambridge: Harvard University Press, 1997.

Barstow, Geoffrey. "Canonical Precedents: The *Laṅkāvatāra* and *Mahāparinirvāṇa Sūtras*." In *The Faults of Meat: Tibetan Buddhist Writings on Vegetarianism*, edited by Geoffrey Barstow. Somerville: Wisdom, 2019.

Barstow, Geoffrey. *Food of Sinful Demons: Meat, Vegetarianism, and the Limits of Buddhism in Tibet*. New York: Columbia University Press, 2019.

Batchelor, Martine. "Even the Stones Smile: Selections from the Scriptures." In *Buddhism and Ecology*, edited by Martine Batchelor and Kerry Brown, 2–17. London: Cassell, 1992.

Bauer-Wu, Susan. *A Future We Can Love: How We Can Reverse the Climate Crisis with the Power of Our Hearts and Minds*. Boston: Shambhala, 2023.

Bender, Frederic L. *The Culture of Extinction: Toward a Philosophy of Deep Ecology.* Amherst: Humanity Books, 2003.

Bennett, Jane. *Vibrant Matter: A Political Ecology of Things.* Durham: Duke University Press, 2010.

Borlée, Floor, C. Joris Yzermans, Bernadette Aalders, Jos Rooijackers, Esmeralda Krop, Catharina B. M. Maassen, François Schellevis, Bert Brunekreef, Dick Heederik, and Lidwien A. M. Smit. "Air Pollution from Livestock Farms Is Associated with Airway Obstruction in Neighboring Residents." *American Journal of Respiratory and Critical Care Medicine* 196 (2017): 1152–61.

Bramwell, Anna. *Ecology in the 20th Century: A History.* New Haven: Yale University Press, 1989.

Brassard, Francis. *The Concept of Bodhicitta in Śāntideva's Bodhicaryāvatarā.* Albany: State University of New York Press, 2000.

Brisman, Avi. "Environmental and Human Rights." *Encyclopedia of Criminology and Criminal Justice,* edited by Gerben Bruinsma and David Weisburd. New York: Springer, 2014.

Brooks, Michael. *Against the Web: A Cosmopolitan Answer to the New Right.* Washington: Zero Books, 2020.

Brown, Charles S. "The Real and the Good: Phenomenology and the Possibility of an Axiological Rationality." In *Eco-Phenomenology: Back to the Earth Itself,* edited by Charles S. Brown and Ted Toadvine, 3–18. Albany: State University of New York Press, 2003.

Brown, Charles S., and Ted Toadvine. "Eco-Phenomnology: An Introduction." In *Eco-Phenomenology: Back to the Earth Itself,* edited by Charles S. Brown and Ted Toadvine, iv–xxi. Albany: State University of New York Press, 2003.

Bryant, Levi R., and Eileen A. Joy. "Preface: Object/Ecology." *O-Zone: A Journal of Object-Oriented Studies* 1 (2014): i–xiv.

Bryant, Levi, Nick Srnicek, and Graham Harman. "Toward a Speculative Philosophy." In *The Speculative Turn: Continental Realism and Materialism,* edited by Levi Bryant, Nick Srnicek, and Graham Harman, 1–19. Melbourne: re.press, 2011.

Butter, Susannah. "Extinction Rebellion's Co-Founder on Bringing London to a Standstill." *The Standard,* 23 July 2019. https://www.standard.co.uk/lifestyle/london-life/extinction-rebellion-co-founder-gail-bradbrook-interview-a4196266.html.

Cabezon, José Ignacio. "Buddhist Theology in the Academy." In *Buddhist Theology: Critical Reflections by Contemporary Buddhist Scholars,* edited by John Makransky and Roger Jackson, 25–52. Richmond: Curzon, 2000.

Callicott, J. Baird. "Animal Liberation: A Triangular Affair." *Environmental Ethics* 2, no. 4 (1990): 311–338.

Callicott, J. Baird. "Animal Liberation and Environmental Ethics: Back Together Again." *Between the Species* 4, no. 3 (1988): 163–169.

Callicott, J. Baird. *In Defense of the Land Ethic: Essays in Environmental Philosophy.* Albany: State University of New York Press, 1989.

Capper, Daniel. *Roaming Free like a Deer: Buddhism and the Natural World.* Ithaca: Cornell University Press, 2022.

Carson, Rachel. *Silent Spring.* Boston: Houghton Mifflin, 1962.

Chen, Zhuo, Ralph W. Hood Jr., Lijun Yang, and P. J. Watson. "Mystical Experience among Tibetan Buddhists: The Common Core Thesis Revisited." *Journal for the Scientific Study of Religion* 50, no. 2 (2011): 328–338.

Chöden Rinpoche. *Mastering Meditation: Instructions on Calm Abiding and Mahāmudrā.* Translated by Tenzin Gache. Somerville: Wisdom, 2020.

Chökyi Nyima Rinpoche. *The Union of Mahāmudrā and Dzogchen.* Translated by Erik Pema Kunsang. Edited by Marcia B. Schmidt. Kathmandu: Rangjung Yeshe, 1989.

Choondassery, Yesudas. "Rights-based Approach: The Hub of Sustainable Development." *Discourse and Communication for Sustainable Education* 8, no. 2 (2017): 17–23.

Clark, John. "On Being None with Nature: Nāgārjuna and the Ecology of Emptiness." *Capitalism, Nature, Socialism* 19, no. 4 (2008): 6–29.

Clayton, Barbra. "Buddha's Maritime Nature: A Case Study in Shambhala Buddhist Environmentalism." *Journal of Buddhist Ethics* 20 (2013): 572–591.

Clayton, Barbra. *Moral Theory in Śāntideva's Śikṣāsamuccaya: Cultivating the Fruits of Virtue.* New York: Routledge, 2006.

Cooper, David E., and Simon P. James. *Buddhism, Virtue and Environment.* Aldershot: Ashgate, 2005.

Cromsigt, Joris P. G. M., Mariska te Beest, Graham I. H. Kerley, Marietjie Landman, Elizabeth le Roux, and Felisa A. Smith. "Trophic Rewilding as a Climate Change Mitigation Strategy?" *Philosophical Transactions of the Royal Society B: Biological Sciences* 373 (2018): 20170440.

Curtin, Deane. "To Live as a Lotus among the Flames: Buddhist Awakening in the Middle of the Climate Crisis." *Worldviews: Global Religions, Culture, and Ecology* 21, no. 1 (2017): 21–40.

Curtin, Deane. "Toward an Ecological Care Ethic." *Hypatia* 6 (1991): 60–74.

Dalai Lama, His Holiness the. *Beyond Dogma: The Challenge of the Modern World.* Translated by Alison Anderson. Edited by Marianne Dresser. New Delhi: Rupa, 1999.

Dalai Lama, His Holiness the. "Principal Commitments," *His Holiness the 14th Dalai Lama of Tibet*. The Office of His Holiness the Dalai Lama, n.d. https://www.dalailama.com/the-dalai-lama/biography-and-daily-life/three-main-commitments.

Dalai Lama, His Holiness the. "Routine Day." *His Holiness the 14th Dalai Lama of Tibet*. The Office of His Holiness the Dalai Lama, n.d. https://www.dalailama.com/the-dalai-lama/biography-and-daily-life/a-routine-day.

Dalai Lama, His Holiness the. *This Fragile Planet: His Holiness the Dalai Lama on Environment*. Edited by Michael Buckley. Manotick: Sumeru, 2021.

Dalai Lama, His Holiness the, and Franz Alt. *Our Only Home: A Climate Appeal to the World*. Toronto: Hanover Square, 2020.

Dalai Lama, the fourteenth. "Nobel Lecture." *The Nobel Prize*. Nobel Prize Outreach AB, 2024. https://www.nobelprize.org/prizes/peace/1989/lama/lecture/.

"The Dalai Lama with Greta Thunberg and Leading Scientists: A Conversation on the Crisis of Climate Feedback Loops." *Mind & Life Institute*. Mind & Life Institute, 2020. https://www.mindandlife.org/event/the-dalai-lama-with-greta-thunberg-and-leading-scientists-a-conversation-on-the-crisis-of-climate-feedback-loops/.

Dalton, Drew M. "Towards an Object-Oriented Ethics: Schopenhauer, Spinoza, and the Physics of Objective Evil." *Open Philosophy* 1 (2018): 59–78.

De Silva, Lily. "Early Buddhist Attitudes toward Nature." In *Dharma Rain: Sources of Buddhist Environmentalism*, edited by Stephanite Kaza and Kenneth Kraft, 91–104. Boston: Shambhala, 2000.

De Silva, Padmasiri. *Environmental Philosophy and Ethics in Buddhism*. Houndmills: Macmillan, 1998.

*Dharma Gaia: A Harvest of Essays in Buddhism and Ecology*. Edited by Alan Hunt Badiner. Berkeley: Parallax, 1990.

Dilgo Khyentse Rinpoche. *The Heart Treasure of the Enlightened Ones*. Translated by Padmakara Translation Group. Boston: Shambhala, 1992.

Dobkin de Rios, Marlene, and Ronni Stachalek. "The *Duboisia* Genus, Australian Aborigines and Suggestibility." *Journal of Psychoactive Drugs* 31, no. 2 (1999): 155–161.

Dominick, Brian A. "Anarcho-Veganism Revisited." In *Anarchism and Animal Liberation: Essays on Complementary Elements of Total Liberation*, edited by Anthony J. Nocella II, Richard J. White, and Erika Cudworth, 23–39. Jefferson: McFarland, 2015.

Dominick, Brian A. *Animal Liberation and Social Revolution*. n.p., 1997.

Dreyfus, Georges B. J. *The Sound of Two Hands Clapping: The Education of a Tibetan Buddhist Monk*. Berkeley: University of California Press, 2003.

Dreyfus, Hubert L., and Stuart E. Dreyfus. "What Is Morality? A Phenomenological Account of the Development of Ethical Expertise." In *Universalism vs. Communitarianism: Contemporary Debates in Ethics*, edited by David Rasmussen, 237–264. Cambridge: MIT Press, 1990.

Dunne, John. "Realizing the Unreal: Dharmakīrti's Theory of Yogic Perception." *Journal of Indian Philosophy* 34, no. 6 (2006): 497–519.

Dzongsar Jamyang Khyentse. *What Makes You Not a Buddhist*. Boston: Shambhala, 2007.

Edelglass, William. "Buddhist Ethics and Western Moral Philosophy." *A Companion to Buddhist Philosophy*, edited by Steven M. Emmanuel, 476–490. Malden: Wiley-Blackwell, 2014.

Edelglass, William. "Moral Pluralism, Skillful Means, and Environmental Ethics." *Environmental Philosophy* 3, no. 1 (2006): 8–16.

Eisen, Michael B., and Patrick O. Brown. "Rapid Global Phaseout of Animal Agriculture Has the Potential to Stabilize Greenhouse Gas Levels for 30 Years and Offset 68 Percent of CO2 Emissions This Century." *PLoS Climate* 1 (2022): e0000010.

Elverskog, Johan. *The Buddha's Footprint: An Environmental History of Asia*. Philadelphia: University of Pennsylvania Press, 2020.

Evernden, Neil. *The Natural Alien*. Toronto: University of Toronto Press, 1993.

*A Feast of the Nectar of the Supreme Vehicle: An Explanation of the Ornament of the Mahāyāna Sūtras — Maitreya's Mahāyānasūtrālamkāra with a Commentary by Jamgön Mipham*. Translated by Padmakara Translation Group. Boulder: Shambhala, 2018.

Fernandez, James W. *Bwiti: An Ethnography of the Religious Imagination in Africa*. Princeton: Princeton University Press, 2019.

Fink, Charles K. "The Cultivation of Virtue in Buddhist Ethics." *Journal of Buddhist Ethics* 20 (2013): 668–701.

Fischer, Roland. "A Cartography of the Ecstatic and Meditative States." *Science* 174, no. 4012 (1971): 897–904.

Forman, Robert K. C. "Introduction: Mysticism, Constructivism, and Forgetting." In *The Problem of Pure Consciousness*, edited by Robert K. C. Forman, 3–49. Oxford: Oxford University Press, 1990.

Forman, Robert K. C. *Mysticism, Mind, Consciousness*. Albany: State University of New York Press, 1999.

*The Foundation for Yoga Practitioners: The Buddhist Yogācārabhūmi Treatise and Its Adaptation in India, East Asia, and Tibet, Volume 1*. Edited by Ulrich Timme Kragh. Harvard Oriental Series 75. Cambridge: Department of South Asian Studies, Harvard University, 2013.

Fox, Warwick. "Approaching Deep Ecology: A Response to Richard Sylban's Critique of Deep Ecology." Hobart: University of Tasmania Environmental Studies Occasional Paper 20, 1986.

Gagliano, Monica, Mavra Grimonprez, Martial Depczynski, and Michael Renton. "Tuned in: Plant Roots Use Sound to Locate Water." *Oecologia* 184, no. 1 (2017): 151–160.

Gamble, Christopher N. Joshua S. Hanan, and Thomas Nail. "What Is New Materialism?" *Angelaki* 24, no. 6 (2019): 111–134.

Gampopa. *The Jewel Ornament of Liberation: The Wish-Fulfilling Gem of the Noble Teachings.* Translated by Khenpo Konchog Gyaltsen Rinpoche. Edited by Ani K. Trinlay Chödron. Boulder: Snow Lion, 1998.

Garfield, Jay L. *Buddhist Ethics: A Philosophical Investigation.* Oxford: Oxford University Press, 2022.

Garfield, Jay L. *Engaging Buddhism: Why It Matters to Philosophy.* Oxford: Oxford University Press, 2014.

Garfield, Jay L. "What Is It Like to Be a Bodhisattva? Moral Phenomenology in Śantideva's *Bodhicaryāvatarā.*" *Journal of the International Association of Buddhist Studies* 33, no. 1–2 (2010): 333–357.

*A Garland of Views: A Guide to View, Meditation, and Result in the Nine Vehicles — Padmasambhava's Classic Text with a Commentary by Jamgön Mipham.* Translated by Padmakara Translation Group. Boston: Shambhala, 2015.

Gelles, David. "How to Meditate." *New York Times: Well.* New York Times, n.d. https://www.nytimes.com/guides/well/how-to-meditate.

Gilligan, Carol. *In a Different Voice: Psychological Theory and Women's Development.* Cambridge: Harvard University Press, 2003.

Goldstein, Joseph. *The Experience of Insight: A Natural Unfolding.* Santa Cruz: Unity, 1976.

Goodman, Charles. *Consequences of Compassion: An Interpretation & Defense of Buddhist Ethics.* Oxford: Oxford University Press, 2009.

Greene, Eric M. "A Reassessment of the Early History of Chinese Buddhist Vegetarianism." *Asia Major* 29, no. 1 (2016): 1–43.

Gruen, Lori. *Entangled Empathy: An Alternative Ethic for Our Relationships with Animals.* New York: Lantern Books, 2015.

Halliwell, Ed. "Of Course the Dalai Lama's a Marxist." *The Guardian.* Guardian News & Media Limited, 20 June 2011. https://www.theguardian.com/commentisfree/belief/2011/jun/20/dalai-lama-marxist-buddhism.

Haraway, Donna J. *Staying with the Trouble: Making Kin in the Chthulucene.* Durham: Duke University Press, 2016.

Harman, Graham. *Prince of Networks: Bruno Latour and Metaphysics.* Melbourne: re.press, 2009.

Harman, Graham. *Tool-Being: Heidegger and the Metaphysics of Objects.* New York: Open Court, 2011.

Harris, Ian. "Buddhism." In *Attitudes to Nature*, edited by Jean Holm and John Bowker, 8–27. New York: Pinter, 1994.

Harris, Ian. "Buddhism and the Discourse of Environmental Concern: Some Methodological Problems Considered." In *Buddhism and Ecology: The Interconnection of Dharma and Deeds*, edited by Mary Evelyn Tucker and Duncan Ryūken Williams, 377–402. Cambridge: Harvard University Press, 1997.

Harris, Ian. "Buddhist Environmental Ethics and Detraditionalization: The Case of EcoBuddhism." *Religion* 25, no. 3 (1995), 199–211.

Harris, Ian. "Causation and Telos: The Problem of Buddhist Environmental Ethics." *Journal of Buddhist Ethics* 1 (1994): 45–56.

Harris, Ian. "How Environmentalist Is Buddhism?" *Religion* 21 (1991): 101–114.

Harris, Ian. "'A Vast Unsupervised Recycling Plant': Animals and the Buddhist Cosmos." In *A Communion of Subjects: Animals in Religion, Science, and Ethics*, edited by Paul Waldau and Kimberley Patton, 207–217. New York: Columbia University Press, 2006.

Harvey, Peter. *An Introduction to Buddhist Ethics: Foundations, Values and Issues*. Cambridge: Cambridge University Press, 2000.

Hayhoe, Katharine, and Tia Nelson. "Climate Change: The Case for Hope and Healing with Katharine Hayhoe and Tia Nelson." *New York Public Library*. New York: New York Public Library, 29 September 2021. https://www.nypl.org/events/programs/2021/09/29/climate-change-case-hope-healing-katharine-hayhoe.

"His Holiness the Dalai Lama Urges Promotion of Vegetarianism, Says the World Can't Do without Animals." *Central Tibetan Administration*, 2020. https://tibet.net/his-holiness-urges-promotion-of-vegetarianism-says-the-world-cant-do-without-animals.

Holbrook, Daniel, "Utilitarianism on Environmental Issues Reexamined." *International Journal of Applied Philosophy* 7, no. 1 (1992): 41–46.

Holder, John J. "A Suffering (But Not Irreparable) Nature: Environmental Ethics from the Perspective of Early Buddhism." *Contemporary Buddhism* 8, no. 2 (2007): 113–130.

Hopkins, Jeffrey. *Jeffrey Hopkins' Tibetan-Sanskrit-English Dictionary*. Taipei: Dharma Drum Buddhist College, 2011.

Hopkins, Jeffrey. *Nāgārjuna's Precious Garland: Buddhist Advice for Living and Liberation*. Boulder: Snow Lion, 2007.

Hopkins, Jeffrey. "A Tibetan Perspective on the Nature of Spiritual Experience." In *Paths to Liberation: The Mārga and Its Transformations in Buddhist Thought*, edited by Robert E. Buswell Jr. and Robert M. Gimello, 225–268. Delhi: Motilal Banarsidass, 1994.

Horgan, Terry, and Mark Timmons. "Moral Phenomenology and Moral Theory." *Philosophical Issues* 15 (2005): 56–77.

*The Hundred Thousand Songs of Milarepa, Volume 1*. Translated by Garma C. C. Chang. Boulder: Shambhala, 1977.

Huxley, Aldous. *The Perennial Philosophy*. New York: Harper & Brothers, 1945.

Igini, Martina. "'Impossible Not to Feel Hopeless'—Guardian Survey of IPCC Scientists Reveals 1.5C Goal Out of Reach." *Earth.org*. Hong Kong: Earth.org, 9 May 2024. https://earth.org/impossible-not-to-feel-hopeless-guardian-survey-of-ipcc-scientists-reveals-1-5c-goal-out-of-reach/.

Ives, Christopher. "Resources for a Buddhist Environmental Ethic." *Journal of Buddhist Ethics* 20 (2013), 541–571.

James, Simon P. "Against Holism: Rethinking Buddhist Environmental Ethics." *Environmental Values* 16 (2007): 447–461.

James, Simon P. *Zen Buddhism and Environmental Ethics*. Burlington: Ashgate, 2004.

James, William. *The Varieties of Religious Experience*. Edited by Matthew Bradley. Oxford: Oxford University Press, 2012.

Jamieson, Dale. "Animal Liberation Is an Environmental Ethic." *Environmental Values* 7, no. 1 (1998): 41–57.

Javanaud, Katie. "The World on Fire: A Buddhist Response to the Environmental Crisis." *Religions* 11, no. 381 (2020): 381–397.

Jigten Sumgon. *Gongchig: The Single Intent, the Sacred Dharma*, with commentary entitled *The Lamp Dispelling the Darkness* by Rigdzin Chökyi Drakpa. Translated by Markus Viehbeck. Munich: Otter Verlag, 2009.

Kabat-Zinn, Jon. *Full Catastrophe Living: Using the Wisdom of Your Body and Mind to Face Stress, Pain and Illness*. New York: Delacorte, 1990.

Katz, Steven T. "Language, Epistemology, and Mysticism." In *Mysticism and Philosophical Analysis*, edited by Steven T. Katz, 22–74. Oxford: Oxford University Press, 1978.

Kaza, Stephanie. *Green Buddhism: Practice and Compassionate Action in Uncertain Times*. Boulder: Shambhala, 2019.

Kaza, Stephanie, and Kenneth Kraft. "Part One: Teachings from Buddhist Traditions—Introduction." In *Dharma Rain: Sources of Buddhist Environmentalism*, edited by Stephanie Kaza and Kenneth Kraft, 11–13. Boston: Shambhala, 2000.

Kellstedt, Paul, Sammy Zahran, and Arnold Vedlitz. "Personal Efficacy, the Information Environment, and Attitudes toward Global Warming and Climate Change in the United States." *Risk Analysis* 28, no. 1 (2008): 113–126.

Keown, Damien. "Buddhism and Ecology: A Virtue Ethics Approach." *Contemporary Buddhism* 8, no. 2 (2007): 97–112.

Keown, Damien. "Keynote One: Damien Keown." *Contemporary Perspective on Buddhist Ethics*. New York: Center for Buddhist Studies, 2007. Accessed 27 Jan. 2022. https://www.cbs.columbia.edu/buddhist_ethics/keynote-one.html.

Keown, Damien. *The Nature of Buddhist Ethics*. New York: Palgrave Macmillan, 1992.

Kern, Robert. "Mountains and Rivers Are Us: Gary Snyder and the Nature of the Nature of Nature," *College Literature* 27, no. 1 (2000): 119–138.

Kheel, Marti. "From Heroic to Holistic Ethics: The Ecofeminist Challenge." In *Ecofeminism: Women, Animals, Nature*, edited by Greta Gaard, 243–271. Philadelphia: Temple University Press, 1993.

Khensur Jampa Tegchok. *Practical Ethics and Profound Emptiness: A Commentary on Nāgārjuna's Precious Garland*. Translated by Bhiksu Steve Carlier. Edited by Bhiksuni Thubten Chodron. Somerville: Wisdom, 2017.

Khunu Rinpoche. *Vast as the Heavens, Deep as the Sea*. Translated by Gareth Sparham. Somerville: Wisdom, 1999.

Kim, Brent F., Raychel E. Santo, Allysan P. Scatterday, et al. "Country-Specific Dietary Shifts to Mitigate Climate and Water Crises." *Global Environmental Change* 62 (2020): 101926.

Kirby, Vicky. *Quantum Anthropologies: Life at Large*. Durham: Duke University Press, 2011.

Kirby, Vicky. *Telling Flesh: The Substance of the Corporeal*. New York: Routledge, 1997.

Kirkham, Nin, and Chris Letheby. "Psychedelics and Environmental Virtues." *Philosophical Psychology* 37, no. 2 (2022): 371–395.

Klein, Anne C. *Knowledge and Liberation. Tibetan Buddhist Epistemology in Support of Transformative Religious Experience*. Ithaca: Snow Lion, 1986.

Knight, Sam. "Does Extinction Rebellion Have the Solution to the Climate Crisis?" *The New Yorker* (21 July 2019). https://www.newyorker.com/news/letter-from-the-uk/does-extinction-rebellion-have-the-solution-to-the-climate-crisis.

Komarovski, Yaroslav. *Tibetan Buddhism and Mystical Experience*. New York: Oxford University Press, 2015.

Kriegel, Uriah "Moral Phenomenology: Foundational Issues." *Phenomenology and the Cognitive Sciences* 7 (2008): 1–19.

Kunsang, Erik Pema, Ives Waldo, Jim Valby, Gyurme Dorje, Thomas Doctor, and Matthieu Ricard. "lta ba." *Rangjung Yeshe Wiki Dharma Dictionary*. Tsadra Foundation, 2021. https://rywiki.tsadra.org/index.php/lta_ba.

Kunsang, Erik Pema, Ives Waldo, Jim Valby, Gyurme Dorje, Thomas Doctor, and Matthieu Ricard. "sgom pa." *Rangjung Yeshe Wiki Dharma Dictionary*. Tsadra Foundation, 2021. https://rywiki.tsadra.org/index.php/sgom_pa.

Leibniz, Gottfried Wilhelm. "Specimen Dynamicum" *Philosophical Papers and Letters, Volume 2*. Translated by Leroy E. Loemker, 435–452. London: Kluwer Academic, 1989.

Leopold, Aldo. *A Sand County Almanac with Essays on Conservation from Round River*. New York: Ballantine Books, 1970.

*The Life of Shabkar: The Autobiography of a Tibetan Yogi*. Translated by Matthieu Ricard. Ithaca: Snow Lion, 2001.

Lobsang Gyatso and Graham Woodhouse. *Tsongkhapa's Praise for Dependent Relativity*. Boston: Wisdom, 2011.

Locke, Jessica. "Making Consciousness an Ethical Project: Moral Phenomenology in Buddhist Ethics and White Anti-Racism." In *Buddhism and Whiteness: Critical Reflection*, edited by George Yancy and Emily McCrae, 161–179. New York: Lexington Books, 2019.

Locke, Jessica. "Training the Mind and Transforming Your World: Moral Phenomenology in the Tibetan Buddhist Lojong Tradition." *Comparative and Continental Philosophy* 10, no. 3 (2018): 251–263.

Longchenpa. *Finding Rest in Illusion: The Trilogy of Rest, Volume 3*. Translated by Padmakara Translation Group. Boulder: Shambhala, 2019.

Longchen Rabjam. *The Practice of Dzogchen: Longchen Rabjam's Writings on the Great Perfection*. Translated by Tulku Thondup. Edited by Harold Talbott. Boston: Snow Lion, 2014.

Lopez Jr., Donald S. "Developments in Buddhist Studies, 2015: A Report on the Symposium 'Buddhist Studies Today,' University of British Columbia, Vancouver, July 7–9, 2015." *Canadian Journal of Buddhist Studies* 11 (2016): 5–36.

Lynas, Mark, Benjamin Z. Houlton, and Simon Perry. "Greater than 99% Consensus on Human Caused Climate Change in the Peer-Reviewed Scientific Literature." *Environmental Research Letters* 16, no. 11 (2021): 1–7.

Mackintosh, Eliza. "A Psychedelic Journey, A Radical Strategy and Perfect Timing. How the World's Fastest-Growing Climate Movement Was Made." *CNN World* (25 Dec. 2019). https://edition.cnn.com/2019/12/25/uk/extinction-rebellion-gail-bradbrook-gbr-intl/index.html.

Macy, Joanna. "The Ecological Self: Postmodern Ground for Right Action." In *Worldview, Religion, and the Environment: A Global Anthology*, edited by Richard C. Foltz, 428–436. Belmont: Wadsworth/Thomson Learning, 2003.

Makransky, John. "The Emergence of Buddhist Critical-Constructive Reflection in the Academy as a Resource for Buddhist Communities and for the Contemporary World." *Journal of Global Buddhism* 9 (2008): 113–153.

Mandelbaum, Maurice. *The Phenomenology of Moral Experience*. Glencoe: Free Press, 1955.

Marietta Jr., Don E. "Back to Earth with Reflection and Ecology." In *Eco-Phenomenology: Back to the Earth Itself*, edited by Charles S. Brown and Ted Toadvine, 121–137. Albany: State University of New York Press, 2003.

Marshall, Paul. *Mystical Encounters with the Natural World: Experiences and Explanations*. Oxford: Oxford University Press, 2005.

Mason, Jim. *An Unnatural Order: Uncovering the Roots of Our Domination of Nature and Each Other*. New York: Simon & Schuster, 1993.

McDonald, Barbara. " 'Once You Know Something, You Can't Not Know It': An Empirical Look at Coming Vegan." *Society & Animals* 8, no. 1 (2000): 1–23.

McMahan, David L. "A Brief History of Interdependence." In *The Making of Buddhist Modernism*, 149–182. Oxford: Oxford University Press, 2009.

Mekonnen, Mesfin M., and Arjen Y. Hoekstra. "A Global Assessment of the Water Footprint of Farm Animal Products." *Ecosystems* 15 (2012): 401–415.

Merchant, Carolyn. *Radical Ecology: The Search for a Livable World*. New York: Routledge, 1992.

Mipham Rinpoche. *The Essence of Mind*. Translated by Adam Pearcey. Lotsawa House, 2016. Accessed 6 June 2021. https://www.lotsawahouse.org/tibetan-masters/mipham/essence-of-mind.

Morton, Timothy. *Dark Ecology: For a Logic of Coexistence*. New York: Columbia University Press, 2016.

Morton, Timothy. *The Ecological Thought*. Cambridge: Harvard University Press, 2010.

Morton, Timothy. "Here Comes Everything: The Promise of Object-Oriented Ontology." *Qui Parle: Critical Humanities and Social Studies* 19, no. 2 (2011): 163–190.

Morton, Timothy. *Humankind: Solidarity with Nonhuman People*. New York: Verso Books, 2019.

Morton, Timothy. *Hyperobjects: Philosophy and Ecology after the End of the World*. Minneapolis: University of Minnesota Press, 2013.

Naess, Arne. "The Deep Ecological Movement: Some Philosophical Aspects." In *Deep Ecology for the 21st Century: Readings on the Philosophy and Practice of New Environmentalism*, edited by George Sessions, 64–84. Boston: Shambhala, 1995.

Naess, Arne. *Ecology, Community and Lifestyle: Outline of an Ecosophy*. Translated by David Rothenberg. New York: Cambridge University Press, 1989.

Naess, Arne. "The World of Concrete Contents." *Inquiry* 28 (1985): 417–428.

Nāgārjuna. *The Root Stanzas of the Middle Way: The Mūlamadhyamakakārikā.* Translated by Padmakara Translation Group. Boulder: Shambhala, 2016.

"The Nobel Peace Prize 1989." *The Nobel Prize.* Nobel Prize Outreach AB, 2024. https://www.nobelprize.org/prizes/peace/1989/summary/.

Norgaard, Kari Marie. *Living in Denial: Climate Change, Emotions, and Everyday Life.* Cambridge: MIT Press, 2011.

Odell, Jenny. *How to Do Nothing: Resisting the Attention Economy.* Brooklyn: Melville House, 2019.

Ogyen Trinley Dorje. *Interconnected: Embracing Life in Our Global Society.* Somerville: Wisdom, 2018.

Ogyen Trinley Dorje, H.H. Seventeenth Gyalwang Karmapa. "Walking the Path of Environmental Buddhism through Compassion and Emptiness." *Conservation Biology* 25, no. 6 (2011): 1094–1097.

Ogyen Trinley Dorje, Karmapa. "Talk on Vegetarianism." Paper presented at the 24th Annual Great Kagyu Monlam, Bodhgaya, India, January 3, 2007. http://www.shabkar.org/download/pdf/Talk_on_Vegetarianism.pdf.

Ohnuma, Reiko. *Unfortunate Destiny: Animals in the Indian Buddhist Imagination.* Oxford: Oxford University Press, 2017.

Pang, Rachel H. "Taking Animals Seriously: Shabkar's Narrative Argument for Vegetarianism and the Ethical Treatment of Animals." *Journal of Buddhist Ethics* 29 (2022): 61–84.

Patrul Rinpoche. *Words of My Perfect Rinpoche.* Translated by Padmakara Translation Group. New Haven: Yale University Press, 2011.

Pellow, David Naguib. *Total Liberation: The Power and Promise of Animal Rights and the Radical Earth Movement.* Minneapolis: University of Minnesota Press, 2014.

Pike, Sarah M. *For the Wild: Ritual and Commitment in Radical Eco-Activism.* Oakland: University of California Press, 2017.

Poore, Joseph, and Thomas Nemecek. "Reducing Food's Environmental Impacts through Producers and Consumers." *Science* 360, no. 6392 (2018): 987–992.

Powell, James. "Scientists Reach 100% Consensus on Anthropogenic Global Warming." *Bulletin of Science, Technology & Society* 37, no. 4 (2017): 183–184.

Prebish, Charles S. *Buddhist Monastic Discipline: The Sanskrit Prātimokṣa Sūtras of the Mahāsāṃghikas and Mūlasarvāstivādins.* University Park: Pennsylvania State Press, 1975.

Priest, Graham. *Capitalism — Its Nature and Its Replacement: Buddhist and Marxist Insights.* New York: Routledge, 2021.

*The Problem of Pure Consciousness.* Edited by Robert K. C. Forman. Oxford: Oxford University Press, 1990.

Purser, Ronald. *McMindfulness: How Mindfulness Became the New Capitalist Spirituality.* London: Repeater Books, 2019.

Rao, Sailesh. "Animal Agriculture Is the Leading Cause of Climate Change—A Position Paper." *Journal of Ecological Society* 33 (2021): 155–167.

"Readout of the President's Meeting with His Holiness the XIV Dalai Lama." *The White House.* The White House Office of the Press Secretary (15 June 2016). https://obamawhitehouse.archives.gov/the-press-office/2016/06/15/readout-presidents-meeting-his-holiness-xiv-dalai-lama.

Regan, Tom. *The Case for Animal Rights.* Berkeley: University of California Press, 2004.

Rhodes, Robert F. "The Four Extensive Vows and Four Noble Truths in T'ien-t'ai Buddhism." *Annual Memoirs of the Otani University Shin Buddhist Comprehensive Research Institute* 2 (1987): 247–266.

Ringu Tulku Rinpoche. "The Bodhisattva Path at a Time of Crisis." In *A Buddhist Response to the Climate Emergency,* edited by John Stanley, David R. Loy, and Gyurme Dorje. Boston: Wisdom, 2009.

Rockstrom, Johan et al. "A Safe Operating Space for Humanity." *Nature* 461 (2009): 472–475.

Rolston III, Holmes. *A New Environmental Ethics: The Next Millennium for Life on Earth.* New York: Routledge, 2012.

Sagoff, Mark. "Animal Liberation and Environmental Ethics: Bad Marriage, Quick Divorce." *Osgoode Hall Law Journal* 22 (1984): 297–307.

Sahni, Pragati. *Environmental Ethics in Buddhism: A Virtues Approach.* London: Routledge, 2008.

Sakya Pandita Kunga Gyaltsen. *A Clear Differentiation of the Three Codes: Essential Distinctions among the Individual Liberation, Great Vehicle, and Tantric Systems.* Translated by Jared Douglas Rhoton. Edited by Victoria R. M. Scott. Albany: State University of New York Press, 2002.

Salleh, Ariel. *Ecofeminism as Politics: Nature, Marx and the Postmodern.* New York: St, Martin's, 1997.

Schmithausen, Lambert. *Buddhism and Nature.* Tokyo: International Institute for Buddhist Studies, 1991.

Schmithausen, Lambert. "The Early Buddhist Tradition and Ecological Ethics." *Journal of Buddhist Ethics* 4 (1997): 1–74.

Schmithausen, Lambert. *The Problem of the Sentience of Plants in Earliest Buddhism.* Studia Philologica Buddhica Monograph Series 6. Tokyo: International Institute for Buddhist Studies, 1991.

Schmunk, Rhianna. "595 People Were Killed by Heat in B.C. This Summer, New Figures from Coroner Show." *CBC News.* CBC News, 1 November 2021. https://www.cbc.ca/news/canada/british-columbia/bc-heat-dome-sudden-deaths-revised-2021-1.6232758.

Sejian, Veerasamy, Iqbal Hyder, T. Ezeji, et al. "Global Warming: Role of Livestock." In *Climate Change Impact on Livestock: Adaptation and Mitigation,* edited by Veerasamy Sejian, John Gaughan, Lance Baumgard, and Cadaba Prasad, 141–169. New Delhi: Springer, 2015.

sGam.po.pa. *The Jewel Ornament of Liberation,* translated by Herbert V. Guenther. Boston: Shambhala, 1986.

Shabkar, Lama. *The Flight of the Garuda.* Translated by Erik Pema Kunsang. Kathmandu: Rangjung Yeshe, 1988.

Shabkar Tsogdruk Rangdrol. *The Emanated Scripture of Manjushri: Shabkar's Essential Meditation Instructions from Lam-Rim to Mahāmudrā and Dzogchen.* Translated by Sean Price. Boulder: Snow Lion, 2020.

Shabkar Tsogdruk Rangdrol. *Food of Bodhisattvas: Buddhist Teachings on Abstaining from Meat.* Translated by Padmakara Translation Group. New Delhi: Shechen, 2008.

Shabkar Tsogdrug Rangdrol. "The View, Meditation, and Action of Mahāmudrā." In *Perfect Clarity: A Tibetan Buddhist Anthology of Mahāmudrā and Dzogchen,* translated by Erik Pema Kunsang. Kathmandu: Rangjung Yeshe, 2012.

Shaviro, Steven. *The Universe of Things: On Speculative Realism.* Minneapolis: University of Minnesota Press, 2014.

Shaw, Julia. "Buddhism and the 'Natural' Environment." In *The Oxford Handbook of Buddhist Practice,* edited by Kevin Trainor and Paula Arai, 213–232. Oxford: Oxford University Press, 2022.

Shaw, Julia. "Religion, 'Nature' and Environmental Ethics in Ancient India: Archaeologies of Human: Non-Human Suffering and Well-Being in Early Buddhist and Hindu Contexts." *World Archaeology* 48, no. 4 (2016): 517–543.

Sherburne, Richard. *The Complete Works of Atīśa Śrī Dīpaṁkara Jñāna, Jo-Bo-rJe: The Lamp for the Path and Commentary, Together with the Newly Translated Twenty-five Key Texts.* New Delhi: Adiya Prakashan, 2000.

Shiva, Vandana, and Maria Miles. *Ecofeminism.* Halifax: Fernwood, 1993.

Simonds, Colin H. "Expanding Sentience: Tibetan Buddhism and the Possibility of Plant, Bacteria, and AI Sentience." *Canadian Journal of Buddhist Studies* 18 (2023).

Simonds, Colin H. "*Lta sgom spyod gsum*: A Tibetan Approach to Moral Phenomenological Praxis." *Journal of Buddhist Ethics* 30 (2023): 93–137.

Simonds, Colin H. "This Precious Human Life: Human Exceptionalism and Altruism in Tibetan Buddhism." *Worldviews: Global Religions, Culture, and Ecology* 25, no. 3 (2021): 239–255.

Simonds, Colin H. "Toward a Buddhist Ecological Ethic of Care." *Religions* 14 (2023): 893.

Simonds, Colin H. *"View, Meditation, Action*: A Tibetan Framework to Inform Psychedelic-Assisted Therapy." *Journal of Psychedelic Studies* 7 (2023): 58–68.

Singer, Peter. *Animal Liberation: A New Ethics for Our Treatment of Animals.* New York: Avon Book, 1975.

Singleton, Mark. *Yoga Body: The Origins of Modern Posture Practice.* Oxford: Oxford University Press, 2010.

Smyer Yü, Dan. "Freeing Animals: Sino-Tibetan Buddhist Environmentalism and Ecological Challenges." *Religions* 14 (2023): 110.

Snyder, Gary. "Buddhist Anarchism." *Journal for the Protection of All Beings #1.* City Lights, 1961. https://theanarchistlibrary.org/library/gary-snyder-buddhist-anarchism.

Snyder, Gary. *Mountains and Rivers without End.* Washington DC: Counterpoint, 1996.

Snyder, Gary. *A Place in Space: Ethics, Aesthetics, and Watersheds.* Washington DC: Counterpoint, 1995.

Snyder, Gary. *The Practice of the Wild.* San Francisco: North Point, 1990.

Snyder, Gary. *The Real Work: Interviews & Talks 1964–1979.* Edited by Wm. Scott McLean. Toronto: George J. McLeod, 1980.

Stace, W. T. *Mysticism and Philosophy.* London: Macmillan, 1961.

Stearns, Cyrus. "The Life and Tibetan Legacy of the Indian Mahāpaṇḍita Vibhūticandra." *Journal for the International Association of Buddhist Studies* 19, no. 1 (1996): 127–172.

Stein, R. A. *Tibetan Civilization.* Stanford: Stanford University Press, 1972.

Stenzel, Julia Caroline. "The Buddhist Roots of Secular Compassion Training: A Comparative Study of Compassion Cultivation in Indian and Tibetan Mahāyāna Sources with the Contemporary Secular Program of Compassion Cultivation Training (CCT)." PhD dissertation. McGill University, 2018.

Suzuki, David. "David Suzuki: The Fundamental Failure of Environmentalism." *The Georgia Straight.* Vancouver: Vancouver Free Press, 1 May 2012. https://www.straight.com/article-674101/vancouver/david-suzuki-fundamental-failure-environmentalism.

Swearer, Donald K. "An Assessment of Buddhist Eco-Philosophy." *Harvard Theological Review* 99, no. 2 (2006).

Thakchoe, Sonam. *The Two Truths Debate: Tsongkhapa and Gorampa on the Middle Way.* Somerville: Wisdom, 2007.

Thich Nhat Hanh. *The Heart of the Buddha's Teaching.* New York: Broadway Books, 1999.

Thich Nhat Hanh. *The Miracle of Mindfulness: An Introduction to Mindfulness.* Boston: Beacon, 1999.

Thich Nhat Hanh. "The Five Mindfulness Trainings." *Plum Village*. Plum Village, 2025. https://plumvillage.org/mindfulness/the-5-mindfulness-trainings.

Thich Nhat Hanh. *Zen and the Art of Saving the Planet*. New York: Harper One, 2021.

Thomson, Iain. "Ontology and Ethics at the Intersection of Phenomenology and Environmental Philosophy." *Inquiry* 47 (2004): 380–412.

Thubten Jinpa. "From Value to Action: A Buddhist Perspective." In *Ecology, Ethics, and Interdependence: The Dalai Lama in Conversation with Leading Thinkers on Climate Change*, edited by John Dunne and Daniel Goleman, 201–221. Somerville: Wisdom, 2018.

Thurman, Robert. *The Jewel Tree of Tibet: The Enlightenment Engine of Tibetan Buddhism*. New York: Free Press, 2006.

Toadvine, Ted. *Merleau-Ponty's Philosophy of Nature*. Evanston: Northwestern University Press, 2009.

Tsele Natsok Rangdrol. *Heart Lamp: Lamp of Mahāmudrā & The Heart of the Matter*. Translated by Erik Pema Kunsang. Kathmandu: Rangjung Yeshe, 2009.

Tsoknyi Rinpoche. "A New Meaning of *Chu* ("Beings") and *No* ("Environment") Has Emerged." In *A Buddhist Response to the Climate Emergency*, edited by John Stanley, David R. Loy, and Gyurme Dorje, 141–146. Somerville: Wisdom, 2009.

Tsong-kha-pa. *Calming the Mind and Discerning the Real: Buddhist Meditation and the Middle View from the Lam Rim Chen Mo*. Translated by Alex Wayman. New York: Columbia University Press, 1978.

Tsongkhapa. *Tantric Ethics: An Explanation of the Precepts for Buddhist Vajrayāna Practice*. Translated by Gareth Sparham. Boston: Wisdom, 2005.

Tulku Urgyen Rinpoche. *Blazing Splendor: The Memoirs of Tulku Urgyen Rinpoche*. Translated by Erik Pema Kunsang. Boudhanath: Rangjung Yeshe, 2015.

Tupper, Kenneth W., Evan Wood, Richard Yensen, and Matthew W. Johnson. "Psychedelic Medicine: A Re-Emerging Therapeutic Paradigm." *Canadian Medical Association Journal* 187, no. 14 (2015): 1054–1059.

Udoudom, Mfonobong. "The Value of Nature: Utilitarian Perspective." *Gnosi: An Interdisciplinary Journal of Human Theory and Praxis* 4, no. 1 (2021): 2714–2485.

Van Shaik, Sam. "The Great Perfection and the Chinese Monk: rNying-ma-pa Defences of Hwa-Shang Mahāyāna in the Eighteenth Century." *Buddhist Studies Review* 20, no. 2 (2003): 189–204.

Van Shaik, Sam. *Tibet: A History*. New Haven: Yale University Press, 2013.

Vasubandhu. *Abhidharmakośabhasyam of Vasubandhu*. Edited by P. Pradhan. Patna: Jayaswal Institute, 1975.

Vélez de Cea, Abraham. "The Dalai Lama and the Nature of Buddhist Ethics," *Journal of Buddhist Ethics* 20 (2013): 500–540.

Vetesse, Troy, and Drew Pendergrass. *Half-Earth Socialism: A Plan to Save the Future from Extinction, Climate Change, and Pandemics.* London: Verso Books, 2022.

Victor, Karen, and Antoni Barnard. "Slaughtering for a Living: A Hermeneutical Phenomenological Perspective on the Well-Being of Slaughterhouse Employees." *International Journal of Qualitative Studies in Health and Well-Being* 11 (2016): 30266.

Wang-ch'ug Dor-je. *The Mahāmudrā: Eliminating the Darkness of Ignorance.* Dharamsala: Library of Tibetan Works and Archives, 1978.

Warren, Karen J. "The Power and the Promise of Ecofeminism, Revisited." In *Environmental Philosophy: From Animal Rights to Radical Ecology,* edited by Michael Zimmerman, J. Baird Callicott, Karen J. Warren, Irene Klaver, and John Clark, 325–343. Upper Saddle River: Pearson Prentice Hall, 2005.

Warren, Mary Anne. "The Rights of the Nonhuman World." In *Environmental Philosophy,* edited by Robert Elliot and Arran Gare, 109–134. New York: University of Queensland Press, 1983.

Wasley, Andrew, and Alexandra Heal. *Revealed: Shocking Safety Records of UK Meat Plants.* London: Bureau of Investigative Journalism, 2018. https://www.thebureauinvestigates.com/stories/2018-07-29/uk-meat-plant-injuries.

Webber, Lama Mark. *Union of Loving-Kindness and Emptiness.* n.p., 2011.

Weston, Anthony. "Beyond Intrinsic Value: Pragmatism in Environmental Ethics." *Environmental Pragmatism,* edited by Eric Karz and Andrew Light, 307–318. London: Routledge, 1996.

Whitehill, James. "Buddhist Ethics in Western Context: The 'Virtues' Approach." *Journal of Buddhist Ethics* 1 (1994): 1–22.

Wilson, Jeff. *Mindful America: Meditation and the Mutual Transformation of Buddhism and American Culture.* New York: Oxford University Press, 2014.

Wilson, Jeff. *Mindful America: The Mutual Transformation of Buddhist Meditation and American Culture.* Oxford: Oxford University Press, 2014.

Wing, Steve, Dana Cole, and Gary Grant. "Environmental Injustice in North Carolina's Hog Industry." *Environmental Health Perspectives* 108 (2000): 225–231.

Wirth, Jason M. *Mountains, Rivers, and the Great Earth: Reading Gary Snyder and Dōgen in an Age of Ecological Crisis.* Albany: State University of New York Press, 2017.

Wohlleben, Peter. *The Hidden Life of Trees: What They Feel, How They Communicate.* Translated by Jane Billinghurst. Vancouver: Greystone Books, 2016.

Wood, David. "What Is Ecophenomenology?" *Research in Phenomenology* 31 (2002): 78–95.

Woodhouse, Emily, Martin A. Mills, Philip J. K. McGowan, and E. J. Milner-Gulland. "Religious Relationships with the Environment in a Tibetan Rural Community: Interactions and Contrasts with Popular Notions of Indigenous Environmentalism." *Human Ecology* 43 (2015): 295–307.

Yeshe Tsogyal. *The Lotus-Born: The Life Story of Padmasambhava.* Translated by Erik Pema Kunsang. Edited by Marcia Binder Schmidt. Boston: Shambhala, 1999.

Žižek, Slavoj. *Heaven in Disorder.* New York: OR Books, 2021.

# Index